Collins
revision guides

TotalRevision
GCSEEnglish

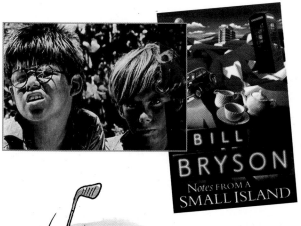

■ **Andrew Bennett**
and Peter Thomas

■ **Series Editor: Jayne de Courcy**

CONTENTS AND REVISION PLANNER

ABOUT THIS BOOK

We have planned this book to make your revision as active and effective as possible.

How?

- by breaking down the skills revision into manageable chunks (Revision Sessions)

- by testing your understanding at every step of the way (Check Yourself Questions)

- by providing extra information to help you aim for the very top grades (A/A* Extras)

- by including a range of extracts to build your confidence (extracts from different genres)

- by giving you expert examiner's guidance about exam technique (Exam Practice)

 **REVISION SESSION**

Revision Sessions

- There are two main skills that you need to revise for your written exams: Reading and Writing.

- Both of these skills are divided into a number of **short revision sessions**. You should be able to read through each of these in no more than 30 minutes. That is the maximum amount of time that you should spend on revising without taking a short break.

- Ask your teacher for a copy of your own exam board's **GCSE English specification**. Tick off on the Contents list each of the revision sessions that you need to cover. It will probably be most of them.

CHECK YOURSELF QUESTIONS

- At the end of each revision session there are some Check Yourself Questions. By trying these questions, you will immediately find out whether you have understood and remembered what you have read in the revision session. **Answers** are at the back of the book, along with **extra hints and guidance**.

- If you manage to answer all the Check Yourself Questions for a session correctly, you can confidently tick off this skill in the box provided in the Contents list. If not, you will need to tick the 'Revise again' box to remind yourself to return to this topic later in your revision programme.

⚡ A/A* EXTRA

These boxes occur in most of the revision sessions. They highlight what you need to do in order to demonstrate that particular skill at **a very high level**. This will help you to achieve the highest grades in your exam.

Extracts from different genres

In order to do well in your English exam, you need to be able to comment confidently on a wide range of fiction and non-fiction.

The authors, who are practising examiners, have carefully selected extracts from as wide a range of different genres as possible. This means you are revising your skills and consolidating your understanding of different genres.

Exam Practice

■ This unit gives you **invaluable guidance on how to answer exam questions well**.

■ There are **typical exam papers** from each of the three main Exam Boards for you to try answering.

■ There are **sample answers** for you to check your own answers against, plus examiner's comments showing what you need to do to score **high marks**.

■ Working through this unit will give you an excellent grounding in exam technique. If you feel you want further exam practice, look at *Do Brilliantly GCSE English*, also published by Collins Educational.

Assessment objectives

Your written papers will test your Reading and Writing skills. Speaking and Listening skills (and some Reading and Writing skills) are tested through your coursework. All Exam Boards have to test the same skills or assessment objectives. This books covers all these assessment objectives, so it is relevant to you whatever specification you are following.

Assessment objectives for Reading

- Read with insight and engagement, making appropriate references to texts and developing and sustaining interpretations of them.
- Distinguish between fact and opinion and evaluate how information is presented.
- Follow an argument, identifying implications and recognising inconsistencies.
- Select material appropriate to the purpose, collate material from different sources and make cross-references.
- Understand and evaluate how writers use linguistic, structural and presentational devices to achieve their effects, and comment on ways language varies and changes.

Assessment objectives for Writing

- Communicate clearly and imaginatively, using and adapting forms for different readers and purposes.
- Organise ideas into sentences, paragraphs and whole texts using a variety of linguistic and structural features.
- Use a range of sentence structures effectively with accurate punctuation and spelling.

Your exam papers

Summarised below are what the exam papers consist of from 2004 for the most popular specification offered by each Exam Board in England.

AQA A (see pages 121 and 127 for sample Papers 1 and 2)

Paper 1, Section A
This tests your Reading skills in relation to non-fiction and media texts. You will be expected to answer a number of questions on a passage or passages.

Paper 1, Section B
This tests your Writing skills. The Writing tasks in this section are 'Writing to argue', 'Writing to persuade' and 'Writing to advise'. There will be one writing task on each type and a fourth task that combines two of these types. You can select the task that you think you will perform best.

Paper 2, Section A
This again tests your Reading skills, this time in relation to poems from different cultures and traditions. The poems will be in your pre-release anthology. You will be offered a choice of one from two questions.

Paper 2, Section B
This again tests your Writing skills. This time, the Writing tasks will be based on 'Writing to inform', 'Writing to explain' and 'Writing to describe'. There will be one writing task on each type and a fourth task that combines two of these types. You can select the task that you think you will perform best.

OCR specification 1900 (Opening Minds)

This summary is for Higher-tier candidates.

Unit 1   Non-fiction, Media and Information
(see page 138 for a sample paper)

Section A
You will be given two or more pieces of material, at least one non-fiction and one media.
Task 1 will expect you to distinguish between fact and opinion, to select and collate material and to cross-refer between texts.
Task 2 will expect you to follow an argument, to identify implication and inconsistencies and/or to evaluate how information is presented.

Section B
You will be asked to produce a piece of writing that informs, explains or describes, on a topic broadly linked to the reading material provided.

Unit 2   Different Cultures, Analysis and Argument

Section A (open book)
You will take into the exam the text that you have studied. You will be expected to complete one task on it, exploring the way that writers use language and structure to create character, setting and theme.

Section B
In response to stimulus material provided, you will be expected to produce two pieces of writing: one to analyse, review or comment; one to argue, persuade or advise.

Unit 3   Literary Heritage and Imaginative Writing

Section A (open book)
In response to stimulus material, you will have to complete one task, producing one or two pieces of writing to explore, imagine or entertain.

Section B (open book)
You will have to complete two tasks: one on the Shakespeare text you have read and one on the poetry selection you have read.

(As an alternative to Unit 3, you can do Unit 4, which is coursework rather than exam based.)

Edexcel Specification A

This summary relates to Higher candidates.

Paper 4H	*The Craft of the Writer: Poetry and Non-fiction (pre-released material)*
Section A	A choice of questions based on the modern poetry in the pre-released anthology.
Section B	A question based on the non-fiction section of the anthology.
Section C	A choice of writing tasks to inform, explain or describe.
Paper 5H	*(see page 148 for a sample paper)*
Question 1	A question based on the reading of an unprepared non-fiction text or texts.
Question 2	A choice of writing tasks to analyse, review or comment.
Question 3	A choice of writing tasks to argue, persuade or advise.

READING

Fact and opinion

KEY EXAM SKILLS

- You need to be able to distinguish fact from opinion in non-fiction texts.

- If you can identify the use of both fact and opinion, you will be able to comment on the writer's purpose and methods.

◉ What is factual writing?

- Very little writing – even if it is labelled 'non-fiction' – is purely factual. Writers find it very hard to keep their **opinions** and **judgements** out of what they write:

- Some of the description is factual and some is opinion.

- Sometimes the two are mixed up in one statement, like the very first one where the **fact** is that the house is detached, but the statements that it is 'magnificently situated' and 'individual' are a matter of opinion.

Facts
- detached house
- south-facing views over the golf course and out to sea
- central heating
- 4 bedrooms
- 2 reception rooms
- bathroom
- shower room
- cloakrooms

Opinions
- magnificently situated
- individual
- superb
- approx. 1 acre

SAUNTON

NEW INSTRUCTION

£249,000
- Magnificently situated individual detached house
- Superb south-facing views over the golf course and out to sea • Central heating • 4 bedrooms
- 2 receptions • Bathroom • Shower room
- Cloaks • Detached garage • Approx 1 acre

- 'Approx. 1 acre' is in the Opinions column because what one person regards as close to one acre may be seen as considerably less than one acre by someone else! This illustrates the problem concerning fact and opinion: the more you think about some examples, the less clear-cut they become.

◉ Buried opinions

- Opinions may be buried within facts. This is a passage from Paul Theroux's account of a journey around the coast of Great Britain, *The Kingdom by the Sea*:

In 1791, the Royal Sea-Bathing Infirmary was founded on the western cliffs of Margate. But nothing improved the tone of the place. In 1824, a traveller wrote, 'From an obscure fishing village, Margate, in the of little more than half a century, has risen into a well-frequented, if not fashionable, watering-place.' A hundred years later, Baedeker's *Great Britain* described Margate as 'one of the most popular, though not one of the most fashionable watering-places in England.' So it had always been crummy and Cockneyfied, just like this, people down from London for the day shunting back and forth on the front in the cold rain, and walking their dogs and gloomily fishing and looking at each other.

In Theroux's opinion, Margate is 'crummy and Cockneyfied'.

- It is a fact that the 1824 traveller and the Baedeker guidebook include the statements Theroux quotes, but those statements are themselves only opinions.
- There are some obvious facts: the whole of the first sentence, and some of the last – that there were Londoners in Margate when Theroux visited; that it was raining; that some people were walking dogs and some were fishing.
- It is only Theroux's opinion that Margate was 'crummy and Cockneyfied'.
- You can't really call a descriptive word like 'shunting' a fact, since its exact meaning is subjective.
- It is subjective as to whether the rain was cold and all the people fishing were 'gloomy'. The latter could just be a case of the writer transferring his own feelings about the place to other people.

◎ Buried facts

■ Even autobiography may at times contain very few facts. Take this passage from Roald Dahl's *Going Solo*:

It would seem that when the British live for years in a foul and sweaty climate among foreign people, they maintain their sanity by allowing themselves to go slightly dotty. They cultivate bizarre habits that would never be tolerated back home, whereas in far-away Africa or in Ceylon or in India or in the Federated Malay States, they could do as they liked. On the SS Mantola, just about everybody had his or her own particular maggot in the brain, and for me it was like watching a kind of non-stop pantomime throughout the entire voyage.

- There isn't a single fact in the whole extract, but some can be inferred – that is, read between the lines.

- 'Buried facts' of that kind would be:
  - Roald Dahl had (possibly) visited Africa, Ceylon, and the Federated Malay States;
  - he had been on a ship called the SS Mantola;
  - there were men and women on the ship;
  - he considered his fellow passengers to be 'slightly dotty'.

Check Yourself Questions

Q1 Look at the leaflet below about Granary Wharf in Leeds. On a piece of paper, head two columns 'Facts' and 'Opinions' and copy all the written information from the leaflet into the appropriate column.

Q2 **a** How do you think the writer hopes readers will react to this leaflet?

b How does the writer attempt to achieve this reaction?

G R A N A R Y   W H A R F

A unique place

Entertainments, special events, music, workshops, canal walks, boat trips and eating facilities for all tastes...there's always plenty to see and do at

Granary Wharf. It's friendly, it's fun and it's free.

G R A N A R Y   W H A R F

FESTIVAL MARKET

30 shops, open 7 days a week

A fascinating selection of original goods and gifts, and a festival market (up to sixty additional stalls) every Saturday, Sunday and Bank Holiday Monday. Shops open 10.00am to 5.30pm.

Right in the centre of Leeds

Granary Wharf is behind the Hilton Hotel in Neville Street, just two minutes walk from Leeds Railway Station.

Access is via the 'Dark Arches'; look out for a small illuminated sign under the railway bridge. Ample parking. Special arrangements for coaches.

GRANARY WHARF THE CANAL BASIN
LEEDS LS1 4BR TEL (0113) 2446570

Design: Ian Cave 0113 27-0104

Answers are on page 157.

How information is presented

■ Information can be presented in a variety of ways in non-fiction texts.

■ You should be able to recognise how an author chooses to convey his or her message and comment on its effectiveness.

◎ Autobiography and biography

■ In writing about their own or other peoples' lives, authors often use pictures, especially photographs, both to make the text look more attractive and to allow the reader to visualise people, places and events more accurately. In *Going Solo*, Roald Dahl uses a variety of pictorial material, including the following copy of a flying assessment:

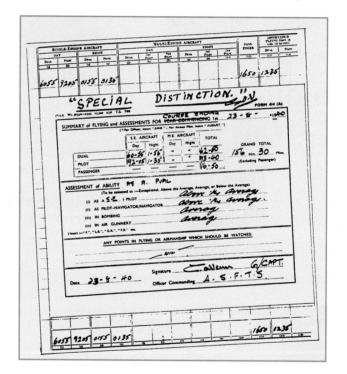

Roald Dahl might have used that photocopied sheet because:
● it would be quite complicated to describe in words;
● the detail would not interest everyone;
● anyone particularly interested can read it carefully for themselves;
● he might not have wished to seem vain by writing directly about his 'Special Distinction'.

◎ Journals, diaries and letters

- Writers sometimes move away from straightforward text because they want to convey a particular feeling or strong emotion.

- Edward Lear, the nineteenth-century author of nonsense rhymes and other humorous texts such as *The Owl and the Pussycat*, started a letter to someone called Mr Fortescue like this:

My dear 4oscue,

    I came to 'leave a card' on you, as you axed me to the dinner yesterday – here it is –

- • Lear's personality would be hard to convey by conventional written means!

- George Bernard Shaw conveys a very different emotion in a letter to his friend Stella Campbell. Shaw had heard of the death of Stella's son in the First World War; he sent a typed letter of sympathy to her which finishes in this way:

Oh damn, damn, damn, damn, damn, damn, damn, damn, DAMN

DAMN!

    And oh, dear, dear, dear, dear, dear, dearest!
                    G.B.S.

- • The large handwritten 'DAMN!' gains its effect by contrasting with the neatly typed text around it.

⚡ A/A* EXTRA

▸ You need to be able to give 'sustained and developed views about how presentational devices achieve their purpose'.

▸ You could say that both Edward Lear and George Bernard Shaw break the conventions of typewritten letters.

▸ Lear achieves humorous effects through a drawing and through the odd spelling of his friend's name, not unlike present day text messaging on mobile phones.

▸ Shaw achieves a tragic effect by the personal nature of the handwritten word which emphasises the genuine nature of his feelings.

Travel writing

- Although travel writing is usually classed as non-fiction, it often presents very personal opinions and views. In that way, it is similar to biography and autobiography.

- It tends to make similar use of pictures, maps and charts to add interest to the text and sometimes to hint at the author's ideas.

Leaflets

- Many leaflets contain information that could be quite difficult to understand. It may therefore be presented in various ways so that different people can understand it (see *Check Yourself Questions* on page 8).

- Some people prefer to read charts, while others prefer to read text if given the choice. Presenting the same information but in different ways means that more people will understand it.

Newspaper articles

- Newspaper articles often use a range of graphic devices to present information. An article in *The Guardian* about the pop-music industry contained the graphs shown on the left.

- The most obvious reason for using graphs is that it saves the newspaper a vast amount of space. Explaining in words all the information given in these graphs, and all the possible interpretations of it, would take up several pages of print.

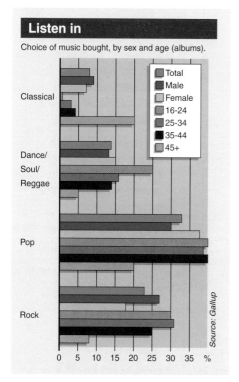

Listen in

Choice of music bought, by sex and age (albums).

Legend: Total, Male, Female, 16-24, 25-34, 35-44, 45+

Categories: Classical, Dance/Soul/Reggae, Pop, Rock

Axis: 0 5 10 15 20 25 30 35 %

Source: Gallup

American pie

Sales by UK artists in US market.

Years: 1989, 1990, 1991, 1992, 1993

Legend: Singles, Albums

Axis: 0 5 10 15 20 %

Source: BPI Surveys

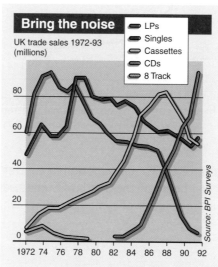

Bring the noise

UK trade sales 1972-93 (millions)

Legend: LPs, Singles, Cassettes, CDs, 8 Track

Axis: 80 60 40 20 0

1972 74 76 78 80 82 84 86 88 90 92

Source: BPI Surveys

Who gets what

Breakdown of money from the sale of a typical £12.99 CD.

Retailer £3.25
Record company £4.66
THE ENGLISH DOGS
Greatest Hits
Producer 44p
VAT £2.27
Manufacturer £1.05
Artist 88p
Publisher 44p

◎ Factual and informative material

■ All kinds of text come under this heading, including instructions for assembling or using items.

■ This is an extract from the instructions for an answering machine:

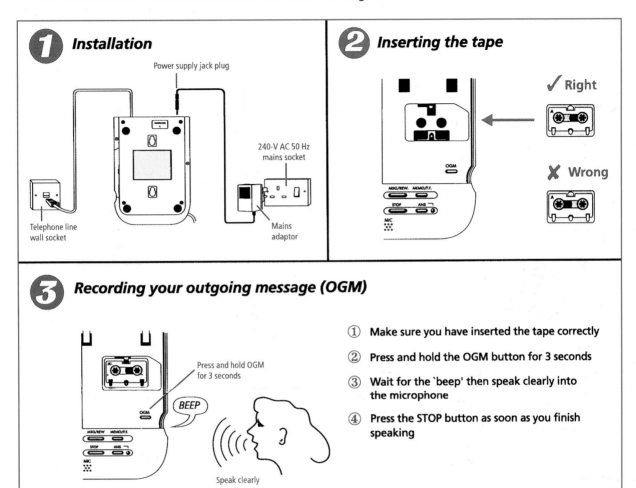

1 Installation

Power supply jack plug

240-V AC 50 Hz mains socket

Telephone line wall socket

Mains adaptor

2 Inserting the tape

✓ Right

✗ Wrong

OGM

3 Recording your outgoing message (OGM)

Press and hold OGM for 3 seconds

BEEP

Speak clearly

① Make sure you have inserted the tape correctly

② Press and hold the OGM button for 3 seconds

③ Wait for the `beep' then speak clearly into the microphone

④ Press the STOP button as soon as you finish speaking

- The pictures are helpful, although the two pictures of tapes in Panel 2 are very similar, and it is difficult to tell what is right and wrong.
- When words and pictures are used together in Panel 3, it is potentially confusing, as the talking head does not appear to be speaking into the microphone, as required in the instructions!
- Diagrams and charts can help, but they can be as confusing as words.

CHECK YOURSELF QUESTIONS

Look at the following extract from a booklet called 'Beach Safety Guidelines'.

Q1 What is the purpose of this information?

Q2 In what different ways does it try to achieve its purpose?

Q3 What effect would the writer want it to have on its readers?

Q4 What different audiences might this booklet be aimed at?

THE WATER SAFETY CODE

Don't go alone

- Swim with a friend – **Never go on your own**.

- Make sure there are other people around - you never know when help might be needed.

Learn how to help

- If you see someone in difficulty, tell somebody, preferably a Lifeguard if there is one nearby, **or**

- Go to the nearest telephone, dial **999**, ask for the **Coastguard**

- You can learn lifesaving and rescue skills.

Contact:

The Royal Life Saving Society UK on **01527 853943** or

The Surf Life Saving Association of Great Britain on **01392 254364**

FLAGS AND SIGNS TO LOOK OUT FOR

Learn what these flags mean

Red and yellow flags means Lifeguards are on patrol. You should only swim or boogie board in the area between the flags.

The red flag means it is dangerous to bathe or swim and you should not go into the water.

The quartered black and white flag indicates the area zoned for surf craft and malibu boards. It is not safe for swimmers and bathers.

Signs for your safety should look like these

These pages are reproduced by kind permission of the RNLI's Sea Safety Initiative, and a copy of the free booklet entitled 'Beach Safety Guidelines' is available by phoning 01202 663174.

Answers are on page 157.

Following an argument

> ■ You must be able to follow the development of an argument in non-fiction text. You need to comment on whether it is logical or not and whether ideas are stated openly or implied.
>
> ■ Interpreting and analaysing the structure of an argument is a sure way of demonstrating high-level reading skills.

◉ The purpose and structure of a leaflet

■ Look at the leaflet on pages 10–11. Its **purpose** is to sell Urathon cycle tyres. To achieve this purpose, the leaflet has to **persuade** you of several things.

> You need to be persuaded that:
> - you need the tyres
> - they're suitable for your bicycle
> - they're easily available, easily fitted, not too expensive, etc.

■ The **structure** of the argument is made clear in a variety of ways.

> - The reader's attention is captured by the text on the cover: 100% PUNCTURE-PROOF TYRES! Cyclists would almost certainly be attracted by this promise.
> - On the inside of the leaflet, there are two columns of print either side of a large photograph (page 11). The print is divided into five sections, each with a bold headline.
> - The headlines go through the argument and set out the reasons why someone should buy these tyres.
>   - The first section states that the tyres are available for all kinds of bicycles, and in a range of 'different' colours.
>   - The next section sets out technical details of the tyres' construction, backed up by a diagram, then returns at the end to the reassurance that punctures are a problem of the past.
>   - The third section moves on to the issue of safety, and links this to the coloured tyres, so these are no longer seen as just a fun idea, but a sensible choice.
>   - Section four develops the safety theme, reminding the reader of what might happen if there is a puncture.
>   - The last section explains how simple it is to have a bicycle fitted with these tyres. ▶

GUARANTEED FROM £13.95 100% PUNCTURE PROOF

GUARANTEED NOT TO LET YOU DOWN

Years of research and development have meant that we can now offer this revolutionary new tyre to fit all standard sizes of bike wheel.

Virtually identical in ride and performance to normal tyres, URATHON Tyres are GUARANTEED NOT TO PUNCTURE and what is more they will outlast normal tyres!

THE PRICE IS RIGHT

From £13.95 a tyre (with fitting FREE), URATHON Tyres are no more expensive than a conventional tyre. But they last longer and we guarantee that punctures will never stop you again!

Just call into your nearest ATS centre and say goodbye to punctures!

URATHON BIKE TYRES - The toughest tyres on the planet.

ATS.

YOUR LOCAL ATS CENTRE IS :

If you have difficulty finding URATHON PUNCTURE-PROOF TYRES call the TYRELINE on **01249 760 585.**

Urathon
BIKE TYRES -
guaranteed not to let you down!

Urathon

100% PUNCTURE PROOF TYRES!

AVAILABLE TO FIT YOUR BIKE

Whether you are fitting them to a Kid's BMX or an adults off-road bike URATHON tyres will be the perfect fit. With tread patterns to suit most aspects of cycling, all you have to do is tell the trained ATS technician which ones you want and leave it up to him! URATHON Tyres come in Conventional Black, but if it's something different that you are looking for, check out Flouro Yellow..Hot Pink or Tornado Red! They're especially popular with the kid's !

HOW IT'S DONE

URATHON Tyres are made from the very latest technology which encapsulates an air-bubble foam core within a tough, resistant Urathane skin. Integral reinforcing bands ensure a firm grip on the wheel. Preset to tyre pressures recommended by professionals, the foam core consists of millions of minute air bubbles to ensure that the ride is virtually identical to a conventional tyre, while the tough outer skin deflects the toughest of objects. So, even if a nail or piece of glass should penetrate the tyre, NOTHING WILL HAPPEN! **Say goodbye to puncture kits, pumps and hassle !**

BRIGHT COLOURS ARE FUN...BUT THEY ARE SAFE TOO

When the short days are with us there is nothing more frightening than the dark roads. URATHON SAFETYBRITE Tyres actually reflect light in cars headlights, making the cyclist visible ...and safer. URATHON SAFETYBRITE Tyres are exactly the same as the black version, but the bright colours make them more fun and safer! Avoid winter road accidents and fit the URATHON

DON'T FORGET THE SAFETY ASPECT

Changing a tyre and fixing a puncture is a hassle, but consider the safety aspect. You may be out on a bike ride, or your kid's cycling around to the local shop when a puncture strikes. It's inconvenient, it's a nuisance and it's dangerous. With URATHON Bike tyres, there's no danger, you just keep on cycling !

FREE FITTING AND TECHNICAL ADVICE

ATS are already the country's leading Car Tyre sales and fitting company. Now you can get URATHON Bike Tyres at every ATS centre. Just visit your local centre - no appointment is necessary - and one of the skilled ATS technicians will advise you on the best Tyre for your requirements and fit it FREE, while you wait.

It couldn't be simpler !

- On closing the leaflet, there is a further section of text which offers a guarantee and mentions an attractively low price; then, on the back face of the leaflet, there is a brief recapitulation of price, properties of the tyres and advice about how to obtain more details (page 10).

◎ Identifying implications

- The leaflet is structured according to its purpose. The **language** of the text is mostly straightforward, and the **sequence of the sections is logical**.

- Overall, the **layout** of the leaflet reinforces the structure and logic of the argument.

- There are **implications** in the text. In other words, there are things it is suggesting; how it sets about really persuading the reader that these tyres are what he or she needs.

- For what appears to be a simple leaflet, it is actually quite sophisticated.

- The **first section** cunningly mentions both adults and children, and also the role of the ATS 'technician' to emphasise that these tyres are serious, not just a fun or fashion item. If they have to be fitted by a 'technician', the implication is that they are complicated technological items, and are not just bicycle tyres. However, so as not to risk becoming too serious, mention of the fluorescent colours is brought in.

- The **second section** follows a similar pattern. This is where the language of the leaflet is less straightforward – purposely so, because the manufacturer wants the reader to be impressed by the technology behind the tyres. Leaflets of this kind will risk almost losing readers in these circumstances, because they know that most people would not admit to being confused by the technical information, but would pretend to understand and be impressed by it. However, the writer does not push this technical language too far, and returns to the good news of no punctures, making sure that the reader's attention is fully restored by using upper-case letters and bold print.

- The **third section** uses one of the commonest tricks in advertising: fear. The implication here is that anyone who doesn't fit fluorescent tyres to their bicycle (or to their children's bicycles) is more likely to have an accident. So while coloured tyres might have initially appeared to be a rather silly idea, this changes that image.

- Having worried the reader, the **fourth section** continues to play on the fear of accidents. A puncture may not be just inconvenient or a nuisance – it may be dangerous. The implication is that if a child has a puncture, he or she may be at the mercy of – what? The leaflet doesn't spell it out, but the implication is clear: if they can 'just keep on cycling', they can escape any undefined threat.

- By the time the reader reaches the **fifth section**, he/she is probably pretty sure these tyres are necessary, so details of fitting are provided. Although the cost of the actual tyres has not yet been mentioned, the leaflet says (in upper case again, to make sure it's noticed) that fitting is free (and simple, underlined) – so wouldn't it be silly not to get some?

- Turning over the page, the price is shown for the first time, and it probably seems very cheap. But note that it is 'from £13.95', the implication being that full-sized tyres for adult bicycles will be much dearer.
- One other point on this page: it says that the Urathon tyres are 'virtually identical in ride and performance to normal tyres': this repeats an implication first suggested in the second section, that they may not actually be as comfortable as conventional pneumatic tyres.

◎ Inconsistencies

■ Although this is a well-structured leaflet of its kind, there are some inconsistencies in the message it gives.

- Are the tyres really a fun item for children (especially the fluorescent ones) or a serious accessory for adults? The leaflet is at pains to emphasise that Urathon tyres are available in 'Conventional Black', but makes considerable play on the safety aspect of the coloured tyres. If the colour is so important, why make black ones at all? Presumably because most adults would not buy them, and the company wants to sell as many tyres as possible.
- The large and dominating photograph is also of a youngish boy, which appears to reinforce the fun/child aspect of the tyres – and it is inconsistent with the safety message of the leaflet, as he is not wearing a helmet or protective elbow and knee pads. There is a real tension in the whole text between safety and fun, young people and adults.

Q1 **a** Look at the page from the Oxfam appeal leaflet. Analyse it in a similar way to the Urathon tyre leaflet and explain the argument.

b Look at the leaflet again and explain the implications.

c Finally, explain any inconsistencies in the leaflet.

Answers are on page 158.

How can your £2 a month help poor people to help themselves?

Photo: Nick Fogden/Oxfam

These days, £2 won't buy very much. But if you give £2 a month to Oxfam, your donation is stretched much further. We support people who are helping themselves, so they contribute their hard work, their time and energy to make every penny go further.

Support a health worker for over 6 months

In India, £2 a month would help train a voluntary health worker for over 6 months safeguarding HUNDREDS of people.

Plant 670 trees

Your £2 a month could supply 670 seedlings every year, which will be planted out by Ethiopian volunteers to help re-green their land.

Photo: Sarah Errington/Oxfam

Clean water for a whole community

In Sudan, £2 a month will help provide enough tools for villagers to dig a well and give their whole community a permanent supply of clean, safe water.

People in the Third World don't want to live on hand-outs. All they want is the opportunity to work them-selves out of poverty – and the chance to live dignified and independent lives.

Photo: Jenny Matthews/Oxfam

OXFAM

274 Banbury Road, Oxford OX2 7DZ
Registered Charity No. 202918

KEY EXAM SKILLS

- You need to be able to describe the similarities and differences between non-fiction texts, both in terms of content and layout.

- By referring to more than one text at a time, through quotation and comparison, you will demonstrate an ability to analyse texts in greater depth.

◎ Collating

- **Collating** means 'comparing in detail' when it is used in relation to more than one text. In other words, looking for similarities and differences, both obvious and more subtle. This can include following arguments and recognising implications and inconsistencies.

◎ Cross-referencing

- **Cross-referencing** simply means referring to actual details in two or more texts, sometimes by direct quotation, to support your argument.

- **High-level cross-referencing** moves to and fro between texts, rather than looking first at one, and then separately at another.

◎ Collating and cross-referencing print

- These two extracts are taken from a feature in *The Observer* in which two men talk about their work.

The lighthouse keeper

AT THE LIZARD lighthouse, my Saturday shift begins at 8 p.m. and I'm on for eight hours until four o'clock in the morning. First, I go down to relieve the watchman, have a chat and check everything is OK. Then I'm up to the lantern to clean the lens before switching on the power. It's an 800,000-candle-power light with a range of 25 miles, and it flashes every second. We're the only legalised flashers in the country, so to speak.

Every half an hour or so, I check that the lamp's sequence and speed are correct; then, every two hours, I check the weather and send the details to the national weather centre at Bracknell. People don't realise how weather reports are done; it's little stations like us that provide the data. I also keep a sharp eye out for fog during the night. If I see it, I start the fog signal: two blasts every minute. It can be heard for eight miles. This is one of the busiest shipping lanes in the world, so if any lights come too close, I warn them off with another blast. If anyone is in real trouble, I call out the coastguard.

The seafront attendant

WHEN THE WEATHER is good, Sunday is the busiest day of the week. It has been for the last 12 summers I've worked here. My job is to look after the bandstand and promenades during the summer season for Eastbourne Borough Council. I arrive at the bandstand between 7.30 and 8 a.m. Turning up so early is my choice: it means I avoid the morning traffic and it gives me a chance to relax with a cup of tea in one of our deckchairs and enjoy the sight of the sun rising over the sea in front of me. Weather permitting, that is.

At this time of day, I see the occasional passer-by strolling along, who, without exception, says 'Good morning' with a smile. It's all so nice and civilised. The other seafront staff arrive at 9 a.m., at the same time as a police search team, including a dog and his handler, to check the bandstand.

Sunday is the first day for the incoming military band, which plays every day for a week. For 12 weeks during the holiday season, different bands provide entertainment. After the search, which is purely a routine precautionary measure, I join the two full-time seasonal bandstand staff to tidy up, if needs be, and check out the microphones and see to any other of the band's requirements.

▸ You need to be able to 'make a clear and detailed comparison' of different pieces of writing.

▸ You could develop the fact that while there are challenging aspects to the work that both men do, they are both able to shift responsibility to others — the lighthouse keeper to the coastguard, and the seafront attendant to the police. Although they are both apparently proud of what they do, they are fairly relaxed about their own accountability.

- When preparing to write about the **similarities** and **differences** in these men's working lives, it is useful to make a few notes in two columns headed 'similarities' and 'differences' under headings such as:
  – their jobs
  – what they feel about these jobs
  – contact with other people
  – how attractive their lives sound

- Here is a sample of a comparison resulting from those lists:

The lighthouse keeper and the seafront attendant

Both men work in jobs which are close to the sea, but the seafront attendant seems to enjoy the sea more; the keeper is aware of the dangers of the sea, watching over 'one of the busiest shipping lanes in the world', especially for fog at night. Indeed, the weather is important to both men: the keeper has to send in regular reports, as well as warning shipping of fog, and the seafront attendant will be more or less busy depending on how good the weather is. Apart from the watchman he relieves, the keeper spends his shift alone, but the seafront attendant talks to passers-by and other staff. The seafront attendant's job sounds easier and more pleasant than the keeper's: the keeper has to watch hard and concentrate on the sea, the weather and shipping all the time. However, the attendant has to be present when police check for explosives under the bandstand. Both men sound proud of the work they do, and take their duties seriously.

- This is a good, detailed answer; the introduction and conclusion both draw together similarities in the men's working lives and their attitudes, but the central part of the answer develops the differences. The only additional detail which could have been included to make this an even fuller answer is a reference to when the lighthouse keeper has to contact the coastguard; the words 'and unless he needs to call out the coastguard' could have been inserted after 'he relieves'. It is not necessary to quote from the text in an exercise of this kind, but one example is included here to show how a direct quotation can be worked into an answer.

CHECK YOURSELF QUESTIONS

Look at the following holiday advertisements which appeared in a London evening newspaper.

Q1 Write a brief comparison of the two holidays in the form of an article (between 150 and 200 words long) which might appear on the travel page of the newspaper. Draw attention to any similarities or differences between what is offered for the price in each case, and suggest what kind of person each holiday might suit.

THE NILE IN STYLE

Eight days, full-board cruise with excursions £399 per person (GLC £389 pp).
Departures 10, 17 August and 7 September

JOIN the Nile Pearl for a wonderful journey through the ancient land of upper Egypt. The exclusive ship has 21 air-conditioned cabins, swimming pool, sun decks, restaurant and bar. There are ten excursions included in the price, and all are accompanied by a qualified Egyptologist.

The price of just £399 per person (GLC: £389) includes return flights, transfers, excursions, all meals and on-board accommodation in a cabin with private facilities.

Why not extend your holiday in Egypt and take advantage of the sunshine, arrange some excellent resort diving or just simply relax? Readers (and GLC members) may choose to extend this holiday with an extra seven nights in Egypt, with a week at the Luxor Hilton with breakfasts each day for an additional £99 per person including transfers, or four nights at the Luxor Hilton and three nights at the Cairo Hilton including transfers and a pyramids and museum excursion for an additional £259 per person.

For full details of the Nile Pearl cruise holiday and optional extensions, call Goldenjoy Holidays on 020 7794 9818, quoting Evening Standard Offer (and GLC members' last four digits of membership number).

SWITZERLAND IN SUMMER

Eight days half board, departing Tuesdays or Wednesdays in August.
Just £299 per person (GLC £289)

SPEND a week in Lugano, where the flamboyant warmth of Italy combines with the cool efficiency of southern Switzerland. This region enjoys a lovely climate and unique cultural mix.

Accommodation is at a three-star hotel two minutes from the lakeside, with indoor and outdoor swimming pools, sauna, bar and sun terrace, in a room with private facilities. This exclusive offer price includes scheduled flights from Heathrow or Stansted to Zurich, half-board accommodation and rail transfers Zurich-Lugano.

For further details call Highlight Travel on 0990 143425. (GLC members quote last four digits of membership number for additional £10 discount.)

Answers are on page 158.

Uses of language

■ All texts are written for a purpose, and writers try to influence how readers respond through a variety of techniques.

■ You need to be able to recognise and analyse how writers use language in non-fiction texts to achieve their purpose.

SAUNTON

£249,000

· Magnificently situated individual detached house
· Superb south-facing views over the golf course and out to sea · Central heating · 4 bedrooms
· 2 receptions · Bathroom · Shower room
· Cloaks · Detached garage · Approx 1 acre

◎ Sly persuasion!

■ Single words which convey the writer's opinion can masquerade as facts. This device can often make the reader believe that what he/she is told is the truth. Examples are:
  - the house advertisement which used words such as 'magnificent' and 'superb' (page 1)
  - Paul Theroux describing Margate as 'crummy' (page 2)
  - the leaflet about Granary Wharf which, amongst many examples, used words such as 'unique' and 'fascinating' (page 3)

■ This technique is used frequently by advertisers or people who are trying to sell something.

■ Using **casual language** – or even slang – makes the reader even more likely to believe it, as it sounds friendly and trustworthy.

◎ Feelings

■ The Theroux piece on Margate also provides an example of how writers sometimes use physical descriptions to evoke feelings in readers. He writes about:

> people down from London for the day shunting back and forth on the front in the cold rain

  - Theroux is saying quite a lot in these apparently simple words: 'shunting' (rather than, say, 'walking' or 'strolling') suggests people going to and fro, like railway carriages in a siding, creating a miserable, aimless feel.
  - The mention of 'the cold rain' gives the impression that Margate is really a pretty dreadful place, full of sad, wet people.

◎ Nothing but the truth?

■ Advertisers in particular are skilled at not telling the whole truth, while not exactly lying. In the leaflet on pages 10–11), the bicycle tyres were advertised as costing 'from £13.95', and giving a ride 'virtually identical' to normal tyres. No lies are told, but it's not quite the whole truth either.

- A similar technique is when a writer avoids saying exactly what he or she means. This may be because they are frightened of the consequences (if, for example, they are writing about someone still alive who might accuse them of libel) or because they are trying to sound clever or inventive. This is part of an obituary for Dame Violet Dickson:

> wholly without intellectual pretensions
>
> - The author actually means that she was not very clever.

◎ Appealing to our worst instincts

- Some statements can imply **snobbery**. The tyre leaflet refers to the 'technicians' who will fit the tyres. This is rather like calling dustmen 'refuse disposal operatives': it doesn't change the job they do, but makes it sound grander.

- Snobbery is also present in the 'Nile in Style' holiday advertisement (page 17), where words and phrases such as 'exclusive' and 'accompanied by a qualified Egyptologist' are designed to capture the interest of those easily persuaded that certain lifestyles can be bought for a few hundred pounds.

- The other holiday advertisement offers the same kind of temptation, referring to:

> where the flamboyant warmth of Italy combines with the cool efficiency of southern Switzerland.
>
> - This is also an example of the first technique – opinion masquerading as fact – but only very confident, well-travelled readers would dispute the descriptions of the flamboyant warmth of Italy or the cool efficiency of southern Switzerland: most would unthinkingly accept this as true.

- A variation on the straightforward approach to snobbery is the use of what has been called 'technobabble' – language which the reader may not quite understand, but which sounds very impressive. The tyre leaflet shows an example of this when it says that the puncture-proof tyre:

> encapsulates an air-bubble foam core within a tough resistant Urathane skin.
>
> - The advertisers want people to believe that anything described in such terms must be good.

⚡ A/A* EXTRA

- ▸ You need to be able to 'analyse a range of uses of language and their effect'.

- ▸ Language can be used to create all kinds of group identity, not just snobbery or 'technobabble'.

- ▸ Advertisements for holidays for young people, such as Club 18–30, may use crudely suggestive language to shock and exclude anyone who might feel uncomfortable with the sort of holiday being promoted.

◎ Colourful phrases and other devices

- Writers use **original**, **colourful phrases** in a genuine effort to persuade the reader of an idea or to create a particular picture. Roald Dahl does this when he writes of the passengers on the boat in the extract from *Going Solo* on page 2:

> just about everybody had his or her own particular maggot in the brain ...
>
> - This is both amusing and, the more you think about the image, disturbing. It is certainly a more creative use of language than that used in the tyre leaflet or holiday advertisements.

- Writers use a number of devices to draw attention to what they are saying. As well as the sort of images Roald Dahl uses, they use rhymes, puns, deliberate misspellings and so on.

- Sometimes the simplest of methods can be used to convey the intensity of feeling of the writer. The repetition used by George Bernard Shaw in the letter to Stella Campbell on page 5 is one example. The Granary Wharf leaflet (page 3) uses a similar technique:

> It's friendly, it's fun and it's free.
>
> - Here, there is repetition backed up by alliteration.

◎ Dear Reader

- There are some techniques used in non-fiction writing which make it seem that the writer is addressing the reader directly, to try and sound more sincere.

- Sometimes the reader is directly questioned, drawn into a mental discussion and made to think about the subject matter of a text. This technique was used in the Oxfam leaflet on page 14:

> How can your £2 a month help poor people to help themselves?

- A similar, but more direct approach is to address the reader in the tones of a command. This can cause a feeling of being wilfully awkward if the command is not obeyed.

- Another aspect of this technique is to adopt a very friendly, conversational style (sometimes called a 'colloquial' style), to make it sound as though the reader is being spoken to directly by someone who then begins to sound like a personal friend and so becomes very hard to ignore. Good examples of this occur in the accounts of the daily routines of the seafront attendant ('Weather permitting, that is') and the lighthouse keeper on page 15:

We're the only legalised flashers in the country, so to speak.

- You may groan at the feeble pun, but it probably makes you feel friendly towards him and, indeed, remember what he has said.

◎ Humour

- **Humour** is often used by writers who are trying to engage the interest of their readers. Jokes may be both **linguistic** and **visual** – as, for example, in Edward Lear's letter to Mr Fortescue (page 5).

- The early twentieth-century comic writer, P.G. Wodehouse, wrote the following to his adopted daughter, Leonora (whom he calls Snorky):

Darling Snorky,
You may well imagine the excitement your letter caused in the home. Mummie was having a bath when she got it and rushed out with a towel round her shrieking for me. Winks barked, 1 shouted, and a scene of indescribable confusion eventuated.

- The comedy is partly in the **situation** but also in the **language**, which uses the 'smart' talk of the 1930s. **Exaggeration** adds to the humorous effect.

? CHECK YOURSELF QUESTIONS

Q1 Read the following extract from Bill Bryson's account of a journey around Great Britain, *Notes from a Small Island*. He is in a small hotel in Bournemouth.

Write down one example in this passage of each of the following writing techniques:
- opinion made to sound like fact
- humour
- addressing the reader
- effective descriptive language

Among the many hundreds of things that have come a long way in Britain since 1973, and if you stop to think about it for even a moment, you'll see that the list is impressively long, few have come further than the average English hostelry. Nowadays you get a colour TV, coffee-making tray with a little packet of modestly tasty biscuits, a private bath with fluffy towels, a little basket of cotton-wool balls in rainbow colours, and an array of sachets, little plastic bottles of shampoo, bath gel and moisturizing lotion. My room even had an adequate bedside light and two soft pillows. 1 was very happy. 1 ran a deep bath, emptied into it all the gels and moisturizing creams (don't be alarmed; I've studied this closely and can assure you that they are all the same substance), and, as a fiesta of airy bubbles began their slow ascent towards a position some three feet above the top of the bath, returned to the room and slipped easily into the self-absorbed habits of the lone traveller, unpacking my rucksack with deliberative care, draping wet clothes over the radiator, laying out clean ones on the bed with as much fastidiousness as if 1 were about to go to my first high-school prom, arranging a travel clock and reading material with exacting precision on the bedside table, adjusting the lighting to a level of considered cosiness, and finally retiring, in perky spirits and with a good book, for a long wallow in the sort of luxuriant foam seldom seen outside of Joan Collins movies.

Answers are on page 159.

Structural and presentational devices

■ Writers can achieve specific effects through the structure and presentation of their work.

■ You need to be able to comment on the ways in which writers do this, their purpose and how effective they are.

◎ Structures

■ **Structural** devices are those which affect *how* the text is written.

BREAKING UP THE TEXT

■ Writers of non-fiction usually try to present **easily digested text**. There are some exceptions to this – private letters and diaries, for example, may be quite difficult for outsiders to interpret – but the point of most non-fiction is to convey information to the reader.

■ It is important for information to be presented clearly. Many non-fiction texts are structured in '**bite-size chunks**'.

■ Writers may use some or all of the following techniques:
  • short sections of text with **headings**, e.g. the Granary Wharf leaflet (page 3)
  • small amounts of text spread about a page, often arranged around one or more **illustrations**, e.g. the inside of the Urathon tyres leaflet (pages 10–11)
  • **key words or phrases in a list** (often 'bullet-pointed') rather than continuous prose, e.g. the house advertisement (page 1)
  • **charts**, **graphs** or **maps**, which, if well presented, can take the place of many words, e.g. the information about music sales (page 6)

HEADINGS

■ **Headings** have different purposes, depending on the nature of the material. The heading of the house advertisement (page 1) is the name of the village where the house is situated. The headings in the Granary Wharf leaflet (page 3) are there to **attract attention** ('A unique place'), then to convey that it's convenient ('30 shops, open 7 days a week') and easy to reach ('Right in the centre of Leeds'). Some people might not even read the rest of the print: those three headlines alone would be enough to persuade them to visit Granary Wharf.

GRANARY WHARF

GRANARY WHARF

A unique place

Entertainments, special events, music, workshops, canal walks, boat trips and eating facilities for all tastes...there's always plenty to see and do at Granary Wharf.

It's friendly, it's fun and it's free.

FESTIVAL MARKET

30 shops, open 7 days a week

A fascinating selection of original goods and gifts, and a festival market (up to sixty additional stalls) every Saturday, Sunday and Bank Holiday Monday.
Shops open 10.00am to 5.30pm.

Right in the centre of Leeds

Granary Wharf is behind the Hilton Hotel in Neville Street, just two minutes walk from Leeds Railway Station. Access is via the 'Dark Arches'; look out for a small illuminated sign under the railway bridge. Ample parking. Special arrangements for coaches.

GRANARY WHARF THE CANAL BASIN
LEEDS LS1 4BR TEL (0113) 2446570

- The headings in the Urathon tyre leaflet (pages 10–11) are there for a similar reason – there is hardly any need to read the rest of the words, except in one important place: the section headed 'HOW IT'S DONE', where the manufacturers would clearly quite like the reader to be dazzled by details of the technology.

- Headings can be used to **make the reader think**, or even to feel guilty in the hope that the writer's message will make its point. The Oxfam leaflet (page 14) has a main heading which attracts attention by asking a question (and assuming that the reader would want to know the answer) and then three sub-headings which answer this question in different ways. This technique ensures that even the quickest glance at the page will get the message across.

Presentational devices

- **Presentational** devices are to do with the *appearance* of the text on the page.

- Among the most common presentational devices are:
  - frames
  - illustrations
  - colour
  - different print styles and sizes
  - logos, symbols, etc.

FRAMES

- A frame can be put around text to make it stand out on the page. At its most simple, this can be seen in the house advertisement (page 1).

ILLUSTRATIONS

- Illustrations serve a number of purposes. Above all, they make text look more **attractive** and **interesting**, and at the same time present an **image** of the information, product or idea being featured.

- The photograph of the house in the advertisement (page 1) is intended to **attract** the reader; the photograph of the boy riding his bike in the Urathon leaflet (page 11) is intended to **show** that the tyres are fashionable and appealing to a certain group of people; and the photographs of the people in the Oxfam leaflet (page 14) are intended to **make the reader feel involved**: he or she could contribute to this sense of well-being by contributing to the charity.

- Advertisements, or publicity of any kind which has **selling something** as its main purpose, will often employ illustrations. More informal drawings may be used to make a book look more attractive, or to help explain aspects of the text.

SAUNTON

NEW INSTRUCTION

£249,000
- Magnificently situated individual detached house
- Superb south-facing views over the golf course and out to sea • Central heating • 4 bedrooms
- 2 receptions • Bathroom • Shower room
- Cloaks • Detached garage • Approx 1 acre

▸ You need to be able to give 'sustained and developed views about how presentational devices achieve their purpose'.

▸ When commenting on font sizes and styles, you could suggest how the reader's eye is drawn to different parts of the text in a particular sequence.

▸ You might say how similar fonts may be used to link parts of a text and so help the reader follow the argument (or, often, to trap the reader into agreeing with the writer's point of view!).

COLOUR

■ **Colour** can add to (or sometimes detract from) the effect of a text. Full-colour printing is expensive, and non-fiction materials may not always use full colour.

■ A limited use of colour can still be eye-catching. The use of just black, white and yellow in the Urathon leaflet is effective. The Oxfam leaflet may look a little dowdy and cheap, but even this can be an advantage. People who are thinking of giving to the charity wouldn't want to see their money being spent on colourful leaflets.

PRINT

■ Many different **styles and sizes of print** are used in non-fiction writing. When responding to this aspect of texts, consider:
  - the use of different **font sizes**, for example, larger print in a heading and smaller print for information which the writer may feel is not so important (e.g. the Granary Wharf information on page 3);
  - the use of different **font styles** to create particular effects or images. The Urathon tyres leaflet uses a 'clean', modern font which reinforces the modern scientific/technological aspects. With a huge range of fonts available on modern word-processing systems, writers often use them to create particular effects, such as 'old English' or 'medieval' fonts to suggest something tried, tested and traditional;
  - the use of **devices** such as upper case, or bold and/or italicised writing to draw the reader's attention.

LOGOS AND SYMBOLS

■ Just as illustrations may take the place of words, or help to explain words, writers of non-fiction may use **logos** and **symbols** to strengthen their message.

■ Logos are mostly used to try and fix the image of a company or an organisation in the reader's mind, so that he or she instantly identifies it when seen again, such as the ATS logo in the Urathon tyres leaflet and the Oxfam logo at the bottom of the appeal sheet.

■ Symbols are an economical way of either **explaining** or **instructing**. In the answerphone instructions, arrows, ticks and crosses help to explain the written instructions, while on the Oxfam appeal (page 14), a small pair of scissors shows that, on the original leaflet, there was a page to complete, cut off and send away if you wished to contribute to the appeal.

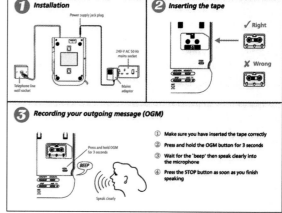

CHECK YOURSELF QUESTIONS

Q1 Look at the Lodge Inns leaflet reproduced below. Write a brief paragraph which comments on its effectiveness, mentioning aspects of the structure and presentation, such as:

- use of headings
- fonts and sizes of typeface
- use of colour
- use of photographs
- overall layout
- audience

LODGE INNS

Where comfort costs less...
Just £37.50 per room, per night.

At Lodge Inns we recognise you expect exceptional standards as well as excellent value for money. Whether you are on the move on business, or with friends or family, you can rest assured that every Lodge Inn location will offer the very best in affordable accommodation.

All of our sites offer the same high standards of facilities.

- Full en suite bathroom with power shower
- Double bed with sheets and quilted bedcover
- Family rooms with additional sofa bed*
- Remote control TV and radio alarm
- Tea and coffee
- Well lit working area with desk and chair

All Lodge Inns also offer cots, a choice of smoking or non-smoking rooms, rooms with connecting doors for families with older children and rooms adapted for disabled guests as well as conveniently located payphone cubicles.

*Our double sofa beds are ideal for younger children to share up to the age of 12. Rooms with interconnecting doors are available for those with older children. Please ask for this service when booking.

EASY TO DO BUSINESS WITH.

Making a reservation is easy – you can book up to 1 year in advance by either calling us direct or phoning Central Reservations Office on the number below. You can check in from 2pm onwards, and as our Receptionists are available until 11pm, later guests will find our friendly staff waiting. Payment at Lodge Inns is made upon arrival and we accept cash, Access, Visa, American Express, travellers cheques, Switch or Diners cards. We also offer the advantage of payment via Company Account – please ask for details.

THE BEST PUBS & RESTAURANTS.

Whichever Lodge Inn you choose you'll always find a pub-restaurant conveniently located immediately next door – the perfect choice for a relaxing drink or meal.

THERE'S ONE NEAR YOU...

HUDDERSFIELD – The Nags Head
New Hey Road, Fixby, Huddersfield, HO2 2EA.
Tel: 01422 373 758 Fax: 01422 370 441

Situated ½ mile from junction 24 of M62. At large roundabout take the A643 Brighouse Road, turn first left after 300 yards. Go to the end of Grimescar Road, turn right.

Next to our Country Carvery Pub Restaurant. Traditional British Fayre served in informal surroundings. Hors d'oeurves from the starter bar, freshly carved roast meats and tempting desserts.

CENTRAL RESERVATIONS OFFICE 0990 39 38 39
OPEN DURING OFFICE HOURS MONDAYS TO FRIDAYS.

2/97

Answers are on page 159.

Different types of non-fiction

KEY EXAM SKILLS

- There are many different types of non-fiction text.
- You need to be able to recognise and comment on the main features and qualities of each type, their purpose and their effect on the reader.

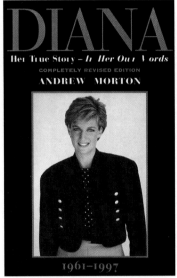

Biography: fact or opinion?

◎ Autobiography/biography

- **Autobiographies** and **biographies** are treated as non-fiction texts, although because they are books about people's lives, they are bound to contain judgements or opinions alongside facts.

> • See Revision session 1 on how to assess fact and opinion (page 1).

- Sometimes **fact and opinion will be mixed**: an author may give a factual account of an event, but then claim to know what was going through the minds of the people involved, or what it tells us about their personalities.

- The author may put forward a particular point of view or argument, for example, that he or she was treated badly by relatives or that a well-known person was dishonest. There are often **implications** and **inconsistencies** in what the author says.

> • See Revision session 3 on following and analysing arguments (page 9).

- Autobiographies and biographies are the category of non-fiction which is closest to fiction in terms of structure, style and imagination, so responding to the author's **use of language** is particularly important.

> • See Revision session 5 on use of language (page 18).

◎ Journals/diaries/letters

- **Journals**, **diaries** and **letters** have similarities to autobiography, but it may be even more difficult to distinguish between fact, opinion and lies.

- If they were written without publication in mind, they will probably be mostly truthful, but may still contain a good deal of opinion.

- If they were written with a view to publication, they will probably be as carefully crafted as an autobiography or a novel.

> • The issues raised in Revision sessions 1, 3 and 5 are all relevant (pages 1, 9 and 18).

- In texts which were intended to be private, writers may use a number of techniques or presentational devices (e.g. jokes, sketches) which they might not have used in a more formal situation. These may give particular insights into the attitudes and intentions of the writer.

> • Revision sessions 2 and 5 give guidance on analysing and commenting on the author's purpose (pages 4 and 18).

◎ Travel writing

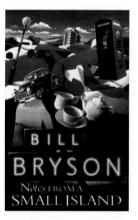

- **Travel writing** frequently has an autobiographical element to it, or aspects of biography if a modern writer is retracing the footsteps of someone from an previous era.

- It can also have the intimacy of a journal, and may even be written in the form of letters or a diary.

- Identifying fact and opinion and considering the author's use of language are particularly important when analysing travel writing.

> • Look at Revision sessions 1, 2 and 5 for more on travel writing; fact and opinion; and use of language (pages 1, 4 and 18).

◎ Leaflets

- **'Leaflet'** covers a variety of texts, ranging from pure information which might be published by a government department, through a mixture of information and advertising, to pure advertising.

- Whatever the purpose of the leaflet, it will always be trying to **convey information** to you as powerfully as possible. The information may contain fact, opinion, arguments, inconsistencies, striking language and a whole range of structural and presentational devices.

> • See Revision sessions 3, 5 and 6 (pages 9, 18 and 22).

◎ Newspaper articles/other factual and informative materials

- When responding to newspaper articles, or any other form of non-fiction which claims to be setting out facts or giving information, go through a mental checklist, such as:
  - Who's it for?
  - What's the balance of fact and opinion?
  - How is it written?
  - Is it successful?
  - What's it for?
  - How is it presented?
  - What's it all about?
  - What do I feel about it?

- Ask yourself 'why?' when answering each of the above questions so that you can find evidence in the text.

> • See Revision session 8 for more on newspapers (page 28).

Different types of media texts

- You should be able to recognise different types of media texts.

- You need to be able to comment on the audiences they are targeted to reach, and how their structure and presentation aim to reach these different audiences.

⚡ A/A* EXTRA

▶ You need to be able to analyse 'patterns and details of language, presentational devices and visual images' in different types of media texts.

▶ You need to show that you understand the different social, gender or age groups media texts are aimed at.

▶ The Diana biography (see page 26) would probably appeal to quite a range of readers because the appeal is to young people who admired her beauty or who sympathised with her problems, as well as to middle-aged or older people with a general interest in the royal family.

▶ The large photo and the words 'Her true story' 'hook' both audiences.

◎ What are media texts?

- Media texts are **radio**, **film**, **television**, **magazines** and **newspapers**.

- There is some overlap between non-fiction texts and media texts, particularly in print-based media (such as newspapers and magazines).

- Response to media is all about how particular effects are achieved and the success of a text in relation to its **target audience** and **intended purpose**.

- For practical reasons, GCSE written exams tend to limit themselves to print-based materials in media response questions.

◎ Audiences

- A great deal of non-fiction writing is addressed to particular **audiences**: those who like travel, those who are interested in charities, those who want to read about the lives of other people, etc.

- In media terms, audiences tend to be broader groups, categorised by income and/or occupation in addition to, rather than by, interest

- Some media texts are aimed very much at broad groups which might be labelled low-, middle- or high-income.

- Until recently, the media were often known as 'the mass media', and this usefully conveys the idea that writers working in the media need to identify carefully which members of a potentially huge audience they intend to target.

- On the next page is the lead article from a 1997 edition of a magazine called *Countryside*, which is distributed to members of the National Farmers Union. The nature of the audience is not in doubt, given the content of the article.

NFU
COUNTRYSIDE
The Journal for NFU Countryside Members　　　　June 1997

British food is clearly the best, and how to prove it beyond doubt to supermarkets, caterers and the general public, is the aim of a new industry-wide farm standards initiative being promoted by NFU. Alison Pratt reports.

Our livestock industry, and the whole of agriculture, learned some salutary lessons in 1996. The BSE crisis so alarmed our customers that they now want to know, more than ever, that the animals and crops which provide their food have been grown, reared and produced to the highest possible standards.

NFU has undertaken to support and promote high quality food production and husbandry standards in conjunction with industry bodies such as the Meat and Livestock Commission (MLC), the Milk Development Council and representatives from the arable and horticulture sectors. The NFU has also held discussions with the multiple retailers many of which run their own assurance schemes.

NFU is currently looking at a single "baseline" standard which would ensure that farmers and growers comply with all relevant food hygiene, health and safety, animal welfare and agrochemical usage regulations. NFU President, Sir David Naish said, "Such a baseline standard would ensure that, in a few years time, the bulk of food and raw materials leaving British farms would have been produced under independently-audited farm assurance schemes."

Inspection, enforcement and auditing are the key aspects of a standardised farm assurance scheme. How else are consumers to know that they are certain to be served the quality they expect from British food? The extra layers of the scheme could, of course, impact upon producers' costs when measures such as registration, inspection and self-assessment are introduced. But the possibility of expanding into new markets and ensuring customer loyalty to British produce can only benefit the industry.

NFU and indeed, the whole of the food production industry, is at the beginning of a long process, consulting and formulating the new standards and structures to ensure the new scheme will be acceptable to producers, processors, retailers and, especially, the consumer.

"It is not enough any more to blithely say that we produce food of the highest quality to some of the toughest standards in the world," said Sir David Naish. "BSE has shown us that such a claim counts for nothing if we cannot prove it. We must show to the satisfaction of all that the very highest standards are being pursued at all times."

British food is the best by far

- Someone seeing just the map and the headline in the above article might have expected it to be about restaurants or traditional dishes rather than farming. Knowing where the article was published and reading the actual content is necessary to make proper sense of it.

- Because the particular audience for this article will have certain expectations, it does not need to be balanced in its views. Many people not involved in food production would feel that the article puts forward a very **biased** view, offering opinions as facts.

- It appeals to the patriotism of readers both in the frequent references to Britain and in the eye-catching map with part of the Union Jack overlaid onto it.

- In case readers do not want to study the whole text, the argument is summed up in the brief, bold paragraph at the start. For those who do wish to read the whole article, their eyes are led to the start by the large, green initial capital.

- Although it is an article which is fighting the corner for farmers, the very subtle background to the page is an idyllic rural scene, again mostly in restful, calm shades of green.

◎ Media language

■ When analysing and responding to the language used in media texts, consider:

- **single words or phrases** which try to influence how the reader feels, often dressing opinion as fact
- **evocative phrases** which influence the reader's feelings but which do not stand up to close analysis
- **claims which are truthful up to a point**: for example, a disinfectant which 'kills all known germs' is not in fact claiming to kill all germs, though the advertisers hope that is what you will think
- **snobbery** and its opposite, **fear**: for example, frequent uses of terms like 'exclusive' or 'executive', and all those television advertisements which try to make people worry about how white their washing is
- **direct appeals to the reader**/listener/viewer: for example, eye contact in television advertisements or documentaries can draw the viewer into the action and make it difficult to ignore or disagree with the speaker
- **humour**, such as punning newspaper headlines

Content and purpose

- Media texts direct their **content** as well as their **language** and their **presentation** at target audiences. The NFU magazine is an obvious example, and the tabloid press, particularly papers such as *The Sun*, the *Daily Mirror* and the *Star* base their content around what might be called 'human interest stories' rather than British politics or international news.

- **Headlines** in the tabloids are often jokey and not always 'politically correct' especially if dealing with international affairs.

- The media often display a **stereotypical** view of their audience and its interests: men's and women's magazines have very different content. Some broadsheet papers run special pages or articles for women readers which assume they, and not men, are interested in matters such as fashion, health and emotional well-being.

- Think about the content of media texts in relation to their **target audience** in order to judge how effective they are likely to be in achieving their purpose, whether that purpose is reinforcing strongly held views through the content of the text or capturing the interest of an audience through the use of a headline.

Structural and presentational devices

- In a magazine, the use of **headings**, **lists**, **frames**, **illustrations**, **different font styles** and **sizes** will often be more extreme than in, for example, an information leaflet. The magazine, as a commercial publication, is out to catch the interest (and the money) of an audience and so will set out for maximum visual effect (and maximum linguistic effect through highly emotional – or intriguing – headlines).

- Many of the techniques referred to in Revision session 6 (page 22) also apply to media texts.

- A similar contrast can be seen between **tabloid** newspapers, which more and more exhibit magazine-like qualities to the almost total exclusion of 'serious' news, and the **broadsheet** papers which use fewer illustrations, a more consistent typeface, longer stories, analytical features, and less contrived headlines.

Q1 Look closely at the following two magazine covers. Write down:

a what the covers have in common

b what makes them different

c what the cover of each magazine suggests about its contents

d what the intended audience is for each magazine.

Give as many details and as much evidence for your answers as you can. Write paragraphs of 60–80 words in answer to questions a) and b) and of about 100–120 words in answer to questions c) and d).

Answers are on page 160.

Poetry – sound effects and imagery

■ Poets use sound and imagery to convey ideas, feelings and levels of meaning.

■ You need to be able to explain how poets use sound and imagery to create different effects.

KEY EXAM SKILLS

◎ Exploiting sound effects

CONSONANTS

■ Alexander Pope wrote this six-line lesson in choosing words for their **sound effects**:

> But when loud surges lash the sounding shore,
> The hoarse, rough verse should like the torrent roar.
> When Ajax strives, some rock's vast weight to throw,
> The line, too, labours, and the words move slow;
> Not so, when swift Camilla lightly scours the plain,
> Flies o'er th' unbending corn, and skims along the main.

- Pope chooses words with 's' and 'sh' sounds in the first line, to make the reader's lips work at the hissing noises of the sea, then words with 'r' sounds in the second line, making the reader's throat do some rasping work. These are forceful, vigorous sounds for a physically violent scene.
- He creates a calmer effect by using words which contain 'm' and 'n' sounds, produced by letting air out through the nose, not working the throat, lips, tongue or teeth. These sounds are more soothing and mellow, fit for a description of gentle lightness.

⚡ A/A* EXTRA

▸ You need to demonstrate close textual analysis of the poet's use of language.

▸ You might write that Pope uses short vowel sounds in 'swift Camilla' and 'skims' to create a sense of speed, and long, open vowels in 'words move slow' to create a very different sense of pace.

■ Tennyson, wanting to recreate the drowsy heat of a summer day in his poem *In Memoriam*, wrote of:

> The moan of doves in immemorial elms
> And the murmuring of innumerable bees

- Making repeated use of chosen consonants is called **alliteration**.

VOWELS

- The main **vowels** are 'a', 'e', 'i', 'o' and 'u', but 'w' and 'y' can also sometimes act as vowel sounds.

- Vowels are all made with an open mouth, but they can each be pronounced in two different ways, called **'short'** and **'long'**. Short vowels together tend to give pace to a line, producing a hurrying effect. Long vowels can slow a line down, or make it sound more sad and weary. Each of the five main vowels can be short and long, as in the following examples:

SHORT	cat	get	fit	box	gut
LONG	staple	be	fine	nose	use

- If a writer wants to suggest **sadness** and **grief**, long vowels help:

> Oh, woe is me, with hurt I moan and cry
> Life holds no more, I'll surely die

- If a writer wants to suggest **brisk, light-hearted energy**, short vowels will help:

> I'm back, and glad, no longer in the pits
> Yippee, I'm chuffed and thrilled to bits

- Play on vowels is called **assonance**.

VOWELS AND CONSONANTS TOGETHER

- Gerard Manley Hopkins combines long vowels and repeated 'l' sounds in this line from *Spring* which suggests flowing growth:

> When weeds, in wheels, shoot long and lovely and lush

- Jon Silkin mixes short vowels and consonants in this description from the poem *Dandelion*:

> Slugs nestle where the stem,
> Broken, bleeds milk.
> The flower is eyeless: the sight is compelled
> By small, coarse, sharp petals,
> Like metal shreds. Formed,
> They puncture, irregularly perforate
> Their yellow, brutal glare.
> And certainly want to
> Devour the earth.

- Silkin uses consonants which are produced at the back of the mouth ('g' and 'c') or exploded as compressed air from shaped lips ('p' and 'b' sounds) help to suggest violence and ugliness.

- Verbal sound effects help to **create mood** and **suggest character**. When you read a poem or write about it, remember to look for ways in which the poet repeats sound patterns or chooses words for sounds which match the sense.

◎ Imagery

- Anyone asked to explain or describe something new to someone else will usually begin by comparing it with something the other person knows or can easily imagine. Saying that the sea is 'as calm as a pond' or that someone moves 'as elegantly as a pig on ice' helps the listener by creating an image he or she can relate to. The simplest form of linking by likeness is simile.

SIMILE

- A **simile** is a stated likeness, using 'like a' or 'as ... as a ...' to make a comparison. Similes are a common part of everyday speech, such as when people refer to 'shaking like a leaf', being 'like a fish out of water' or 'like two peas in a pod'.

- Rupert Brooke wanted to suggest that going off to war was as invigorating and refreshing as diving into fresh water:

> like swimmers into cleanness leaping

- Wilfred Owen used a simile to compare the feeling of what it was like to be caught in the brutality of war with the helpless sensation of being burnt by either flames or quicklime:

> like a man in fire or lime

- Seamus Heaney uses a simile in *Trout* to make an explicit comparison of the rapid fish-movement with something shot from a gun:

> darts like a tracer-
> bullet back between the stones

METAPHOR

- **Imagery** can come from all areas of life: from athletics, we get the expression 'toe the line'; from swimming, we get 'jump in at the deep end'; war and soldiering have left us with 'sticking to your guns', to name but a few.

- Using expressions which belong literally to something else in a different context means they cannot be literally true. There is no 'deep end' in an argument for us to jump into. We call these expressions **metaphors** and their strength lies in the suggestiveness.

- When Wilfred Owen described the dawn on the day of an attack during the first world war, he wrote that:

> dawn masses in the east
>
> - This suggests that dawn is like a hostile army, 'massing' itself ready for an attack.

- Tony Harrison described his family as a unit held together with a kind of electric energy, but this stopped when he broke away from his parents:

> I'd be the one to make that circuit short.

- Gareth Owen writes of a rocket launch like this:

> Out of the furnace
> The great fish rose
> Its silver tail on fire

- Look at this excerpt from Seamus Heaney's poem *Trout*:

> Where water unravels
> over gravel beds he
> is fired from the shadows
> white belly reporting
>
> flat; darts like a tracer-
> bullet back between the stones
> and is never burnt out
> A volley of cold blood
>
> Ramrodding the current
>
> - Heaney makes the creature seem powerful and dangerous by using words connected with gunfire and weaponry.

ANIMATING AND PERSONIFYING

- In the previous poem, a living creature was compared with mechanical objects, inanimate things, to create a specific impression. Metaphorical language can also create vivid effects by making **inanimate objects** seem as if they are **alive**.

- If the writer chooses words which are usually associated with animals or human beings, it can make a place or object seem to come to life. Reread the lines on page 17 which come from Jon Silkin's poem *Dandelion*. Notice how he chooses words which give it qualities associated with animals or humans. It is described as tough and determined to survive. Verbs like 'puncture', 'perforate' and 'devour' all make the plant seem an active and destructive creature. Also, the dandelion is described as 'bleeding', as if wounded, and 'eyeless'.

- Thomas Hardy thought that human beings were helpless creatures suffering under the cruel play of Time. He was used to living in the country, where he saw pheasants hatched and raised by a gamekeeper ready for the shooting season. This gave him a metaphor for Time as something that seems to be on our side, but has its own purpose:

> Sportsman Time but rears his brood to kill.

- Giving human intentions to something abstract like Time humanises it. This is usually called **personification**.

EXTENDED METAPHOR

- A poem can be full of all sorts of different images, or it may play with one image, which becomes an **extended metaphor**, where the poet deliberately tries to work the comparison as far as it will go.

- In his poem *Mastering the Craft*, Vernon Scannell shows that poetry and boxing have lots in common, not only because they both need practice and skill, but because both can involve a surprising knockout:

> To make the big time you must learn
> The basic moves: left jab and hook,
> The fast one-two, right-cross; the block
> And counter-punch; the way to turn
> Opponents on the ropes; the feint
> To head or body; uppercut;
> To move inside the swing and set
> Your man up for the kill. But don't
> Think that this is all; a mere
> Beginning only. It is through
> Fighting often you will grow
> Accomplished in manúuvres more
> Subtle than the text books know:
> How to change your style to meet
> The unexpected move that might

⚡ A/A* EXTRA

▸ You need to demonstrate close textual analysis of the poet's use of language.

▸ You might write that Vernon Scannell links boxing and poetry by referring to training in skills and manoeuvres which make an impact on the opponent or reader: pace, repetitions and the strongest impact at the end.

Leave you open to the blow
That puts the lights out for the night.

The same with poets: they must train,
Practise metre's footwork, learn
The old iambic left and right,
To change the pace and how to hold
The big punch till the proper time,
Jab away with accurate rhyme;
Adapt the style or be knocked cold.
But first the groundwork must be done.
Those poets who have never learnt
The first moves of the game, they can't
Hope to win.
    Yet here comes one,
No style at all, untrained and fat,
Who still contrives to knock you flat.

■ Imagery is a **literary** device, not a literal one, because it helps to convey meaning without having to be strictly – literally – true. When you are reading, or writing about poems, look for examples of imagery, and say why the imagery is appropriate and how the linkage is effective for you.

CHECK YOURSELF QUESTIONS

Q1 Read this poem, *City Jungle* by Pie Corbett.

  a How does the poet use sound effects and imagery to make a city scene seem jungle-like?

  b What does it make you feel about a city at night?

Rain splinters town.

Lizard cars cruise by;
Their radiators grin.

Thin headlights stare –
shop doorways keep their mouths shut.

At the roadside
Hunched houses cough.

Newspapers shuffle by,
hands in their pockets.
The gutter gargles.

A motorbike snarls;
Dustbins flinch.

Streetlights bare
Their yellow teeth.
The motorway's
cat-black tongue
lashes across
the glistening back
of the tarmac night.

Answers are on page 161.

Poetry – purpose, tone and attitude

KEY EXAM SKILLS

- Poets use a variety of devices to convey their purpose and feelings towards the subject of their poem.

- You need to be able to explain how poets use language to convey feelings and levels of meaning and to influence the reader's attitude.

◎ Purpose

- Many poets think it is their business to surprise the reader, to say 'Hey – look at this!' They try to take away the dulling effect of familiarity, and show us something interesting about things we take for granted. And what does the poet rely on to pull off this trick? Just words.

- In his poem, *Fishing Harbour Towards Evening*, Richard Kell shows a violent side to nature, rather than a pretty, picture-postcard view:

> Slashed clouds leak gold. Along the slurping wharf
> The snugged boats creak and seesaw. Round the masts
> Abrasive squalls flake seagulls off the sky:
>
> - The poem uses words which suggest violence in a scene which, from the title, may have been a picturesque one.
> - There is a contrast between the 'snugged' boats along the wharf and the sky above, which is not blue with fluffy clouds, but violent, where the clouds appear wounded ('slashed') and 'leaking' as if bleeding, with winds 'abrasive' like a kitchen cleaner, sweeping gulls away.

- Many poets want to change the way we see things, so they choose to write about familiar objects or events in a way that gives a new perspective. When you read poems, or write about them, look for words, comparisons and ideas which change a common view, or challenge a cliché or stereotype.

◎ Tone

- The **tone**, or how the writer addresses the reader, is what conveys the attitude of the writer to the reader.

- Some poems are written as if the writer is speaking confidentially to their reader. Others may be very direct in telling the reader what needs to be said.

- In his poem *Weeds*, Norman Nicholson takes a direct approach to telling the reader what he thinks:

> Some people are flower lovers. I'm a weed lover.
>
> Weeds don't need planting in well-drained soil;
> They don't ask for fertiliser or bits of rag to scare away birds.
> They come without invitation;
> And they don't take the hint when you want them to go.
> Weeds are nobody's guests:
> More like squatters.

- Some poems may have the tone of telling the reader what to think. Dylan Thomas writes as someone urging the reader to listen and take advice about coping with old age. He is being instructive, telling his reader how to behave:

> Do not go gentle into that goodnight. Old age should rage against the dying of the light

◎ Attitude

- Poets do not always write their poems from their own point of view. They may adopt a persona, just as prose writers may let a character speak directly. In this extract from the poem *Dress Sense* by David Kitchen, the poet creates a character unlike himself, giving the character speech to make a point about parental attitudes:

> You're not going out in that, are you?
> I've never seen anything
> More ridiculous in my whole life.
> You look like you've been dragged
> Through a hedge backwards
> And lost half your dress along the way.
>
> What's wrong with it?
> You're asking me what's wrong with that?
> Everything: that's what.
> It's loud, it's common,
> It reveals far too much of your ...
> Your ... well your 'what you shouldn't be revealing'.
>
> No, I'm not going to explain;
> You know very well what I mean, young lady
> But you choose to ignore
> Every single piece of reasonable helpful advice
> That you are offered.

It's not just the neckline I'm talking about
– And you can hardly describe it as a neckline,
More like a navel-line
If you bother to observe the way that it plunges
Have you taken a look at the back?
(What little there is of it.)
Have you?

Boys are only going to think
One thing
When they see you in that outfit.
Where in earth did you get it?
And don't tell me that my money paid for it
Whatever you do.

You found it where?

Well, it probably looked different on her
And, anyway, you shouldn't be going through
Your mother's old clothes.

? CHECK YOURSELF QUESTIONS

Q1 Read the following poem, *Thistles* by Ted Hughes.

   a How does Ted Hughes try to make the reader see thistles afresh?

   b What attitude does he have towards these plants?

   c What do you think about *Thistles* now you have read it?

Against the rubber tongues of cows and the hoeing hands of men
Thistles spike the summer air
Or crackle open under a blue-black pressure

Every one a revengeful burst
Of resurrection, a grasped fistful
Of splintered weapons and Icelandic frost thrust up

From the underground stain of a decayed Viking.
They are like pale hair and the gutturals of dialects.
Every one manages a plume of blood.

Then they grow grey like men.
Mown down, it is a feud. their sons appear,
Stiff with weapons, fighting back over the same ground.

Answers are on page 161.

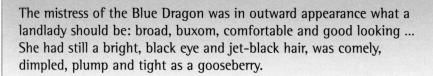

KEY EXAM SKILLS

- In fiction, authors use a range of different methods to create and reveal characters.

- You need to be able to comment in detail on these different methods

◎ Telling

- Authors have different ways of making characters seem real on the page. Sometimes, they may give information about them directly as part of the story:

> He was a bad-tempered, ungrateful man who hated children and only showed feelings for his cats.

- This is explicit information.
- The reader is told what to think about the character.

- Writers often use **appearance** to suggest character, without referring to what the characters do and say. The effect on the reader depends on the choice of vocabulary, which may be **positive** or **negative**, as you can see from this extract from *Martin Chuzzlewit* by Charles Dickens:

> The mistress of the Blue Dragon was in outward appearance what a landlady should be: broad, buxom, comfortable and good looking ... She had still a bright, black eye and jet-black hair, was comely, dimpled, plump and tight as a gooseberry.

- The words used to describe the landlady make her seem friendly and good company because they are to do with smiling and good eating.
- She is not skinny, bony and bad tempered, but 'buxom', 'dimpled' and 'plump', which makes us think that she smiles a lot and would be good for a cuddle.

◎ Showing through action

- An author can convey the same information about a character by describing **behaviour** and letting the reader form a **judgement** about the person based on what he or she does. In other words, the writer shows **character through action**:

> He gave no thanks for the help and scowled at the boys who had returned his cat, going inside, speaking softly to the wet animal.
>
> - The reader has to infer.
> - He 'scowls' at the boys; this is a negative signal.
> - He speaks 'softly' to the animal; this implies tenderness.
> - The reader's judgement is based on what he does, not what the author tells us explicitly.

- Look at the passage below from *Great Expectations*, where Charles Dickens uses the simplest of domestic activities to suggest the attitudes, manner and personality of Pip's older sister, who is his foster-parent:

> My sister had a very trenchant way of cutting our bread and butter for us that never varied. First, with her left hand, she *jammed* the loaf hard and fast against her bib – where it sometimes got a pin in it, and sometimes a needle, which we afterwards got into our mouths. Then, she took some butter (not too much) on a knife and spread it on the loaf, in an apothecary kind of way, as if she were making a plaister – using both sides of the knife with a slapping dexterity, and trimming and moulding the butter off round the crust. Then, she gave the knive a final smart wipe on the edge of the plaister, and then *sawed* a very thick round off the loaf; which she finally, before separating from the loaf, *hewed* into two halves, of which Joe got one and I the other.
>
> - The words in italics make you think of force and physical exercise. They are not words that would normally come to mind when making a snack.
>   - The verb 'jammed' suggests fierce and violent movement with a purpose.
>   - The verbs 'sawed' and 'hewed' suggest physical activities you would associate with a strong, labouring man.
> - The vocabulary suggests that, although she is doing something domestic, she attacks it with fierce and unfeminine energy.
> - The verbs 'trimming' and 'moulding' suggest exact, almost scientific precision.
> - She does not allow them 'too much' butter, which suggests meanness.
> - She gets pins into food, hinting that she is not very soft hearted or careful about their comfort.

◎ Showing through speech

■ Another way authors can create character without simply describing them is to let the reader judge them from what they say:

> 'Yes, that's my cat,' he said irritably.
> 'She's wet and hungry,' said Robert.
> 'I can see that myself,' he snapped, 'I don't need a nosy kid to tell me that!'
> 'I hope she'll be all right.'
> 'Yes. Now clear off.'

- This writer puts in further prompts about the character in the choice of speech-verb ('snapped') and adverbs ('irritably'). Other writers think this makes it too obvious, and let the reader pick up what they can from the speech alone.
- The boy's speech indicates concern about the cat's welfare, so the reader's sympathy is less likely to be with the man.

■ In the following extract from *Emma*, Jane Austen creates an impression of Mrs Elton by recording only what she says, adding no direct narrative comment or guidance to the reader:

> The whole party were assembled, excepting Frank Churchill, who was expected every moment from Richmond; and Mrs Elton, in all her apparatus of happiness, her large bonnet and her basket, was very ready to lead the way in gathering, accepting or talking. Strawberries, and only strawberries, could now be thought or spoken of. 'The best fruit in England – everybody's favourite – always wholesome. These the finest beds and finest sorts. Delightful to gather for one's self – the only way of really enjoying them. Morning decidedly the best time – never tired – every sort good – hautboy infinitely superior – no comparison – the others hardly eatable – hautboys very scarce – Chili preferred – white wood finest flavour of all – price of strawberries in London – abundance about Bristol – Maple Grove – cultivation – beds when to be renewed – gardeners thinking exactly different – no general rule – gardeners never to be put out of their way – delicious fruit – only too rich to be eaten much of – inferior to cherries – currants more refreshing – only objection to gathering strawberries the stooping – glaring sun – tired to death – could bear it no longer – must go and sit in the shade.

- Mrs Elton starts off full of enthusiasm, giving everyone the benefit of her superior opinions, then gets tired and ends up contradicting everything she has said previously.
- Jane Austen does not record every word of what Mrs Elton says – she just gives us 'sound-bites'.

◎ Showing through the unspoken

■ Sometimes it's what's **not** spoken that tells you more about the character's mood, manner or motive:

Are you quite sure?'
'Well ... yes ... I mean ... I, er, I'm sure, I am really.

- **Hesitations** suggest doubt and uncertainty, and although what the character says explicitly is that she is sure, the implied message is the opposite.
- The reader needs to ask the question 'Why is the speaker hesitating?' then find a motive which explains the behaviour.

◎ Using a mixture of techniques

■ Most writers use a mixture of different methods to reveal character. In this extract from *Martin Chuzzlewit*, Dickens uses narrative and speech to reveal Sarah Gamp's character:

She wore a very rusty black gown, rather the worse for snuff, and a shawl and bonnet to correspond. In these dilapidated articles of dress she had, on principle, arrayed herself, time out of mind, on such occasions as the present; for this at once expressed a decent amount of veneration for the deceased, and invited the next of kin to present her with a fresher suit of weeds [mourning clothes]: an appeal so frequently successful, that the very ghost of Mrs Gamp, bonnet and all, might be seen hanging up, any hour in the day, in at least a dozen of the second-hand clothes shops about Holborn. The face of Mrs Gamp – the nose in particular – was somewhat red and swollen, and it was difficult to enjoy her society without becoming conscious of a smell of spirits. [...]

If certain whispers current in the Kingsgate Street circles had any truth in them, she had indeed borne up surprisingly; and had exerted such incommon fortitude as to dispose of Mr Gamp's remains for the benefit of science. [...]

You have become indifferent since then, I suppose?' said Mr Pecksniff. 'Use is second nature, Mrs Gamp.'

'You may well say second nature, sir,' returned that lady. 'One's first ways is to find such things a trial to the feelings, and so is ones' lasting custom. If it wasn't for the nerve a little sip of liquor gives me (I never was able to do more than taste it), I never could go through with what I sometimes has to do. "Mrs Harris," I says, at the very last case as ever I acted in, which it was but a young person, "Mrs Harris," I says, "leave the bottle on the chimley-piece, and don't ask me to take none, but let me put my lips to it when I am so dispoged, and then I will do what I'm engaged to do, according to the best of my ability." "Mrs Gamp," she says, in answer, "if ever there was a sober ▶

Mrs Gamp

▶ You need to be able to analyse methods and effects of presentation of character.

▶ Dickens makes Mrs Gamp's speech sound as if she has a swollen nose by pronouncing 'disposed' as 'dispoged' and 'chimney' as 'chimley'.

▶ Drawing attention to her pronunciation reminds us that her nose is swollen from too much drinking.

creetur to be got at eighteen pence a day for working people, and three and six for gentlefolks – night watching,"' said Mrs Gamp, with emphasis, "'being an extra charge – you are that invallable person." "Mrs Harris," I says to her, "don't name the charge, for if I could afford to lay all my feller creeturs out for nothink, I would gladly do it, sich is the love I bears 'em. But what I always says to them as has the management of matters, Mrs Harris"' – here she kept her eye on Mr Pecksniff – "'be they gents or be they ladies, is, don't ask me whether I will, but leave the bottle on the chimley-piece, and let me put my lips to it when I am so dispoged."'

• Dickens' narrative gives us the impression of someone who is:
  – not sentimental about her dead husband (she sold his body for medical research);
  – quick to turn situations to financial advantage (she tries to get second-hand clothes passed on to her, and then sells them);
  – fond of drink (red nose, smelling of spirits).
• Mrs Gamp's speech gives the impression that she is:
  – very fond of drink, even though she pretends it's only to help her do her work;
  – craftily careful to set out her charges, especially for any extras;
  – long winded and repetitive;
  – keen to impress people with her honesty and sincerity.
• The dialogue section of the extract amplifies the preceding information given in the narrative, using a more naturalistic method of making the reader feel that he or she has been on the receiving end of Mrs Gamp's tongue.

CHECK YOURSELF QUESTIONS

Q1 What do you learn about Jenny from the following?

'Now tell me honestly, and don't try to hold anything back. Were you there when the police arrived?' Jenny studied her shoes intently.

Q2 What is the author suggesting about Fothergill in the following sentence?

'Fothergill picked his way carefully between two swaying bag-ladies, drawing his coat-collar tight and flicking some dust off his sleeve.

Q3 What impression do you get of these two characters from what they say and how they say it?

"With respect, Mr Cornwall, may I humbly suggest that your memory of the event may not be entirely perfect, and that you may have practised some economy with the facts?'

'I, er ... that is ... I, certainly not! I have told you everything as accurately as I can!'

Answers are on page 162.

Prose – responding to setting

- ■ Authors use setting to reveal characters and reflect their moods.
- ■ You need to be able to explain what makes a setting vivid and interesting and how a setting is used in a passage.

Using setting to create a meaning

■ Read the following description of a country scene in Dorset, taken from *Return of the Native* by Thomas Hardy. It is not the kind of factual geographical account you would expect to find in an information book:

> The sombre stretch of rounds and hollows seemed to rise and meet the evening gloom in pure sympathy, the heath exhaling darkness as rapidly as the heavens precipitated it ... the place became full of a watchful intentness now; for when other things sank brooding to sleep, the heath appeared slowly to awake and listen.

- ● Hardy makes the environment seem like a living thing by choosing words which we normally associate with animals, not places.
- ● 'Rise' and 'meet' suggest the ability to move, and 'exhaling' is a feature of living creatures.
- ● 'Watchful', 'awake' and 'listening' are all things which animals do, and not things which are usually associated with landscape.
- ● Hardy animates the environment. He makes it seem as if it has actions, feelings and intentions, like a living thing.

■ Hardy made the setting active and powerful because he believed that the natural environment is an influence on human behaviour. It is rather like a character always in the background of his novels.

Using setting to reveal character

■ An author may use the description of setting in order to **convey something about the character** observing it. In this extract from Charles Dickens' *Great Expectations*, a small boy is shown gazing over the landscape near his home:

> Ours was the marsh country, down by the river, within, as the river wound, twenty miles of the sea. My first most vivid and broad impression of the identity of things seems to me to have been gained on a memorable raw afternoon towards evening. At such a time I found out for certain that this bleak place overgrown with nettles was the churchyard; and that Philip Pirrip, late of this parish, and also
>
> ▶

Georgiana, wife of the above, were dead and buried; and that Alexander, Bartholomew, Abraham, Tobias and Roger, infant children of the aforesaid, were also dead and buried; and that the dark flat wilderness beyond the churchyard, instersected with dykes and mounds and gates, with scattered cattle feeding on it, was the marshes; and that the low leaded line beyond was the river; and that the distant savage lair from which the wind was rushing was the sea; and that the small bundle of shivers growing afraid of it all and beginning to cry was Pip.

- The scene is presented through the eyes of the child, and mingled with his feelings.
- As his gaze travels further and further into the distance, away from the comfortable closeness of his familiar home, it becomes quite frightening to the child, as if the wider world is hostile and menacing, making the child suddenly feel vulnerable and afraid.

◎ Using setting to reflect a character's mood

■ A person's character may be basically stable and consistent, but there can be changes in his or her **mood**, depending on what is happening in the story. In this extract from *Jake's Thing* by Kingsley Amis, Jake is in a bleak mood, on his way to see his doctor about a worrying problem:

The bus passed between the tiled façade of Mornington Crescent station and the roughly triangular paved area with the statue of Cobden near its apex, pitted and grimy and lacking its right hand, Richard Cobden the corn-law reformer and worker for peace and disarmament, too famous for his Christian name and dates to be needed in the inscription. Almost at the foot of the plinth what looked like the above-ground part of a public lavatory, black railings draped with black chicken-wire, bore a notice saying London Electricity Board – Danger Keep Out and gave a limited view of a stairway with ferns growing out of it and its walls. Two bollards painted in rings of black and white were to be seen not far off, their function hard even to guess at. Weeds flourished in the crevices between the paving-stones, a number of which had evidently been ripped out; others, several of them smashed, stood in an irregular pile.

Elsewhere, there was a heap of waterlogged and collapsed cardboard boxes and some large black plastic sheets spread about by the wind. Each corner of the space was decorated with an arrangement of shallow concrete hexagons filled with earth in which grew speckled evergreen bushes and limp conifer saplings about the height of a man, those at the extreme ends crushed by traffic and the greenery run into the soil along with aftershave cartons, sweet-wrappers, dog-food labels and soft-drink tins. Turning south, the bus stopped at its stop across the road from Greater London House, through the windows of which fluorescent lighting glared or flickered all day. It stood on ground filched from an earlier generation of dwellers in the Crescent who had woken one morning to see and hear their garden being eradicated.

Fifteen minutes later Jake was walking down Harley Street, buffeted by damp squalls as he went.

- The details of this setting reflect the way Jake feels about life. It is described in a way which emphasizes all the depressing and gloomy aspects.
- The author's purpose is to reflect the jaded view of the character observing it. As in real life, what people notice about a scene reflects the positive or negative way they feel about life and themselves.

■ In summary, setting is not just background. It can be something which **reflects** or **has an effect** on the character or the mood. When reading about a setting, ask yourself if it's there to explain what happens, or to reflect what's happening: is the description a **cause** or a **result** of what a character has done?

? CHECK YOURSELF QUESTIONS

Q1 Here is a description of a setting taken from Laurie Lee's *Cider with Rosie*. How is the reader given a sense of the observer and not just the place?

Radiating from that house, with its crumbling walls, its thumps and shadows, its fancied foxes under the floor, 1 moved along paths that lengthened inch by inch with my mounting strength of days. From stone to stone in the trackless yard 1 sent forth my acorn shell of senses, moving through unfathomable oceans like a South Sea savage island-hopping across the Pacific. Antennae of eyes and nose and grubbing fingers captured a new tuft of grass, a fern, a slug, the skull of a bird, a grotto of bright snails.

From the harbour mouth of the scullery door 1 learned the rocks and reefs and the channels where safety lay. 1 discovered the physical pyramid of the cottage, its stores and labyrinths, its centres of magic, and of the green, sprouting island-garden upon which it stood. My mother and sisters sailed past me like galleons in their busy dresses, and 1 learned the smells and sounds which followed in their wakes, the surge of breath, carbolic, song and grumble, and smashing of crockery.

The scullery was a mine of all the minerals of living. Here, 1 discovered water – a very different element from the green crawling scum that stank in the garden tub. You could pump it in pure blue gulps out of the ground, you could swing on the pump handle and it came out sparkling like liquid sky. And it broke and ran and shone on the tiled floor, or quivered in a jug, or weighted your clothes with cold. You could drink it, draw with it, froth it with soap, swim beetles across it, or fly it in bubbles in the air. You could put your head in it, and open your eyes, and see the sides of the bucket buckle, and hear your caught breath roar, and work your mouth like a fish, and smell the lime from the ground. Substance of magic – which you could wear or tear, confine or scatter, or send down holes, but never burn or break or destroy.

Here too was the scrubbing of floors and boots, of arms and necks, of red and white vegetables. Walk in to the morning disorder of this room and all the garden was laid out dripping on the table. Chopped carrots like copper pennies, radishes and chives, potatoes dipped and stripped clean from their coats of mud, the snapping of tight pea-pods, long shells of green pearls, and the tearing of glutinous beans from their nests of wool.

Answers are on page 163.

Prose – narrative devices

- There are various narrative devices which authors can use to tell a story.

- You need to be able to explain how a narrative works, to comment on the style and structure and to evaluate the use of narrative conventions.

Third-person narrative

- The **narrative** of a story is usually written in the kind of language you expect an educated author to use – third person, past tense, Standard English:

Reginald Fanshaw was twenty-three and feeling older. It was a wet Wednesday in Widnes, and Reginald held in his hand the latest in a long line of rejections from a publisher, together with the dog-eared copy of the masterpiece that was to make him rich and famous.

- There are, however, various other narrative techniques that can be used.

First-person narrative

- An author may choose to write in the style of an **invented character**. The purpose is to make the author seem **invisible**, and make the reader feel they are being spoken to by someone who is not a professional writer, but someone just like themselves. Here is the beginning of a teenage novel, *Push Me, Pull Me* by Sandra Chick:

Everyone likes Christmas Eve. I don't. Would never admit it, though. Wouldn't be fair on the others to play selfish and dampen the spark. Truth is, I get jealous of the fun everybody else is having. Only like the presents, just pretend to enjoy the rest. Can't stand pushing myself forward, I s'pose. You know, stupid games, dancing, that kind of thing. Makes me feel clumsy and embarrassed, makes my cheeks flush and a sort of cramped sensation belts me in the stomach. I wish I didn't feel that way. I'd like to join in, be the one who's always there, in the centre, but I can't force myself. The more people try to encourage me, the bigger idiot I feel. Prefer my Own company – quite happy but in a different way.

It was chilly out, still had my jacket on, collar turned up to cover my ears, hands pushed up inside the front – didn't have pockets or gloves. I let my tongue taste the clearness that crept down on to my lip from my nose, cold and itchy – always do that and hope no one ever sees. When it's really freezing, my eyes go funny, and they were sort of stiff from the bitter wind.

- The informality and naturalness of this passage come from the way it is written as if it were conversation.
- It uses the present tense and sentences are incomplete.
- The writer doesn't always start a sentence with 'I'.
- There's a tone of intimate confession about private habits that seems to take the reader into the writer's confidence.

◎ Narrator and persona

■ This device adopts the **persona of a main character** as the tale-teller. In *The Catcher in the Rye*, an adult writer, J.D. Salinger, writes the book as if it is told by the main, teenage, character:

If you really want to hear about it, the first thing you'll probably want to know is where I was born, and what my lousy childhood was like, and how my parents were occupied and all before they had me, and all that David Copperfield kind of crap, but I don't feel like going into it. In the first place, that stuff bores me, and in the second place, my parents would have about two haemorrhages apiece if I told anything pretty personal about them. They're quite touchy about anything like that, especially my father. They're nice and all – I'm not saying that – but they're also touchy as hell. Besides, I'm not going to tell you my whole goddam autobiography or anything. I'll just tell you about this madman stuff that happened to me around last Christmas before I got pretty run-down and had to come out here and take it easy.

© J.D. Salinger, 1945, 1946

- The writer uses informal, youthful words such as 'lousy', 'goddam' and 'crap'.
- The tone is personal, directly addressing the reader as 'you'.
- It is written as conversation, with corrections of meaning added – 'I'm not saying that' – that make it sound spontaneous.
- Because it's written in the first person, it addresses the reader as second person, giving an intimate tone.

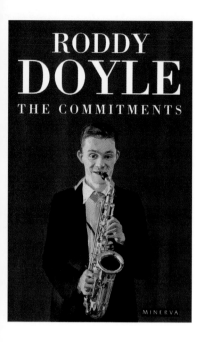

RODDY
DOYLE
THE COMMITMENTS

MINERVA

◎ Mixing dialogue with narrative

■ Some authors feel that writing in the third person can be more immediate if they use a lot of **dialogue** and make the narrator an **unidentified** part of the events.

■ This can make the writing seem **immediate** and **authentic**, as if overheard directly, not reported, but without having to use 'I' or make the narrator take part in the events, as shown in the following extract from *The Commitments* by Roddy Doyle:

—We'll ask Jimmy, said Outspan. —Jimmy'll know.
Jimmy Rabbitte knew his music. He knew his stuff all right. You'd never see Jimmy coming home from town without a new album or a 12-inch or at least a 7-inch single. Jimmy ate *Melody Maker* and the *NME* every week and *Hot Press* every two weeks. He listened to Dave Fanning and John Peel. He even read his sisters' *Jackie* when there was no one looking. So Jimmy knew his stuff ...

The last time Outspan had flicked through Jimmy's records he'd seen names like Microdisney, Eddie and the Hot Rods, Otis Redding, The Screaming Blue Messiahs ... groups Outspan had never heard of, never mind heard. Jimmy even had albums by Frank Sinatra and The Monkees. So when Outspan and Derek decided, while Ray was out in the jacks, that their group needed a new direction, they both thought of Jimmy. Jimmy knew what was what.

● The narrator is an unidentified character – someone the reader doesn't know, but who knows the other characters – such as Jimmy – in the story and can describe them.
● The third-person narrator describes but doesn't explain – references to groups and magazines are included as part of the accepted culture that don't need spelling out to the reader.

◎ Using two or more characters as narrators

■ An author may present a story through the eyes and voices of two (or more) of the characters in it. What they think, feel and say about a situation may vary enormously.

■ The following two extracts are alternate chapters from *Daz 4 Zoe* by Robert Swindells, written as if by the two main characters.

■ Daz is a Chippy, living in a squalid, run-down slum, and Zoe is a Subby, living in a respectable, well-off area fenced off from Chippyville. Normally, these two would not meet because of their different social backgrounds:

Zoe

What happened was, Larry saw this girl. Chippy girl. She was with another girl and two guys. She was pretty and he was smashed and he caught her eye and smiled and started making signs for her to leave the others and come on over. The girl kept smiling, but it was the sort of smile people put on when they're embarrassed and don't know what else to do. I could see that, but not Larry. Oh no. He thought she fancied him and redoubled his efforts.

Daz

So this crash com and Cal's away i open the door a crack and luck owt and its wot i fought. Subbys. i knew ther be trubble tonite wiv them in. Stanstareeson dunnit.

i luck and i fink, sod em. They blew it 4 me. Let em get topped. Then i seen the girl. The 1 i bin watching. She luck scairt. 2 hunnerd peeple want me ded, i luck scairt. i seen her and i cant let em do it. The uvvers i don't give a monkeys abowt but i cant let em top her.

- Robert Swindells has made the two narrators very distinct by using different speech, pronunciation and writing patterns.
- Daz does not speak Standard English, and in his speech he does not sound all syllables, as in his rendering of 'It stands to reason, doesn't it?' – notice how Swindells uses non-standard spelling and punctuation to convey this.

◎ Dialogue as dramatic narrative

- Some writers have a gift for using dialogue to **create character** and **replace explicit narrative**.

- In this extract from *Emma*, Jane Austen gives the reader a vivid sense of being in Miss Bates' company by recording her conversation:

Everybody's words were soon lost under the incessant flow of Miss Bates, who came in, talking, and had not finished her speech until many minutes after her being admitted into the circle at the fire. As the door opened, she was heard—

'So very obliging of you!—No rain at all. Nothing to signify. I do not care for myself. Quite thick shoes. And Jane declares—Well! (as soon as she was within the door), well! This is brilliant indeed! This is admirable! Excellently contrived, upon my word. Nothing wanting. Could not have imagined it. So well lighted up! Jane, Jane, look! did you ever see anything? Oh, Mr Weston, you must really have had Aladdin's lamp. Good Mrs Stokes would not know her own room again. I saw her as I came in; she was standing in the entrance. "Oh, Mrs Stokes," said I—but I had not time for more.' She was now met by Mrs Weston. 'Very well, I thank you, ma'am. I hope you are quite well. Very happy to hear it. So afraid you might have a headache! seeing you pass ▶

by so often, and knowing how much trouble you must have. Delighted to hear it indeed.—Ah! dear Mrs Elton, so obliged to you for the carriage; excellent time; Jane and I quite ready. Did not keep the horses a moment. Most comfortable carriage. Oh! and I am sure our thanks are due to you, Mrs Weston, on that score. Mrs Elton had most kindly sent Jane a note, or we should have been. But two such offers in one day! Never were such neighbours. I said to my mother, "Upon my word, ma'am." Thank you, my mother is remarkably well. Gone to Mr Woodhouses's.'

- This brings out Miss Bates' garrulous character and allows the reader to know who is in the room and what they are doing.
- Jane Austen uses the flow of talk to make the reader supply details of the other characters' responses to Miss Bates.
- Throughout the non-stop talk, we get an impression of the whole company of people being inspected by Miss Bates, chatted to and then passed on for the next. All that we can imagine about their reaction comes from what Jane Austen implies, not what she states.

Putting the reader in the character's shoes

■ Sometimes there is a **distinct narrator** who wants the reader temporarily to identify with a character.

■ This can be done very subtly by making the reader feel as if he or she is in the position of one character facing another.

■ Jane Austen does this in an episode involving Mrs Elton when she comes to visit, taking it on herself to advise Emma about improving her social life:

'You have many parties of that kind here, I suppose, Miss Woodhouse, every summer?'

'No; not immediately here. We are rather out of distance of the very striking beauties which attract the sort of parties you speak of; and we are a very quiet set of people, I believe; more disposed to stay at home than engage in schemes of pleasure.' [...]

'I perfectly understand your situation, however, Miss Woodhouse (looking towards Mr Woodhouse), your father's state of health must be a great drawback. Why does not he try Bath?—indeed he should. Let me recommend Bath to you. I assure you I have no doubt of its doing Mr Woodhouse good.'

'My father tried it more than once, formerly, but without receiving any benefit; and Mr Perry, whose name, I daresay, is not unknown to you, does not conceive it would be at all more likely to be useful now.'

'Ah! that's a great pity; for I assure you, Miss Woodhouse, where the waters do agree, it is quite wonderful the relief they give. In my Bath life I have seen such instances of it! And it is so cheerful a place that it could not fail of being of use to Mr Woodhouses's spirits, which, I understand, are sometimes much depressed. And as to its recommendation to you, I fancy I need not take much pains to dwell on them. The advantages of Bath to the young are pretty generally understood.

- Jane Austen chooses not to write a dialogue in which the two characters clash and show their feelings, but to put the reader at the receiving end, imagining how Emma must feel about Mrs Elton's patronising advice and comments.
- If the reader begins to feel desperate or furious, or wants to get a word in, he or she will sympathise with Emma.
- At this point Jane Austen wants the reader to take Emma's side.

■ Elsewhere in the story, Jane Austen wants the reader to see Emma's faults, which she describes in the narrative mode:

The real evils indeed of Emma's situation were the power of having rather too much of her own way, and a disposition to think a little too well of herself.

■ If the author makes you sometimes **identify** with the hero and sometimes **feel against** him or her, the hero is being treated in a lifelike way.

■ Writing which makes the reader have **mixed feelings** is usually more realistic than writing which always shows the hero in a flattering light. Also, if we know that Emma usually has her own way and thinks highly of herself, we react to the scene with Mrs Elton with mixed feelings – it's about time she met some opposition, but Mrs Elton is an awful person.

■ In this way, we are kept changing and balancing our view of Emma. The author is making us feel undecided or ambivalent about her, just as we may do about people in real life.

? CHECK YOURSELF QUESTIONS

Q1 Penelope Lively is a writer who wants to look under and behind the appearance of things. What she reveals is less ideal and simple than the reader may want to find. In this extract from *The Darkness Out There*, the character appears to be a sweet, old lady, but there is more to her than we think at first reading.

a Which *narrative* details make her seem sweet and cosy?

b Which *dialogue* details make her seem sweet and cosy?

c What narrative hints are there that she may be something else?

She seemed composed of circles, a cottage-loaf of a woman, with a face below which chins collapsed one into another, a creamy smiling pool of a face in which her eyes snapped and darted.

'Tea, my duck?' she said. 'Tea for the both of you? I'll put us a kettle on.' The room was stuffy. It had a gaudy lino floor with the pattern rubbed away in front of the sink and round the table; the walls were cluttered with old calendars and pictures torn from magazines; there was a smell of cabbage. The alcove by the fireplace was filled with china ornaments: big-eyed, flop-eared rabbits and beribboned kittens and flowery milkmaids and a pair of naked, chubby children wearing daisy chains.

The woman hauled herself from a sagging armchair. She glittered at them from the stove, manoeuvring cups, propping herself against the draining board. 'What's your names, then? Sandra and Kerry. Well, you're a pretty girl, Sandra, aren't you. Pretty as they come. There was – let me see, who was it? – Susie last week. That's right, Susie.' Her eyes investigated, quick as mice. 'Put your jacket on the back of the door, dear, you won't want to get that messy. Still at school, are you?'

The boy said, 'I'm leaving, July. They're taking me on at the garage, the Blue Star. I been helping out there on and off, before.'

Mrs Rutter's smiles folded into one another. Above them, her eyes examined him.

'Well, I expect that's good steady money if you'd nothing special in mind. Sugar?'

There was a view from the window out over a bedraggled garden with the stumps of spent vegetables and a matted flower bed and a square of shaggy grass. Beyond, the spinney reached up to the fence, a no-man's land of willow herb and thistle and small trees, growing thicker and higher into the full density of woodland. Mrs Rutter said, 'Yes, you have a look out, aren't I lucky – right up beside the wood. Lovely it is in the spring, the primroses and that. Mind, there's not as many as there used to be.'

Answers are on page 163.

THE HENLEY COLLEGE LIBRARY

▰ Reading beneath the surface ▰

- There is usually more to meaning than meets the eye – there are often additional or alternative interpretations that emerge only after a second reading of a passage.

- You need to be able to explain how and why writers use literary language to create different levels of meaning.

◎ Surface meaning and ambiguity

- **Literal language** has all its meaning on the surface. It calls a spade a spade and a pen a pen. **Literary language**, on the other hand, deliberately exploits varieties of meaning, through suggestiveness, ambiguity and metaphor.

- Literary language may try to make the reader think of similarities between a spade and a pen by linking them, as in these lines from Seamus Heaney's poem *Digging*:

> Between my finger and my thumb
> The squat pen rests.
> I'll dig with it.

- Ambiguity can be unintentional or intentional, making the reader react to a word in a way different from usual:

> His smooth hands waved persuasively and his plump features broke into a genial smile as he predicted the company's profits from the export of landmines.

- Usually, words like 'plump' and 'smooth' have a positive effect, suggesting comfort and cosiness, but a writer can use these words in a way which makes the reader react against comfort and cosiness.
- Because the character is pleased with making money out of something that hurts people, the reader may see his smoothness and comfort as unattractive.
- The use of these words is no longer positive, but negative, provoking the reader into a moral judgement.

SURFACE FINISHES FOR CONCRETE

The surface finishes produced by tamping or striking off with a sawing action are perfectly adequate for a skid-proof, workmanlike surface for a *pad, drive or pathway, but you can produce a range of other finishes using simple handtools once you have compacted and levelled the concrete.*

Float finishes
Smooth the tamped concrete by sweeping a wooden float across the surface, or make an even finer texture by finishing with a trowel (steel float). Let the concrete dry out a little before using a float or you will bring water to the top and weaken it, eventually resulting in a dusty residue on the hardened concrete. Bridge the formwork with a stout plank so that you can reach the centre, or hire a skip float with a long handle for large pads.

Exposed-aggregate finish
Embedding small stones or pebbles in the surface makes a very attractive and practical finish but it takes a little practice to be successful.
   Scatter dampened pebbles onto the freshly laid concrete and tamp them firmly with a length of timber until they are flush with the surface (1). Place a plank across the formwork and apply your full weight to make sure the surface is even. Leave the concrete to harden for a while until all surface water has evaporated, then use a very fine spray and a brush to wash away the cement from around the pebbles until they protrude (2). Cover the concrete for about 24 hours, then lightly wash the surface again to clean any sediment off the actual pebbles. Cover the concrete again and leave it to harden thoroughly.

Make a smooth finish with a wooden float

Brush finishes
Make a finely textured surface by drawing a yard broom across the setting concrete. Flatten the concrete initially with a wooden float, then make parallel passes with the broom held at a low angle to avoid 'tearing' the surface.

1 Tamp pebbles into the fresh concrete

Texture the surface with a broom

2 Wash the cement from around the pebbles

Brush-finishing concrete

Exposed-aggregate finish

Literary and literal language have very different purposes.

◎ Reading beneath the story

■ Think back to the description of the marshes by Pip in *Great Expectations* (pages 47–8), especially the passage where he begins to feel frightened by the vastness all around him. Dickens' purpose is to show how frightening an environment can be to an impressionable child:

> ... the dark flat wilderness beyond the churchyard, intersected with dykes and mounds and gates, with scattered cattle feeding on it, was the marshes; and that the low leaded line beyond was the river; and that the distant savage lair from which the wind was rushing was the sea; and that the small bundle of shivers growing afraid of it all and beginning to cry was Pip.

- Dickens uses 'wilderness' to make the area seem unlike home, and 'savage' to make the noise of the wind frightening; but the word that really creates a sense of menace is 'lair'.
- It is not literally true that the wind lives in a cave, but the word 'lair' suggests that it does.
- Statement and metaphor work together to help the reader understand what lies beneath the surface of the story.
- The metaphorical meaning – the theme – *below* the story is about a child as the vulnerable prey of a predatory wider world.

◎ Metaphor

■ **Metaphorical language** works in prose just as it does in poetry. You need to understand how it works, as it can help you comment on the author's **ideas** and **attitudes** which lie beneath the story.

■ Thomas Hardy believed that human beings, however educated or civilised, were as much influenced by natural impulses as the animals and plants. When, in *Tess of the D'Urbervilles*, he wanted to suggest that human beings were moved by Nature's force to grow, blossom and reproduce, he described Nature's energy and fertility as something powerful enough to touch and hear:

> Amid the oozing fatness and warm ferments of the Froom Vale, at a season when the rush of juices could almost be heard below the hiss of fertilisation, it was impossible that the most fanciful love should not grow passionate.

- Hardy magnifies the processes of growth, as if holding a microphone to amplify and record the 'rush' and 'hiss' of biological processes.
- By showing characters affected by these natural forces, he is implying something about human beings in general.
- His linking of plant and human life gives us a clue to his thinking. Hardy was influenced by Darwin's view that we have evolved like everything else, and are not so different from other products of nature.

◎ Symbolism

■ Writers can exploit **connections** made by words.

■ If they keep up a pattern of choosing words which remind the reader of something else, the result can be deliberately **symbolic**. In the following passage from *Lord of the Flies*, William Golding describes the death of Simon, murdered by the other boys in a savage ritual:

> The tide swelled in over the rain-pitted sand and smoothed everything with a layer of silver. Now it touched the first of the stains that seeped from the broken body, and the creatures made a moving patch of light as they gathered at the edge. The water rose further and dressed Simon's coarse hair with brightness. The line of his cheek silvered and the turn of his shoulder became sculptured marble. The strange, attendant creatures, with their fiery eyes and trailing vapours, busied themselves round his head. The body lifted a fraction of an inch from the sand and a bubble of air escaped from the mouth with a wet plop. Then it turned gently in the water.

● Golding builds an image of holiness using references to light ('moving patch of light', 'brightness', 'silvered') and suggests that Simon's body is like a marble statue.
● The description of a luminous gathering around his head suggests a halo, symbolising Simon's saintliness.

SYMBOLIC WRITING AND AUTHORS' IDEAS

■ An author's **ideas** can often be identified by reading beneath the events of a story.

■ Thomas Hardy saw agricultural life in the nineteenth century changing as a result of technology. In *Tess of the D'Urbervilles*, he showed how farm workers had to work harder to match the pace of new machinery, and describes a mechanical thresher and its operator as a harsh, unnatural influence on rural life:

> Close under the eaves of the stack, and as yet barely visible, was the red tyrant that the women had come to serve – a timber-framed construction, with straps and wheels appertaining – the threshing machine which, whilst it was going, kept up a despotic demand upon the endurance of their muscles and nerves.
>
> A little way off, there was another indistinct figure; this one black, with a sustained hiss that spoke of strength very much in reserve ... By the engine stood a dark, motionless being, a sooty and grimy embodiment of tallness, in a sort of trance, with a heap of coals by his side: it was the engineman ...
>
> He was in the agricultural world, but not of it. He served fire and smoke, these denizens of the field served vegetation, weather, frost and sun. He travelled with his engine from farm to farm, from county

▶

▸ You need to be able to exploit patterns and details of language for implication or suggestion.
▸ The use of words like 'tyrant', 'despotic' and 'serve' show that the female labourers are the subjects of a powerful force.
▸ Hardy uses words such as 'served', 'compelled' and 'master' in relation to the engineman as well.
▸ He suggests that in this new, harsh industrial world, both workers and the people above them are equally dominated by the power of the machine and industrial processes.

to county. … He spoke in a strange northern accent: his thoughts being turned inward upon himself, his eye on his iron charge, hardly perceiving the scenes around him, and caring for them not at all: holding only strictly necessary intercourse with the natives, as if some ancient doom compelled him to wander here against his will in the service of his Plutonic master.

- The words 'tyrant' and 'despotic' in the first paragraph suggest ruthless dictatorship.
- The engineer is 'motionless' and does not communicate with the workers.
- He speaks like a foreigner and deals with fire and smoke, not Nature.
- The reference to Pluto could either suggest that he is only interested in money (as Pluto was the god of wealth) or that he is a servant of the Lord of Hell.
- The latter reference, together with the black and red colouring, suggest that the machinery is devil-like, a hellish intruder into the scene.

◎ Irony

- Recognising **irony** is a vital part of commenting on an author's purpose, because irony is usually an attempt to make us **laugh** at something foolish or to make a **moral comment**.

- Irony usually works by saying something that is the **opposite** of what the writer means.

IRONY IN ATTITUDE

- Arthur Clough wanted to criticise the way people put too much value on wealth. In *The Latest Decalogue*, he wrote as if recommending the worship of money:

Thou shalt have one God only; who
Would be at the expense of two?
No graven images may be
Worshipped, except the currency.

- He means the opposite of what he literally says.
- He uses irony and biblical language to make the reader feel shocked by a frank statement of what may be true, but is not admitted.

IRONY IN SITUATION

- In this extract from *A Kestrel for a Knave*, Barry Hines describes a school assembly:

Then a boy coughed – 'Who did that?'
Everybody looked round.
'I said WHO DID THAT?'
The teachers moved in closer, alert like a riot squad.

'Mr Crossley! Somewhere near you! Didn't you see the boy?'
Crossley flushed, and rushed amongst them, thrusting them aside
in panic.
'There, Crossley? That's where it came from! Around there!'
Crossley grabbed a boy by the arm and began to yank him into the open.
'It wasn't me, Sir!'
'Of course it was you.'
'It wasn't, Sir, honest!'
'Don't argue lad, I saw you.'
Gryce thrust his jaw over the front of the lectern, the air whistling
down his nostrils.
'MACDOWALL! I might have known it! Get to my room, lad!'
Crossley escorted MacDowall from the hall. Gryce waited for the doors
to stop swinging, then replaced his stick and addressed the school.
'Right! We'll try again. Hymn one hundred and seventy-five.'
The pianist struck the chord. Moderately slow, it said in the book, but
this direction was ignored by the school, and the tempo they produced
was dead slow, the words delivered in a grinding monotone.

> 'New ev-ry morn-ing is the love
> Our waken-ing and uprising prove;
> Through sleep and dark-ness safely brought,
> Re-stored to life, and power, and thought.'

- The Headmaster's behaviour is made even more gross and unfair by
  being contrasted with the words of the hymn, and the supposedly
  religious purpose of an assembly.
- Hines' ironic treatment of the scene contrasts the joy and love and
  safety mentioned in the hymn with the atmosphere of brutal harshness
  in the school.

IRONY IN SPEECH

- Writers who want their readers to see something as **ridiculous** or
  unacceptable may avoid direct statement, and try to suggest a reaction
  by using language **ironically**. Irony is a powerful tool for making readers
  understand that there is more to what is being said than the literal
  meaning.

- Siegfried Sassoon attacked the way some people treated casualties of
  the war by exaggerating a 'never mind' attitude. He does not mean
  what he says, but expresses ideas which he wants to criticise:

> Does it matter? Losing your sight?
> There's such splendid work for the blind:
> And people will always be kind.

Siegfried Sassoon (1886–1967)

IRONY IN NARRATIVE

■ Irony does not always have to be conveyed in dialogue. Alexander Pope lists what can be seen on a young woman's dressing table:

> Puffs, powders, patches, bibles, billet-doux

● By casually including 'bibles' (she has several!) in a list of cosmetics and personal trifles, Pope makes her attitude to religion appear trivial, no more important to her than the other things cluttering her table.

CHECK YOURSELF QUESTIONS

Q1 In this extract from William Thackeray's *Vanity Fair*, Becky Sharp, a lady fallen on bad times, is visited by a former close friend. As you read through, think about her motives and how she treats Jos. Think particularly about the underlined words. What impression do you get of Becky Sharp in this passage?

Becky's little head peeped out full of <u>archness</u> and <u>mischief</u>. She lighted on Jos. 'It's you,' she said, coming out. 'How I have been waiting for you! Stop, not yet – in one minute you shall come in.' In that instant she put a rouge-put, a brandy bottle and a plate of broken meat into the bed, gave one smooth to her hair and finally let in her visitor.

She had, by way of morning robe, a pink domino, a trifle faded and soiled, and marked here and there with pomatum [*scented oil*]; but her arms shone out from the loose sleeves of the dress very white and fair, and it was tied round her little waist, so as not ill to set off the trim little figure of the wearer. She led Jos by the hand into her garret. 'Come in,' she said. 'Come, and talk to me. Sit yonder on the chair;' and she gave the Civilian's hand a little squeeze, and laughingly placed him upon it. As for herself, she placed herself on the bed, – not on the bottle and plate, you may be sure – on which Jos might have reposed, had he chosen that seat; and so there she sat and talked with her old admirer.

'How little years have changed you,' she said with a look of <u>tender</u> interest. 'I should have known you anywhere. What comfort it is amongst strangers to see once more the frank honest face of an old friend' ... 'I should have known you anywhere,' she continued; 'a woman never forgets some things. And you were the first man I ever – I ever saw.'

'Was I, really?' said Jos. 'God bless my soul, you – you don't say so.'

'When I came with your sister from Chiswick, I was scarcely more than a child,' Becky said. 'How is that dear love? Oh, her husband was a sad, wicked man, and of course it was of me that the poor dear was jealous. As if I cared about him, heigh-ho! when there was somebody – but no – don't let us talk of old times,' and she passed her handkerchief with the tattered lace J across her eyelids.

'Is not this a strange place,' she continued, 'for a woman, who has lived in a very different world too, to be found in? I have had so many griefs and wrongs, Joseph Sedley, I have been made to suffer so cruelly, that I am almost made mad sometimes. I can't stay still in any place, but wander about always restless and unhappy. All my friends have been false to me – all. There is no such thing as an honest man in the world. I was the truest wife that ever lived, though I married my husband out of pique, because somebody else, – but never mind that. I was true, and he trampled upon me, and deserted me. I was the fondest mother. I had but one child, one darling, one hope, one joy, which I held to my heart with a mother's affection, which was my life, my prayer, my – my blessing; and they – they tore it from me – tore it from me,' and she put her hand to her heart with a passionate gesture of <u>despair</u>, burying her face for a moment on the bed.

The brandy bottle inside clinked up against the plate which held the cold sausage. Both were <u>moved</u>, no doubt, by the exhibition of so much grief.

Answers are on page 164.

Making effective comparisons

■ You need to be able to compare features of language, theme and attitude.

◎ Comparison within a passage

■ When reading a passage or a poem, ask yourself if the writer makes the same point, or uses the same kind of language, throughout the text. If you find that there is a range of ideas, and a variety of language, you can **compare attitudes** or **ideas** or **language** within the text you are dealing with.

■ You may want to compare two parts of a story where a character behaves in a similar way (allowing you to sustain a statement about character) or two parts where a character behaves differently or is changed (allowing you to develop a point about complexity of development of character). An example of the latter might be:

> He goes from being shy and nervous to being more confident. In the first paragraph, he is surprised that everybody is so happy, and he is surprised that they welcome him. For example, he thought the staff were 'remarkably cheerful' and he was 'reassured' to find a desk to work with his name on it. But later, he had got used to this and began to expect more, when he said, 'I don't see why I should stay late because the place is in chaos.'

You may want to compare two parts of a story where a character behaves differently or is changed.

◎ Comparisons between texts

■ You may want to show a similarity or a difference between two separate accounts:

> In both of these passages, you can see how parents influence their children, and how children react to problems by getting angry, but they have to learn that sometimes it's better to be calm and think before doing anything rash. The first one shows you how the mother has strong feelings but hides them, but the other one only gives you the child's feelings.

■ You may also want to compare two characters responding to a situation. Your comparison will be more effective if you deal with differences *and* similarities, as this shows that you can explore and evaluate:

They have different ideas about education and children. The Headmistress thinks kids need to be kept in order, and the teacher thinks they need freedom. She doesn't trust them, and he does. Anyway, you realise that he's too soft when they are rude behind his back and make up excuses for not doing their work and she's a bit hard when she won't listen to the kids. They're both a bit right and a bit wrong.

◎ Structured comparison

- A **structured comparison** needs to make clear which things are alike and which are not; this will give your comments a sense of range and discrimination.

- It is also worth saying something about **style** as well as meaning. For example, it is more effective to write:

Although both of these poems are written in blank verse and modern language (and one is a sonnet and the other one is a double sonnet), they give a very different impression of war.

than:

These two poems take a different view of the subject of war.

- Commenting on style as well as subject matter shows that your study is not of the war itself, but of poetry written about the war.

◎ Extended comparison

- Sometimes you may be asked to compare two poems which are similar, and sometimes to **contrast** two poems which are different. The similarity or difference may be in one or a combination of the following:
  - ideas
  - attitudes
  - feelings
  - purpose
  - use of language
  - verse form

- In linking your comments about similarity and difference, there are some simple but very powerful words and phrases that will help you to go from a sustained response to a developed one, and to evaluate different qualities and responses. Starting a sentence with one of the following **linking phrases** shows that you can handle conflicting evidence or interpretation, and draw conclusions from evidence.

Although ...   *On the other hand, ...*
Alternatively, ...   *Perhaps ...*
Also, ...   *So ...*
Because ...   *Some people may think ...*
Despite ...   *This could mean ...*
Even if ...   *This may be ...*
However, ...   *This suggests ...*

Comparing ideas, attitudes and feelings

- Anything you read will contain feelings and attitudes, and will also produce feelings and attitudes in you. Try to deal with both of these aspects in your comparison, so that you show understanding of what the writer feels and thinks, and explore your response to those feelings and ideas.

- Remember that other people may respond differently. Anything you add to show how others may respond – or may have responded at the time of writing – will improve your comments, as shown in the following example:

> Rupert Brooke's poem (1914) makes war exciting and almost refreshing and fun when he writes about it like 'swimmers into cleanness leaping'. Wilfred Owen (in 'Dulce et Decorum Est') doesn't see it as sport, though, and he makes out that it's like falling into something which kills you, so you're 'drowning' and choking for breath. When you read Rupert Brooke's poem, you think 'Yes, I'll have a go' but then you read Wilfred's and you think, 'I'm not going to risk that happening to me,' so he's warned you off. When they were writing, young men were being encouraged to join up, and Brooke's poem would have made them feel good about it.

Owen's poem gave a more accurate picture of the horrors of war.

Comparing purpose, language and form

- As well as commenting on *what* a poet has to say, you need to comment on the *how* and *why*.

- The previous example does some of this, but it's worth making sure that you've said something about the **author's intentions**. You may not be certain about this –and there's usually no way of telling if you're right –but you should explore an author's reasons for choosing to write in the first place, and choosing form and words for the purpose:

> He's probably not as strong as his father, or he's no good at physical work like digging. You can tell he admires him when he writes as if he's proud of his Dad, almost boasting about him, 'By God the old man could handle a spade'. When he thinks that his pen is his spade, and he can still be good at something like his Dad, he writes a short sentence as if he's made his mind up and settled something, 'I'll dig with it'.

◎ Comparing your own attitudes

- It is good to show that your own response to a character or situation can develop and change over the course of your reading. This shows that you are an **active reader**, not content with a quick opinion that you stick with for the rest of the book.

- Recording how your view changes can be a useful way of showing response to a poem's structure, or the way a writer has presented an idea:

> When I first read it, I thought she was safe from the lion because she wasn't afraid of it, and the poet's message was that you shouldn't be afraid of things, but it still eats her in the end, which I didn't expect. The poem is called 'A Cautionary Tale' so it's warning you that fear can be a useful thing really.

- Recording the way in which you have two or more attitudes to something shows that you can cope with **complexity** and **ambiguity**. If you can show two ways of responding then decide on one, you will have shown ability to **evaluate alternative responses**.

CHECK YOURSELF QUESTIONS

Q1 Reread Ted Hughes' poem *Thistles* on page 41 and then read the following poem, also called *Thistles*, by Jon Stallworthy. Compare the two poems, showing similarities and differences in their attitude to their subject and the ways they use language and verse.

Thistles

Half grown before half seen,
like urchins in armour
double their size they stand
their ground boldly, their keen
swords out. But the farmer
ignores them. Not a hand

will he lift to cut them down:
they are not worth his switch
he says. Uncertain whom
they challenge, having grown
into their armour, each
breaks out a purple plume.

Under this image
of their warrior blood
they make a good death,
meeting the farmer's blade
squarely in their old age.
White then as winter breath

from every white head
a soul springs up. The wind
is charged with spirits: no –
not spirits of the dead
for these are living, will land
at our backs and go

to ground. Farmer and scythe
sing to each other. He
cannot see how roots writhe
underfoot, how the sons
of this fallen infantry
will separate our bones.

Answers are on page 165.

Selecting and using textual references

KEY EXAM SKILLS

- When you comment on texts, it is very important to support your comments with appropriate and purposeful references, rather than quoting chunks of text.

- If you use textual references well, you can show knowledge and ability to select, illustrate and comment.

◎ Illustrative references (technique)

- When you comment on the way something is written, you need to identify what the writer is doing, and give an example which illustrates it.

- You can use a **technical term** if you wish, but it is more important to **show** how the technique works.

- In the following examples, the students don't mention alliteration or animation, but it is clear that they understand them and can comment on the way they are used:

> He uses words with sounds which are like the sound of water – like 's' and 'sh' sounds in the line 'the shingle scrambles under the sucking surf'.
>
> He doesn't say straight out that the machine is alive, but the words he uses to describe it are words that make you think of a living creature – 'hiss' and 'flank' and 'iron muscles'.

- Don't simply list features. Always pick out some detail and comment on it. There's no point in saying that the writer uses onomatopoeia or a simile and a metaphor without some detail and explanation of how these things create meaning and feeling.

Supportive references (argument)

- When you are stating an opinion as part of an argument or the answer to a question, you need to make a clear statement then follow it with some evidence which fits what you are saying:

> She is quite a fussy person. She doesn't like dirt and she has a dream about living in a perfect country cottage with a perfect country stream and a perfect family. You can tell this because she doesn't just walk down the path, she 'picks her way daintily' and her feet 'wince' on the cinders. She doesn't think much of the garden or the cottage because she doesn't want to live in a place 'like this'. Another thing that tells you about her is the way she thinks the boy is oily and dirty, but he is only like this because he works with cars.

- It's useful to include some details which *don't* support your argument, so that you can show that you have looked at two views before deciding on one:

> Although he offers to help and gives her some money, which could be kind, he's really doing it to keep her quiet and make her think that he's really generous and on her side.

Running reference

- This is a useful way of using quotation without spending time writing out full lines. Use just what you need to show your knowledge:

> The scene has violence in it from the start, because in the opening line the clouds are 'slashed' and the sunlight that peeps through 'leaks' like blood from a wound, and the gulls are 'flaked off' the sky by squalls which are 'abrasive', like a Brillo pad!

Display reference

- This is where you quote a few lines and display them with indentation to make them stand out. This is fine, but don't expect marks if this is all you do!

- Make sure that if you quote a few lines, something in each line has a comment. Examiners will expect you to use more lines in writing your comment than you use to write out your quotation. Look at this example of a commentary following a display:

> Slashed clouds leak gold. Along the slurping wharf
> The snugged boats creak and seesaw. Round the masts
> Abrasive squalls flake seagulls off the sky

There is a lot of violence in this scene, with violent verbs ('slashed' and 'flaked') used to contrast with the cosiness of the harbour ('snugged'), and the gusts of wind are rough and 'abrasive', so that even seagulls can't stay in the sky.

- In this case, the commentary offers no more than the example of running quotation above, so it is worth asking whether the displayed three lines are worth writing out at all.
- If it's not necessary to display quotations, don't. Use time and ink for detailed comment instead.

Making the most of references: SECSI

- If you are making a point about something you have read, it helps to have a purposeful paragraph structure, so that it is clear to your reader what you are doing. SECSI (an acronym of Statement, Evidence, Comment, Scheme of things, Interpretation) is one practical way of making the most of quotation.

*Wilfred Owen
(1893–1918)*

STATEMENT

- You open with your opinion, attitude or idea, for example: 'Wilfred Owen wanted to shock his readers'.

EVIDENCE

- Display your reference, for example:

> Blood comes gargling from the froth-corrupted lungs
> Obscene as cancer, vile as incurable sores on innocent tongues

COMMENT

- You make sustained comments on your reference:

> He chooses images which are frightening and repulsive – not just 'froth-corrupted lungs', which is something you can see, but 'gargling' blood, which is something you can hear. And then he compares it with diseased 'innocent' tongues which makes it seem unfair. All the time he chooses words with ugly, harsh sounds 'g' and 'c (k)' and lots of hissing 's' sounds.

SCHEME OF THINGS

- This is connected with the writer's purpose in ideas, style or attitude:

> He wanted to be realistic and make the reader see real, physical details instead of images of flags and duty and heroic deeds. He was like a documentary poet, not a propaganda poet, and he thought people like Jessie Pope used pretty words to hide ugly facts, so he used ugly words for truth.

▸ You need to be able to integrate references with response and analysis.

▸ The teacher has to put up with 'insults', 'scrawl' and 'indifference', which must make him feel that his work is wasted.

▸ The use of terms such as 'leash', 'hounds' and 'haul' suggests that his students are animals and have to be dragged, rather than led and encouraged.

INTERPRETATIONS

■ Show that ambiguity in the text, or different attitudes in different readers, can result in opposing responses:

> Some people may think this is horrible and disgusting because they don't want to read about people's lungs being frothy with gas when you read a poem, but I think he is saying we shouldn't expect poetry to be pretty and nice, but about real things that are happening that matter. It is the truth and he said he was not concerned with Poetry (big P) but with pity.

■ The SECSI sequence allows you to show engagement with an issue, insight into textual detail, personal response and awareness of effects on different readers.

? CHECK YOURSELF QUESTIONS

Q1 Read the poem *Last Lesson of the Afternoon* by D.H. Lawrence, then write about:

- what the writer feels;
- how his feelings are expressed.

Now compare your answer with the sample answer and the comments on page 166. Is your answer better or worse in:

- developing comment on stated and implied attitudes?
- supporting comment with appropriate textual detail?

What textual details would you choose to support the comments at the numbered points in the answer?

When will the bell ring, and end this weariness?
How long have they tugged the leash and strained apart,
My pack of unruly hounds! I cannot start
Them again on a quarry of knowledge they hate to hunt,
I can haul them and urge them no more.

No longer now can I endure the brunt
Of the books that lie out on the desks; a full threescore
Of several insults of blotted pages, and scrawl
Of slovenly work that they have offered me.
I am sick, and what on earth is the good of it all?
What good to them or me I cannot see!

So, shall I take
My last dear fuel of life to heap on my soul
And kindle my will to a flame that shall consume
Their dross of indifference; and take the toll
Of their insults in punishment? – I will not!
– I will not waste my soul and my strength for this.
What do I care for all they do amiss?
What is the point of all this learning of mine, and of this
Learning of theirs? It all goes down the same abyss.
What does it matter to me, if they can write
A description of a dog, or if they can't?
What is the point? To us both it is all my aunt!
And yet, I'm supposed to care, with all my might.

I do not and will not; they won't and they don't; and that's all!
I shall keep my strength for myself; they can keep theirs as well.
Why should we beat our heads against the wall
Of each other? I shall sit and wait for the bell.

Answers are on page 166.

WRITING

Using accurate spelling

KEY EXAM SKILLS

- Accurate spelling is important, and can be achieved by learning a few basic rules.

- You need to be able to spell a wide range of vocabulary correctly.

◎ Spelling rules

- Although there are many irregular spellings, English does obey rules and patterns for much of the time. If you learn just a few of these, your spelling will improve dramatically.

- There are often a few exceptions to these rules, and it is of course important that you learn them. However, it is the general rules which you most need to remember!

- Examples of simple spelling rules are:

Good spelling is seen as an important social skill.

> - The letter 'q' is always followed by 'u' except in the name of the country 'Iraq'.
>
> - 'i' comes before 'e', except when it follows 'c': e.g. 'priest', 'friend', 'brief' but 'ceiling', 'deceive', 'receive'.
>
> - Note exceptions: when the vowel sound is 'a', as in 'neighbour' and 'weigh'; also 'neither', 'foreign', 'seize', 'sovereign', 'counterfeit', 'forfeit', 'leisure'.

DOUBLING RULES

- 'l', 'f' and 's' are doubled after a single vowel at the end of a one-syllable word: e.g. 'call', 'miss', 'stuff', 'tell', 'toss'.

> - Note a number of exceptions in very common words: 'bus', 'gas', 'if', 'of', 'plus', 'this', 'us', 'yes'.

- Words ending with a single vowel + single consonant double the consonant if adding an ending which begins with a vowel: e.g. 'shop–shopped–shopping'; 'flat–flatter–flattest'; 'swim–swimmer–swimming'.

SINGLING RULES

- ''All' followed by another syllable drops one 'l': e.g. 'also', 'already', 'always', 'although'.

▸ You need to be able to show that you can 'spell accurately a wide range of vocabulary, including irregular polysyllabic words'.

▸ If you use as many of the words as possible in the boxes on page 73 in your examination answers, and spell them correctly, you will be rewarded for your ambition.

▸ Using vocabulary like this will also help you make strong, evaluative points about texts and will enhance the impact of your own writing.

• Note an exception: 'all right' should be written as two words. If you make it 'alright', you are showing understanding of this spelling rule, but are misapplying it.

■ 'Full' and 'till' drop one 'l' when added to another syllable: e.g. 'hopeful', 'useful', 'cheerful', 'until'.

END GAMES

■ An 'i' or 'ee' sound at the end of a word is nearly always spelled 'y': e.g. 'hungry', 'county', 'rugby'.

• Note exceptions such as 'coffee', 'committee' and 'taxi', and some words which are borrowings from other languages (mainly Italian, e.g. 'spaghetti', 'macaroni').

■ Drop the final 'e' from a word before adding an ending which begins with a vowel, but keep it before an ending which begins with a consonant: e.g. 'love–loving–lovely'; 'drive–driving–driver'; 'rattle–rattled–rattling'.

• Note there are some exceptions: e.g. as 'dye' and 'singe', which keep the final 'e' before 'ing' ('dyeing', 'singeing') to avoid confusion with 'die' ('dying') and 'sing' ('singing').

■ If a word ends with a consonant followed by 'y', change the 'y' to 'i' before all endings except 'ing': e.g. 'heavy–heaviness'; 'fun–funnily'; 'marry–married–marrying'; 'hurry–hurriedly–hurrying'.

PLURALS

■ Regular plurals are made by adding 's': e.g. 'dog–dogs'; 'horse–horses'; 'committee–committees'.

■ Words ending 'y' after a consonant make the plural by changing the 'y' to 'ies': e.g. 'lady–ladies'; 'baby–babies'.

■ Add 'es' to words ending with 's', 'x', 'z', 'sh', 'ch', 'ss': e.g. 'bus–buses'; 'fox–foxes'; 'buzz–buzzes'; 'wish–wishes'; 'church–churches'; 'miss–misses'.

■ Most words ending with a single 'f' or 'fe' change the 'f' or 'fe' to 'ves' to form the plural: e.g. 'leaf–leaves'; 'wolf–wolves'; 'knife–knives'; 'wife–wives'.

• Note exceptions: 'dwarf–dwarfs'; 'roof–roofs'; 'chief–chiefs'; 'safe–safes'.
• Some words can take either 's' or 'ves' in the plural: 'hoof', 'scarf', 'wharf'.

'Dwarfs' doesn't follow the usual pattern.

HOMONYMS

■ **Homonyms** are words which have different spellings for different meanings, but sound similar, e.g. 'their', 'there' , 'they're'; 'its', 'it's'; 'birth', 'berth'; 'were', 'where', 'wear', 'we're', 'weir'.

■ Generally speaking, you need to learn the meanings and/or the different grammatical functions of these words: there is advice on some of these in Revision session 3 (page 80).

Common mistakes

■ Some words are often misspelt – make a point of ensuring that you can spell all of these words:

argument	conscience	favourite	persuade
beautiful	deceive	friend	prejudice
beginning	develop	hoping	rhyme
behaviour	dining	immediately	rhythm
believe	disappear	jealous	suspense
business	embarrassed	language	unnatural
character	fascinate	necessary	
conscious	father	occasionally	

■ These words are more ambitious – if you can spell them correctly, you are more likely of making a good impression:

antagonise	economically	onomatopoeia	terrain
atmosphere	environment	oppression	turbulent
channelled	facial	professional	turquoise
committed	hygienic	psychologically	tyrannical
competence	hypocrisy	rumour	villain
condemned	independent	stereotypical	vicious
connive	metaphorically	strikingly	
eccentric	naive	symbolise	

CHECK YOURSELF QUESTIONS

Q1 Which spelling patterns do the following words illustrate?

a chiefs   f although
b deceive   g driving
c shopping   h funnily
d hopeful   i leaves
e weigh   j question

Q2 Rewrite the passage below, correcting the spelling mistakes and noting which of the above rules are involved.

My nieghbour is hopefull of returning to the land of her berth one day, and she is driveing me mad with her constant chater about how much lovelyer than England most other countreys are. She has been all over the far and middle east, including Iraqu, were her best freind lives. I would happyly take a leaf out of her book – several leafs, to tell the truth – and visit foriegn places, but I'm allways kept very busy at my job. I mend rooves, and after this winter's storms I've been busyer than ever. I'm hopeing to get a holiday soon, but it won't be until the better whether comes. I'm dying for a brake, but I'm a bit short of money at the moment – I hardly have enough to keep the wolfs from the door, never mind exciting holidays.

Answers are on page 166.

Using appropriate punctuation

KEY EXAM SKILLS

- There are many different types of punctuation. The main ones are the comma, the semi-colon and colon, dashes, brackets, question marks and exclamation marks, apostrophes and speech marks.

- You need to be able to recognise and use punctuation correctly so that you can interpret texts that you read, and ensure that your own writing conveys the message that you intend.

◎ Punctuating sentences

- This is an extract from William Golding's *Lord of the Flies*:

Lord of the Flies

> He was old enough, twelve years and a few months, to have lost the prominent tummy of childhood; and not yet old enough for adolescence to have made him awkward.

- It is one sentence, so it begins with a **capital** (or **upper case**) **letter** and ends with a **full stop**.
- Sentences usually contain one or two main ideas or actions.
- Because the sentence contains two definite ideas – a contrast between childhood and adolescence – Golding has separated them with a semi-colon; he could have chosen to write two separate sentences, but, as the two ideas are closely linked, he decided that the less complete break shown by the **semi-colon** was more suitable.
- Note how the same thing has been done in the above comment, where the words following the semi-colon develop and explain the first half of the sentence.

- It is a good idea to use semi-colons yourself. Not only does it show your understanding of punctuation, but it helps you to develop and vary the style of your writing.

- **Commas** are used to separate off from the main part of the sentence a group of words (known as a phrase) which add a description. If you read the sentence from *Lord of the Flies* again, but miss out the words between the commas, you will see that it still makes perfect sense.

- The words 'twelve years and a few months' add useful information for the reader and so, although they are included, are marked off with commas to show that they are additional to the main idea of the sentence.

- Sometimes the main purpose of commas is to help the reader by indicating places in a long sentence where a slight pause will clarify the meaning. This sentence is from George Orwell's *Animal Farm*:

Animal Farm

> She knew that, even as things were, they were far better off than they had been in the days of Jones, and that before all else it was needful to prevent the return of the human beings.

- • The sentence is more easily understood if you pause at the commas when reading it.

- Commas are also used to separate items in a list, as in this extract from Harper Lee's *To Kill a Mockingbird*:

> Of all days Sunday was the day for formal afternoon visiting: ladies wore corsets, men wore coats, children wore shoes.

- • Note that Harper Lee has also used a **colon**. This piece of punctuation is particularly useful for introducing a list, as in the above example.

- The **dash** (–) is best used only occasionally, to emphasise an idea or statement. In the second comment on the *Lord of the Flies* excerpt opposite, two dashes have been used to make a point about the idea in Golding's sentence.

- Using dashes too frequently gives writing a rather frantic, breathless appearance and annoys the reader. Used sparingly, however, they can direct the reader's attention to important points.

- **Brackets** (or **parentheses**) are most often used to add an explanation, an example or (as at the beginning of this sentence) an alternative. Brackets are less striking (and less annoying to the reader if used frequently) than dashes.

- A **question mark** goes at the end of any direct question, as in this passage from Mildred C. Taylor's *Roll of Thunder, Hear My Cry*:

> Mama stared into Mr Morrison's deep eyes. 'Whose fault was it?'
> Mr Morrison stared back. 'I'd say theirs.'
> 'Did the other men get fired?'
> 'No, ma'am,' answered Mr Morrison. 'They was white.'

- • The questions are directly quoted in this passage. If, however, a question is merely reported during an account or narrative, a question mark is not used. An example of this (from the same book) is: 'When I asked him if he wanted to come work here as a hired hand, he said he would.'

▸ You need to be able to show that you can use 'a wide variety of appropriate punctuation to enhance clarity and meaning'.

▸ Think about how you can reveal the character of someone in a piece of fiction by using punctuation such as dashes and exclamation marks, and apostrophes of omission when they speak.

▸ While the actual words you use are very important, for example in straightforward description, imaginative punctuation helps the reader 'hear' the character's voice in their own mind.

■ The **exclamation mark**, like dashes, should be used sparingly. It is used to indicate anger, surprise, humour or any strong or unexpected feeling, as in this extract from Rukshana Smith's *Salt on the Snow*:

> Before she could be questioned Julie shouted, 'I know because I was there! That's how my head got bruised. Because he threw a brick at the window.'
> 'It wasn't me, prove it!' yelled Jim.

- The words 'shouted' and 'yelled' give a clue that exclamation marks might be appropriate; but remember that punctuation alone cannot convey feelings – it can only strengthen the impact of well-chosen language.

◎ Apostrophes

■ The two main uses of the **apostrophe** are to indicate missing letters and to show possession. Learn the rules carefully, as it is one of the most frequently misused items of punctuation.

MISSING LETTERS

■ The apostrophe shows where one or more letters have been missed out. The apostrophe is placed where the missing letter would have been.

- In the above passage from *Salt on the Snow*, the apostrophe in the word 'That's' shows that an 'i' has been left out – in a more formal situation, the speaker would have said 'That is'.
- The apostrophe in the word 'wasn't' shows that an 'o' has been left out – if the speaker had used more formal English, he would have said 'was not'.

■ If more than one letter is left out, you still only put one apostrophe into the word. Here is another example from *Salt on the Snow*:

> 'I've been too busy at work to keep an eye on things here, but I'll be watching you from now on.'

- In both instances where apostrophes are used here, two letters have been left out. The spoken version of 'I have' has become 'I've', and the spoken version of 'I will' has become 'I'll'.
- This last example shows how important it is to use apostrophes correctly, or the word 'I'll' might be confused with 'Ill' (meaning unwell), just as 'we'll' ('we will') might be confused with 'well' (not ill!) unless an apostrophe is correctly inserted.
- Watch out for instances where the apostrophe might stand for different letters; for example, 'he's' could be a spoken version of 'he is' or 'he has'.

■ The other main use of apostrophes is to show possession. This is a passage from Barry Hines' *A Kestrel for a Knave*:

> One lap of MacDowell's shirt curved out from beneath his sweater, and covered one thigh, like half an apron. Billy's shirt buttons had burst open all down the front. One button was missing, the corresponding button-hole ripped open. Their hair looked as though they had been scratching their scalps solidly for a week, and their faces were the colour of colliers'.

- The three apostrophes used here all show possession: we are told about the shirt which belongs to MacDowell, and then the shirt which belongs to Billy; the final word in the extract is comparing the colour of their faces to the colour of colliers' (or coal-miners') faces.
- If the writer had not put an apostrophe at the end of the word 'colliers', the meaning would have been quite different – he would have been suggesting that MacDowell's and Billy's faces were the colour of coal-miners, whatever that is!
- The apostrophe makes it clear that the boys' faces are the colour of colliers' faces, as the apostrophe makes the reader mentally refer back to an earlier word in the sentence which could be linked with 'colliers'' ('faces').

■ The apostrophe is also used when a book is ascribed to an author, as in William Golding's *Lord of the Flies* or Rukshana Smith's *Salt on the Snow*. The same is true of pictures (Leonardo da Vinci's *Mona Lisa)*, music (Beethoven's ninth symphony), films (Hitchcock's *Psycho*) and so on.

■ When using an apostrophe to show possession, an 's' is put after the apostrophe if the word does not already end with one.

■ If the word already ends with 's' but is not a plural (for example, 'bus' or the name 'Chris'), it is usual to add another 's' after the apostrophe, so you would have 'The bus's seats were very comfortable' or 'It was Chris's birthday last week'.

■ If the word is a plural – like 'colliers' in the example from *A Kestrel for a Knave* – you only need to put the apostrophe: do not add another 's'. Some words have a plural form which does not end in 's', for example 'women', 'children', 'geese'. In these cases, an 's' should be added after the apostrophe, so we would have 'The women's votes were crucial to the candidate's success' or 'The children's clothes were stolen from the changing rooms'.

■ Make sure you put apostrophes in the right place. In the comments on the extract from *A Kestrel for a Knave* it says:

> the boys' faces are the colour of colliers' faces

- That means 'the faces belonging to the two boys, MacDowell and Billy'. If it had said 'the boy's faces', it would not have made much sense, as it would have meant the two or more faces belonging to one boy!

CONFUSING APOSTROPHES

■ There are two potentially confusing uses of the apostrophe in words which are pronounced similarly but which have different meanings. If you remember that apostrophes generally replace missing letters, you should not have any problems.

I think it's lost its way

It's/Its

■ 'It's' is the shortened version of 'it is' or 'it has' and would be found in sentences such as 'It's a long way from here'.

■ 'Its' (without the apostrophe) means 'belonging to it', for example: 'The dog lost its ball.'

Who's/Whose

■ 'Who's' is the short form of 'who is' or 'who has' and might be found in sentences such as 'Who's going to carry this for me?'

■ 'Whose' (without the apostrophe and with an 'e' on the end) means 'belonging to whom', for example 'Whose house is that?'

- These examples may appear to contradict what has been said above about using apostrophes to show possession, but in this case there is no apostrophe because the words themselves contain the notion of possession. The same is true of 'hers', 'his', 'ours', 'yours', 'theirs'.

◎ Punctuating speech

■ **Speech marks**, sometimes known as **inverted commas** or **quotation marks**, are used to punctuate direct speech. This passage is from *Lord of the Flies*:

> "I don't care what they call me," he said confidentially, "so long as they don't call me what they used to call me at school."
> Ralph was faintly interested.
> "What was that?"
> The fat boy glanced over his shoulder, then leaned towards Ralph.
> He whispered.
> "They used to call me 'Piggy'."

- This extract illustrates the main rules of punctuating speech. These are:
  - put all spoken words inside the speech marks (the speech marks themselves can be double commas, as in the above example, or single commas, as in the previous examples from *Roll of Thunder, Hear My Cry* and *Salt on the Snow*);
  - each new piece of speech must begin with a capital letter, but one piece of speech can be broken up by other words as in Piggy's first sentence above, in which case the speech continues with a small (or lower-case) letter;
  - any punctuation of the speech goes inside the speech marks, for example the comma after 'me' in the first sentence and the question mark at the end of Ralph's reply;
  - if another set of quotation marks is needed within the speech marks, for example when Piggy mentions his nickname, then use single commas if you are already using double commas, or double commas if you are already using single commas;
  - if you start a passage of direct speech with words such as 'she said', 'he asked', then you need to put a comma after these words and before the speech marks, as in this example from *Salt on the Snow*: Rashmi pointed to the ceiling and Julie said, 'Not where, how?'

■ Speech marks are also used in handwritten text for the titles of books, films and works of art.

? CHECK YOURSELF QUESTIONS

Q1 What are the different uses of commas?

Q2 Look at this example of apostrophes:

The women's votes were crucial to the candidate's success.'

How would the meaning change if the second apostrophe were placed after the 's' (candidates')?

Q3 Punctuate this passage from *Animal Farm*:

but the men did not go unscathed either three of them had their heads broken by blows from boxers hoofs another was gored in the belly by a cows horn another had his trousers nearly torn off by jessie and bluebell and when the nine dogs of napoleons own bodyguard whom he had instructed to make a detour under cover of the hedge suddenly appeared on the mens flank baying ferociously panic overtook them

Answers are on page 167.

REVISION SESSION **3** ■ Using different sentence structures

■ The way that you structure sentences is very important, in conveying both the meaning and the tone of what you write.

■ You need to be able to tell the difference between formal and informal language and to structure your sentences appropriately.

◎ Appropriate use of informal/formal written English

FICTION

■ When you start to plan a piece of fictional writing, your first consideration should be whether the context of the writing is **formal** or **informal**.

■ Informal writing generally involves a lot of dialogue and informal language, including slang, to give the effect of addressing the reader directly in a 'chatty', engaging way.

■ More formal writing usually involves a more reflective, descriptive writing, much less like the informality of spoken language.

■ This is an extract from a GCSE student's story called 'Viva España':

> "'ere, Trace, what's the time?"
> "Will you stop asking that, for God's sake? It's just gone two."
> "Don't you think we ought to cover up? We've been out here since half ten this morning." Sharon squinted up at the midday sun and reached for her lipstick, which melted as soon as she applied it to her lips.
> "Hell's bells, Sharon, don't you want to get brown or something?"
> "Yeah, but . . ."
> "But what?"
> "Well, I'm going dead red and I feel sort of sick."

● Informal English is used to good effect to create the two characters. Sharon drops the 'h' in 'here', uses abbreviations (e.g. 'what's', 'don't', 'we've'), misses out words ('half [past] ten') and uses slang ('Yeah', 'dead [red]'), giving the impression of a casual, and perhaps not too bright, young lady.

● Tracey's impatience with her friend is shown by her use of phrases such as 'for God's sake', 'hell's bells' and the incomplete sentence, 'But what?'.

● Note, however, that the writer uses a more formal style in the sentence which describes Sharon putting on her lipstick: the use of the words 'squinted' and 'midday' set the scene precisely, and the use of the word 'applied' shows the writer's ability to use language precisely and to create effective contrasts.

- In fiction writing, different degrees of formality are necessary, depending on the precise purpose and the audience being written for.

- Formal English can be particularly effective in conveying an appropriate atmosphere through description. This is the beginning of a student's story called 'The Outsider':

Wait. It was all she could do. Time was rushing past and there was nothing her old and bony hands could do to hold it back. She did not know the time but knew that this was probably her last night on earth. Meg was to spend her last night alone, as she had spent most of her life.

- This passage is formal in spite of the fact it uses simple words and phrases. All words are given their full forms, and sentences are carefully constructed.
- The first sentence contains one word only which helps it to stand out.
- Note that the phrase 'old and bony' could have been written as 'old, bony' but the use of 'and' gives it a more formal and considered sound.

- Good fictional writing may often use an informal style for particular effects, when appropriate, and formal, precise language to create character and mood.

NON-FICTION

- Non-fiction writing can be informal, for example, a personal memory which includes realistic dialogue or casually expressed thoughts, but it is usually expressed formally, since this kind of writing is usually trying to explain or persuade.

- This is the start of a GCSE student's account of work experience:

The words 'work experience' have always conjured up a host of emotions, from when I first heard them and slotted them somewhere far off in the haze of the future. A mixture of excitement, curiosity, interest and hope mingled with a slight apprehension as the two-week period drew nearer.

- The language and the structure of the sentences is formal – the author is writing for an unknown audience, so a degree of formality is courteous; the purpose is to explain a feeling clearly and without risk of misunderstanding.
- The structure of the sentences is more complex than in Sharon and Tracey's dialogue. You would not write or speak to a friend like this – you'd be more likely to start, 'The thought of work experience really freaked me out, you know!'

The powerful description of Meg conjures up a vivid image.

Types of sentence

■ Achieving the right degree of formality and informality in your writing is not just a matter of avoiding slang or abbreviations. You also need to be able to vary how you structure sentences.

SIMPLE SENTENCES

■ A **simple sentence** contains just one basic thought or idea, and normally includes a subject and a verb:

> I laughed.
>
> • Here, 'I' is the subject, and 'laughed' is the verb.

■ Simple sentences are not necessarily so short; they can be much longer:

> No escaped prisoners of war were found hiding anywhere in the extensive network of underground passages.
>
> • This sentence is defined as 'simple' because it contains only one main verb.

COMPOUND SENTENCES

■ A **compound sentence** joins one or more simple sentences together. For example, you might write in a story:

> She had been gone for only a month. He felt lonely without her.

■ Alternatively, you could join these simple sentences into a compound sentence:

> She had been gone for only a month, but he felt lonely without her.

■ Sometimes, a series of short, simple sentences will convey an atmosphere of excitement or an agitated state of mind. At other times, longer, more complicated sentences will be necessary to explain a difficult idea, to suggest a character's confusion, or give the writing a continuous flow.

COMPLEX SENTENCES

■ **Complex sentences** are different from compound sentences. They join together several ideas by changing the basic grammatical structure of the sentence. Here are two more simple sentences:

> He had lost his interest in fishing. He decided to take up golf.

⚡ A/A* EXTRA

▸ You need to be able to show that you can write in a fluent style using grammar and syntax that is 'elaborate or concise, vigorous or restrained, according to purpose and audience'.

▸ You do not always need to write very complex sentences to impress the examiner. Strong contrasts are often very effective, such as in the extract from 'The Outsider' quoted on page 81.

▸ Different structures may imply different meanings: the example of a compound sentence shown on the right sounds less emotionally involved than the two simple sentences from which it derives. Your choice of which to use in a story would create a quite different impression of the character in question.

- These could be made into a compound sentence:

> He had lost his interest in fishing and decided to take up golf.

- The two simple sentences could also be formed into a complex sentence:

> Because he had lost his interest in fishing, he decided to take up golf.
>
> - The word 'because' makes the connection between the two parts of the sentence clearer.

◎ Using sentence structure

FICTION

- Varying sentence structures can add to the interest of fiction writing. This is the end of 'Viva España', the student's work featured on page 80:

Because he had lost his interest in fishing, he decided to take up golf.

> They stop and sit down on the cool, soft sand. She hugs her knees and looks up at him, the breeze now blustery and blowing her fine hair about. He sits with his legs folded under him, picking up handfuls of sand and letting it trickle slowly back through his fingers. While the waves lap quietly on the sand, distant music can still be heard.
>
> He whispers something in her ear and they laugh. He gently pushes back her hair so that he can see her face clearly; when he moves his hand, the hair falls back into her face. And he kisses her.
>
> - The sentences here are varied effectively. Every time something important happens – when the couple stop and sit down, when he whispers to her, and when they kiss – the sentences are simple and short.
> - In between, when the surroundings or the actions of the couple leading up to the kiss are being described, the sentences are longer, and compound or complex.

- This is a useful technique which helps the action in a story move quickly when necessary, but allows descriptions and reflections to be added which improve the overall effect and create more interest for the reader.

NON-FICTION

- In non-fiction writing, varying sentence structures can be an important way of conveying information clearly.

- Short sentences can be used to make a point as simply and straightforwardly as possible. Longer compound or complex sentences can then be used to elaborate or add detail, as for the descriptions or reflections in a narrative.

■ This is a further extract from the work-experience essay, which shows this technique in factual writing:

> I learned many useful things. One of these was how to use a sewing machine. I was pleased to discover how easy it was. Perhaps, though, I shouldn't have been so blasé! On a number of occasions I forgot to put the foot down, and had to spend the next few minutes surreptitiously (without much success) trying to free the machine from the acres of blue or red or white cotton which had become entangled in its depths.

- The three short, simple opening sentences set the scene.
- The two sentences which follow, both complex and one quite long, add detail and sustain the reader's interest.

INCOMPLETE SENTENCES

■ Sometimes sentences do not appear to obey any rules or conventions of the kind described above. This can be an effective device, but it needs to be used sparingly.

■ In speech, we often use incomplete sentences that do not contain a main verb, and this adds to the reality of the situation. Incomplete sentences are a normal part of how we speak – they can be incomplete because the speaker did not finish his or her thoughts, because of interruption or distraction.

- In 'Viva España', Tracey says to Sharon, 'But what?' This is a shorthand way of indicating that she doesn't think that any possible reason that Sharon might be about to suggest is valid.
- In 'The Outsider', the first sentence consists of just the one word 'Wait'. This makes the reader stop and think, and emphasises the atmosphere of quiet and stillness which the writer is trying to create.

CHECK YOURSELF QUESTIONS

Q1 Link the following groups of sentences into compound or complex sentences. You may miss some of the words out in your sentences.

a In Folkstone I met old Walter Dudlow. I was crossing the Leas. I was heading west.

b I came upon the diary. It was lying at the bottom of a rather battered red cardboard collar-box. I kept my Eton collars in it as a small boy.

Answers are on page 168.

Q2 Rewrite the following passage from a letter to a friend describing part of a week at an outdoor activities centre, in a style appropriate for inclusion in your school or college Record of Achievement. (Tip: think about appropriate language and sentence structures.)

I really got over being frightened of heights too! We climbed and abseiled a lot, and then guess what! The instructor said we were going potholing. I'm dead scared of the dark anyway, never mind being stuck in it! But I even got to lead a group through one tunnel. When we got out he said I'd done well, 'cos some of the others were even more scared than me.

Using paragraphs

- Structuring your writing using paragraphs will help you to convey your meaning clearly and achieve the purpose of your writing.

- You need to be able to use paragraphs, especially opening and closing paragraphs, appropriately in order to convey your meaning.

◉ What are paragraphs?

■ Think of **paragraphs** as part of the overall structure of writing, something which organises meaning and makes texts more accessible to readers.

■ A paragraph might therefore be a number of sentences which are connected by:
  - **topic** or subject, e.g. describing a character in a story or your feelings about one aspect of a controversial topic;
  - **narrative sequence**, e.g. a train journey made by the central character in a story;
  - an **argument**, e.g. reasons why you do or don't believe that the Loch Ness monster exists in an essay on world mysteries.

◉ How long is a paragraph?

■ Paragraphs are **flexible** and can be used not only to help organise writing so that its meaning is clear to readers, but also to contribute to the tone or atmosphere.

■ There are no rules for how long paragraphs should be. They can be as long or as short as they need to be. The following description of a public execution in Jedda appeared in the *Daily Express* in February 1958:

> Instinctively the man started, and in so doing raised his head. On the instant, with a swift and expert blow, the executioner decapitated him.
>
> A long, slow sigh came from the onlookers.
>
> Now a woman was dragged forward. She and the man had together murdered her former husband. She, too, was under thirty and slender.

- Most of the account is written in short paragraphs.
- It is designed to shock and involve the reader by making each aspect of the event stand out.
- We tend to pause at the end of each paragraph when reading, and in this case that pause allows the horror of the situation, the reaction of the crowd and the nature of the crime, to sink in.
- If all this had been written as one paragraph, there would have been a risk of readers hurrying through it without thinking so much about what they had read.

Disturbing scenes are often reported in short paragraphs. Breaking up text in this way encourages the reader to pause and take in the full horror of the situation before reading on.

▸ You need to show that you can 'make effective links within and between paragraphs so that the structure of your writing enhances its meaning and effect'.

▸ It is a good idea to think about the main point of each paragraph. This is sometimes known as the 'topic sentence'.

▸ The topic sentence may come anywhere in the paragraph, but your reader should be able to follow the argument or story simply through the topic sentences. If not, there is a structural problem with your writing!

◎ Beginnings and endings

OPENING PARAGRAPHS

■ The opening paragraph of a piece of writing needs to grab the reader's attention. It may be a strong statement of opinion, a description of a mysterious character or the expression of an original or unusual thought, depending on the type of writing. But whatever it is, it must appeal to the reader.

■ Here are some openings written by GCSE students. The first is from a story called 'Journey to my Father', in which a girl is invited to spend some time with her father. Her parents have divorced recently and she lives with her mother:

> 'Visit him? Why should you want to do that? Don't I give you enough? Haven't we . . .'
> Her voice droned on in the background. He was my father.
> Why shouldn't I see him?

This is a successful opening as it:
- uses direct speech, which always tends to involve the reader;
- conveys the mother's edginess through the repeated questioning;
- suggests the daughter's lack of patience as she lets her mind wander off what her mother is saying;
- sets up a conflict of loyalties in the story to come.

■ The second example is from a piece of non-fiction writing about advertising. It begins:

> I want to write about the way women are treated by the makers of car advertisements. For some reason, they think that they can use women to sell their cars. It makes me furious, the way they treat women.

- In its way, that is also a successful opening, as it:
  - makes a clear statement about the subject of the writing;
  - states the writer's views strongly and boldly.
- On the other hand, it:
  - is repetitive ('women' used three times in as many sentences);
  - is very informal in tone, which might not be appropriate for the intended audience.

CLOSING PARAGRAPHS

■ The ending of Laurie Lee's *As I Walked Out One Midsummer Morning* shows one very common technique in closing paragraphs:

> 'I was back in Spain, with a winter of war before me.

- This shows the one-sentence approach and also the technique of using the ending to leave the reader wanting more. There is a sequel to Laurie Lee's book, and the odds are that anyone who had enjoyed *As I Walked Out One Midsummer Morning* would have their appetite to read the sequel whetted by that final paragraph.
- A final paragraph like that is not really final – it's more of a link to what comes next. It is a technique that leaves readers wondering about what might have happened.

■ This student has used the same technique at the end of a piece of narrative writing called 'The Dare':

> I knew deep inside me that when I opened the door, something terrible would be waiting for me. But I wasn't prepared for this.

- Here, the reader is left to use the power of her or his own imagination to complete the story – not a technique you can use too often, and not because your own imagination has failed!

■ To be successful, an ending like that has to follow powerful and detailed writing, which will have got the reader's mind working, so that the ending they mentally supply is appropriate to what has been written before.

■ Summing-up paragraphs are often used at the end of a piece of non-fiction writing. For example, the student who wrote about the use of women in car advertising finished with this paragraph:

> So I think that advertisers are wrong to use women the way they do. Buying a car is nothing to do with sex, and advertising like this is degrading to everyone involved.

■ Another common style of ending is to use a paragraph which brings events to a tidy conclusion, leaving the reader with a satisfied feeling and a strong image of a central character.

■ This technique is used by Harper Lee at the ending of *To Kill a Mockingbird*:

> He turned out the light and went into Jem's room. He would be there all night, and he would be there when Jem waked up in the morning.

- Here the reader feels the story is closed (note the symbolism of turning out the light on all that has happened, and the new start which the morning will bring).
- The impression of Atticus as the caring, protective father is a reassuring and comforting note on which to end.

Atticus in the film of To Kill a Mockingbird.

■ The story 'Journey to My Father' ends:

> He was my father. However difficult it would make living with mum in the future, I couldn't ignore this kind and thoughtful man. Whatever had gone wrong between my parents was not my fault, and they were not going to punish me for it. To me, they were both good people, both part of me, now and for ever. Never mind the past, I thought, just let me get on with my life, and with both of them.

● This is a satisfying ending, as it draws together the themes and the characters in the story and also has just a touch of the wonder-what-will-happen feel about it, so you are fairly certain that the reader will continue thinking about the story after he or she has actually finished it.

CHECK YOURSELF QUESTIONS

Q1 The following extract from *The Diary of Anne Frank* was originally in six paragraphs. Where would you put the paragraph breaks, and why?

My longing to talk to someone became so intense that somehow or other I took it in my head to choose Peter. Sometimes if I've been upstairs into Peter's room during the day, it always struck me as very snug, but because Peter is so retiring and would never turn anyone out who became a nuisance, I never dared stay long, because I was afraid he might think me a bore. I tried to think of an excuse to stay in his room and get him talking, without it being too noticeable, and my chance came yesterday. Peter has a mania for crossword puzzles at the moment and hardly does anything else. I helped him with them and we soon sat opposite each other at his little table, he on the chair and me on the divan. It gave me a queer feeling each time I looked into his deep blue eyes, and he sat there with that mysterious laugh playing round the lips. I was able to read his inward thoughts. I could see on his face that look of helplessness and uncertainty as to how to behave, and, at the same time, a trace of his sense of manhood. I noticed his shy manner and it made me feel very gentle; I couldn't refrain from meeting those dark eyes again and again, and with my whole heart I almost beseeched him: oh, tell me, what is going on inside you, oh, can't you look beyond this ridiculous chatter? But the evening passed and nothing happened, except that I told him about blushing – naturally not what I have written, but just so that he would become more sure of himself as he grew older. When I lay in bed and thought over the whole situation, I found it far from encouraging, and the idea that I should beg for Peter's patronage was simply repellent. One can do a lot to satisfy one's longings, which certainly sticks out in my case, for I have made up my mind to go and sit with Peter more often and to get him talking somehow or other. Whatever you do, don't think I'm in love with Peter – not a bit of it! If the Van Daans had a daughter instead of a son, I should have tried to make friends with her too.

Answers are on page 168.

THE HENLEY COLLEGE LIBRARY

Presenting your work

- The presentation of your work matters: neatness and clarity are especially important under examination conditions.

- You also need to be able to use a variety of presentational techniques to help clarify your meaning.

◎ Handwriting

- Fluent, legible handwriting is important, as you have to use handwriting in the examination. The ability to write quickly, but still neatly and legibly should be consciously developed.

- People react favourably to neat handwriting. It can be characterful, but it should not be so unusual that it distracts the reader from the content of the work.

- Try to develop handwriting which:
  - is a sensible size – not too large, too small, too cramped or too spread out;
  - keeps the spaces between words to the same size;
  - shapes and joins letters consistently;
  - makes clear distinctions between lower- and upper-case letters;
  - leans one way, if it leans at all.

- It is easier to write neatly with fountain pens or roller balls than with biros, and different shapes and sizes of pens suit different hands. Experiment with styles of writing and pens to settle on a combination which allows you to work comfortably, quickly and neatly.

Experiment with different types of pen.

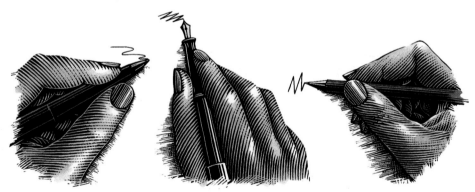

if you're on a YT but you're a special case

If you're a YT trainee, you'll get a weekly training allowance of at least £29.50 if aged 16 or £35 if aged 17 or over. This is more than the Income Support payment for most young people.

But some young people on YT may be able to get Income Support as well as the training allowance. For example, you could qualify if you are –

- A single parent and your child lives with you
- Living with a partner and with a child
- Living with a partner who is 18 or over and who is not working
- Living independently and your YT allowance is less than £36.15.

HOW TO CLAIM

1 Go to your local Social Security office and say you want to claim Income Support.

2 Fill in the form they give you and send it or take it back.

If in doubt about claiming, ask for advice at a Social Security office. See page 16 to find out how to find local offices.

NOTE: If you're on YT but employed full-time by the employer you're placed with, you'll not be able to claim Income Support. But if you have a child, you might be able to claim money from Family Credit. Look for a leaflet in post offices or Social Security offices.

- Note how the colour is used here.
- If you are preparing a piece of writing for coursework, you may be able to use IT to help you produce similar techniques.

◎ Breaking up the text

FICTION

- When writing prose fiction, use paragraphs effectively (see page 85).
- A lengthy narrative might have chapter headings.
- A newspaper or magazine story might have a headline and sub-headings as well as paragraphs.
- When writing poetry, the text should be structured into lines and verses.
- When writing drama scripts for the stage, obey layout conventions which make it easy to follow the dialogue and any stage directions. Radio and TV scripts need additional directions for cameras, microphones and effects of various kinds.

NON-FICTION

- When writing non-fiction, think carefully about using devices such as:
  - titles;
  - underlinings;
  - margins;
  - headings and sub-headings;
  - frames;
  - bullet points and numbers.
- This page from an Income Support claim shows how a few simple techniques can lift the appearance of a page.
- Even in a handwritten examination answer, most of these devices can be used to break up the text and make it both more attractive and more accessible to readers.

◎Illustrations and graphics

FICTION

■ Presentational devices seldom add to the reader's understanding of fiction in the way that they can with non-fiction.

■ Very occasionally, illustration may be crucial to a narrative: in one of his Sherlock Holmes stories, *The Adventure of the Dancing Men*, Arthur Conan Doyle uses the series of drawings shown on the right to help explain the mystery (which involves breaking a code) and to challenge readers' powers of interpretation.

> "I never should,
> the absurd | Mr. Holmes. But my wife does. It is frightening her to death. She says nothing, but I can see terror in her eyes. That's why I want to sift the matter to the bottom."
> drawing," I
> Holmes held up the paper so that the sunlight shone full upon it. It was a page torn from a note-book. The markings were done
> Cubitt, of | in pencil, and ran in this way :—
> k, is very
>
> 𝆏𝆏𝆏𝆏 𝆏𝆏 𝆏𝆏𝆏 𝆏𝆏𝆏
>
> the stairs, | Holmes examined it for some time, and then, red a tall, | folding it carefully up, he placed it in his whose clear | pocket-book.
> life led far | "This promises to be a most interesting He seemed | and unusual case," said he. "You gave me sh, bracing, | a few particulars in your letter, Mr. Hilton

NON-FICTION

■ Using illustrations and graphics in non-fiction writing can be extremely useful, and an awareness of readers' needs in understanding complex material is important.

■ This is an extract from a government leaflet about smoke alarms in the home:

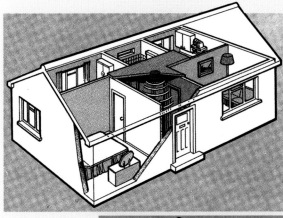

✓ Do make sure your smoke alarm is fixed on the ceiling at least 30 cm (12 inches) from the wall or light fitting. A central position is best. If it's designed for wall mounting, put it between 15 and 30 cm (6 and 12 inches) below the ceiling.

✓ Do put your smoke alarm where you will be able to reach it fairly easily – and safely – for regular testing and maintenance; not above stairwells, for example.

✗ Don't put your smoke alarm in any room which tends to get very hot (a boiler room for example) or very cold (an unheated outhouse).

✗ Don't put your smoke alarm in bathrooms, shower rooms or in cooking areas or garages where the smoke alarm may be triggered by steam, condensation or fumes.

✗ Don't put your smoke alarm next to or directly above heaters or air conditioning vents.

✗ Don't fix your smoke alarm to surfaces which are normally much warmer or colder than the rest of the room. These can include uninsulated exterior walls and ceilings (temperature differences might stop smoke from reaching it).

- There is a lengthy piece of text which goes into considerable detail (not shown), but then the reader is given drawings and a checklist.
- For many readers, this is a helpful and reassuring way of presenting the main points from that section of the leaflet.

◎ Editing and proof reading

- Never forget to check your work.

- **Editing** means re-reading work and thinking about issues raised in this and previous revision sessions such as:

  - **audience**: who is this writing for, and what requirements does that imply?
  - **purpose**: why am I writing this, and what do I want to get across?
  - **topic**: have I included the right information, given the audience and purpose?
  - **structure**: is the content presented logically and in the best order?
  - **presentation**: is it easily understood, and does it look right?

- **Proof-reading** means checking for mistakes in the mechanics of your writing: spelling, punctuation and grammar.

- Look particularly for mistakes which you know you often make, and correct them carefully.

- In coursework, produce a clean, final draft which makes it seem there have never been mistakes.

- In an examination, cross out the error neatly and write the correction above or beside it. The examiner will be impressed that you have proof-read successfully.

? CHECK YOURSELF QUESTIONS

Q1 If an examination question gave you a piece of written information on a subject such as 'Smoking by teenagers' and asked you to re-present it more attractively for a given audience, what sorts of presentational devices might you think of using? Make a list of up to six appropriate devices, and say why each could be useful. (Remember, this is in an examination, so you do not have access to IT.)

Answers are on page 169.

Using vocabulary and stylistic features

> ■ You need to be able to demonstrate a wide and varied vocabulary in all aspects of your work.
>
> ■ You also need to be able to recognise and use different stylistic features to engage and sustain the reader's interest.

KEY EXAM SKILLS

◎ Writing narrative

■ Use apt and imaginative **vocabulary**, choosing words for their precise and appropriate meaning.

■ Match the vocabulary to the needs of the audience and to the settings, characters or ideas being described.

■ Extend your own vocabulary by:
- reading widely, checking the meanings of unfamiliar words in a dictionary;
- thinking about words which have very close meanings: what is the difference between them, and how would you use them appropriately?
- using a thesaurus to find alternatives to words which you overuse, or which do not seem quite right for a particular purpose;
- using a dictionary alongside the thesaurus to check the precise meanings of unfamiliar words.

■ This is the opening of a GCSE candidate's story called 'Discovery':

> The repetitive hum of the helicopter echoed threateningly above them. Their thick, leather boots, toughened by previous use, trekked rhythmically over the difficult terrain. Suddenly they halted, hiding in the shadow of a tree, their hands on the drenched moss, trying to recapture lost breath and regain lost stamina. Rain was beating on the trees above them. A flash of lightning illuminated the forest around them – or was it? Their minds were so confused and exhausted it might have been the strong beam of the helicopter scanning the area for them.

- Very few of the words used here are unusual, but all are chosen carefully to give a precise description of the scene and an impression of the feelings of the hunted people.
- The use of 'repetitive' and 'trekked rhythmically' suggests the weariness of the people and the length of time they have been on the move.
- The effect of the word 'drenched' is made greater by the plainness of the language around it: it is a small detail which brings the scene to life by involving your sense of touch and it prepares you for the mention of the 'beating' rain later.

- It is not always possible to use original, imaginative vocabulary – very few people know great numbers of unusual words, and anyway they would lose their effect if used constantly. Judging when to use a word is as important a skill as knowing the word in the first place.

- Think about different ways of presenting stories and what effect this can have on readers. In *Animal Farm*, for example, George Orwell uses the apparent structure of a children's story about talking animals to tell a fable or parable about modern society.

- Another kind of stylistic feature is for a story to be told by two or more characters so that the reader not only gets to know them well, but sees events through two sets of eyes and has to think about where the truth lies. This can be done by using letters or diaries to tell one or both sides of the story.

- If you were writing about someone confined to one place, such as a prison cell or a hospital bed, or even a boarding school, using a device such as an interchange of letters to tell a story can be realistic as well as effective.

◎ Writing poetry

- When writing poetry, it is important to decide:
  - how the vocabulary used can convey strong feelings or ideas to the reader;
  - what use can be made of devices such as metaphor, simile, alliteration to make the vision vivid;
  - what form to use: rhyme or no rhyme? A regular verse-pattern or not?

- These are the final lines of Seamus Heaney's *Storm on the Island*:

Space is a salvo,
We are bombarded by the empty air.
Strange, it is a huge nothing that we fear.

- The lines show the use of alliteration, onomatopoeia, metaphor and half-rhyme to convey a striking idea, that space is frightening simply because it is 'empty', 'a huge nothing'.
- The words 'space', 'salvo' and 'strange' are linked by the alliteration which therefore joins the words in your mind and helps to form the idea of the peculiar and threatening nature of space, which you may previously have thought of as mere emptiness.
- The use of an onomatopoeic word like 'bombarded' strengthens the threatening quality of the lines, in which the air is seen metaphorically as a force which attacks us.
- The half-rhyme of 'air' and 'fear' is like a discord in music, a jagged sound on which to end an unsettling poem.

■ When writing poetry, aim to write short, concentrated bursts of language. This GCSE candidate conveys the intense feelings of young love:

> Passions ago,
> we walked on grass
> and flowers.
> They have died
> by our heat;
> we stand on
> erosion,
> our feet
> crumble by hours.
> We have kissed away
> greenness, and the colours
> of uncrushed joy.

- The poet starts with an original image: 'passions' ago, rather than days, weeks or months.
- The image is carried on in the suggestion that the love is so intense that it has burnt up the grass and flowers, and this leads to the idea that love is not built on anything secure – 'erosion', an unusual choice of word in this context, and made to stand out even more by the fact that it provides the only rhyme in the poem.
- 'Crumble' is again a strikingly unromantic word in this setting.
- The last three lines express the poet's guilt or loss of innocence, using a pun in 'greenness', which both refers back to the burnt-up grass, but also means innocence.
- The intensity of the language and the stylistic features used by the candidate mean that in just thirty-four words, the reader has been given much to think about.

◎ Writing non-fiction

■ When writing non-fiction, it is often presentational features (see pages 89–92) which contribute much of the effect; however, stylistic devices can be used too.

■ The following headline is from an advertisement for banking services to assist Amnesty International:

Two new weapons to fight oppression.

> ● It uses a metaphor, calling a credit card and cheque book weapons, which is ironically appropriate for an organisation which tries to stamp out torture and abuse and arms dealing.

■ When writing narrative kinds of non-fiction, such as autobiography or travelogue, think about the use of carefully chosen vocabulary and stylistic devices much as you would if writing fictional narrative.

■ This is the start of a GCSE student's memoir of her early life:

> My earliest memories are like the bottom of an old bucket: rusty and damp. Rusty, because I really don't remember them all that well, but damp because I do recall that in our Dartmoor village it seldom seemed to stop raining.

- This is a striking opening, not through the use of any unusual words, but because the simile which compares life to a bucket is original and makes you want to read on.
- The writer has also skilfully chosen three words beginning with 's' at the end of the second sentence, using the alliteration to imitate the sound of the rain which is the chief memory.

CHECK YOURSELF QUESTIONS

Q1 As an exercise in using a range of vocabulary, copy out this passage from William Golding's *Lord of the Flies*, filling in the blanks with appropriate words.

Smoke was rising here and there among the creepers that ......[1] the dead or dying trees. As they watched, a ......[2] of fire appeared at the root of one wisp, and then the smoke thickened. Small flames stirred at the ......[3] of a tree and ......[4] away through leaves and brushwood, dividing and increasing. One patch touched a tree trunk and ......[5] up like a bright ......[6]. The smoke increased, sifted, rolled outwards. The squirrel leapt on the ......[7] of the wind and clung to another standing tree, ...[8] downwards. Beneath the dark canopy of leaves and smoke, the fire laid hold on the forest and began to ......[9]. Acres of black and yellow smoke rolled steadily towards the sea. At the sight of the flames and the ......[10] course of the fire, the boys broke into shrill, excited cheering. The flames, as though they were a kind of wild life, crept as a ......[11] creeps on its ......[12] towards a line of birch-like saplings that ......[13] an outcrop of the pink rock. They ......[14] at the first of the trees, and the branches grew a brief ......[15] of fire. The heart of flame leapt ......[16] across the gap between the trees and then went swinging and ......[17] along the whole row of them. Beneath the ......[18] boys a quarter of a mile square of forest was ......[19] with smoke and flame. The separate noises of the fire merged into a ......[20] that seemed to shake the mountain.

Answers are on page 170.

Writing to explore, imagine and entertain

- You need to be able to recognise certain qualities and use certain techniques when producing creative writing.

What kind of writing is this?

- This category includes most 'imaginative' or 'creative' writing; in other words, usually fiction. It can be in the form of poetry or a play script, but prose is usually expected in examination answers.

- The writing does not have to start with original ideas; if you have read a novel or a play and you decide to write an extra chapter or a 'missing' scene, that would count as 'writing which explores, imagines or entertains', even though you are using someone else's characters and settings.

- The category also includes writing about your own experiences (in other words, non-fiction) if it is used to explore or imagine.

Qualities of prose fiction

- This is the beginning of a rather unusual short story called *There Was Once* by Margaret Atwood:

> – There was once a poor girl, as beautiful as she was good, who lived with her wicked stepmother in a house in the forest.
> – Forest? Forest is passé, I mean I've had it with all this wilderness stuff. It's not a right image of our society, today. Let's have some urban for a change.
> – There was once a poor girl, as beautiful as she was good, who lived with her wicked stepmother in a house in the suburbs.
> – That's better. But I have to seriously query this word poor.
> – But she was poor!
> – Poor is relative. She lived in a house, didn't she?
> – Yes.
> – Then socio-economically speaking, she was not poor.

- It **explores**:
  - the idea of how a traditional fairy-tale might be updated;
  - character, by structuring the story through the different viewpoints of two speakers.
- It **imagines**:
  - what an updated plot or story might be;
  - what an appropriate setting for the modern story might be.
- It **entertains**:
  - by making fun of (or 'parodying') a traditional form or structure;
  - through the relationship of the characters as shown in their language.

Angela Carter reworked and 'updated' many traditional tales. In the Company of Wolves, based on Little Red Riding Hood, was made into a film.

◎ Planning a story

- Some of the features of prose fiction which need to be considered when planning a piece of writing are:
  - **plot** or **story**: what happens? Why? How? In what order?
  - **characters**: who are they? How are they brought alive through description, dialogue and action?
  - **setting**: how important is this to the story? How do you create a sense of place through detailed description and the action of the story?
  - **ideas**: what is the point of the story? What's it all about? Is there a clear 'message'?
  - **structure**: do you tell the story? Is it told by one of the characters involved? Do you use flashbacks? Do you tell part of it through diaries or letters?

- Planning can take the form of outline notes, or you can rough out some actual sentences or paragraphs which might be included in the finished story.

- This title was set on a recent GCSE paper:

> Write a story about a school trip where something unexpected happened.

PLOT

- The starting point must be what happened and why it was unexpected.

- Aim for some originality. Don't write about a pupil getting lost, or the bus breaking down, or someone being ill or losing all their money: these are not unexpected happenings on a school trip!

- On the other hand, don't be absurd – don't write about a pupil finding a paper bag containing a million pounds which he and his friends get to spend, or a famous film or music star coming by and falling madly in love with one of the pupils.

- Think hard about what might happen which is realistic and possible, but not expected, for example a pupil who has always been very shy and quiet performs a heroic deed by helping another pupil, always seen as brave and outgoing, who has become stuck on a ruined castle tower.

CHARACTERS

- Think about the characters who might be involved. In the above example, there are certainly two pupils, of contrasting personality: one apparently quiet and shy, the other bold and noisy. These aspects of their characters could be established through describing part of the bus journey to the castle.

- Don't just write 'Tom sat quietly while Jack made a lot of noise'. You need to give more detail and in more subtle ways. For example, you might describe an incident such as this:

Tom could hear the noise at the back of the coach. Everyone was laughing at Jack's impersonations of the teachers, and at his jokes. Suddenly he felt a sharp pain on the back of his neck: so it had started, throwing things. Next they'd tease him, try to embarrass him. 'Tommy, oh Tommy'. He could hear them now. It would get worse. He continued reading his book, pretending that he couldn't hear.

- This description involves description, dialogue and action.

■ Don't spend so long establishing the characters that you have no time left to describe the central incident.

■ Concentrate on bringing the main characters to life through detail, but where other characters are concerned, remember that just one or two carefully chosen words will make a description work in the reader's mind. So instead of merely writing 'They went into the castle past the attendant's hut', try something like:

They went into the castle past the hut where the attendant sat, watching them suspiciously as if they were an invading army returning after hundreds of years to attack the walls again.

- The sentence quickly conveys the picture of the attendant who's not very keen on school parties, and suggests some of the noisy, and perhaps aggressive, qualities of the children.

SETTING

■ When describing the setting, take the chance to show your powers of description. After all, the setting is crucial to the plot of this story.

■ A poor writer will be content to say something like 'The castle was old and falling down. The walls were high and broken in places. The towers had gaps where you could see right through them'. To create a more atmospheric setting, use more complex sentences, more sophisticated vocabulary and images:

The ancient castle, its harsh grey stone partly covered with green and gold lichen, loomed above them. In places, the walls had tumbled into piles of random boulders, while the towers, still dark and tall against the pale blue spring sky were ragged with holes; they looked like the arms of an old, worn-out jumper stretching towards the clouds.

- The use of colours in description helps the reader visualise a scene more precisely.
- Using similes (such as comparing the castle towers with old sleeves) or other figures of speech adds even more to the atmosphere.

IDEAS

- Decide what the story is about. The above example is making the point that true bravery does not always make a loud show, or that people's true characters and qualities are only revealed under stressful circumstances.

- Do not express this as a kind of 'moral' tacked on to the end of the story; credit your readers with the intelligence to work that out for themselves, provided you nudge them gently in the right direction.

- The final paragraph might be something like this:

> Tom sat silently in his seat on the coach. Not in the way that he had sat that morning, but with a glow of calm satisfaction. Yes, he knew they were talking about him again; but he knew that they wouldn't be throwing anything and that the talk would no longer be mocking. Jack was sitting quietly too, he noticed.

- An understated ending like that leaves the reader to think over what the story has been about, keeping interest engaged right to – and beyond – the end of the written words.

STRUCTURE

- The above example assumes that the story would be told in the order in which it happened and in the third person (that is, as though you were someone outside the action watching it and describing it).

- Other possible approaches are:
  - telling the story from the point of view of one of the characters and so telling it in the **first person**;
  - telling parts of the story in **flashback**, remembering what happened during the journey back to school at the end of the day.

- Be careful not to overdo such features. An examination answer is often too brief to allow clever structural tricks – longer pieces of coursework are really the place for that.

- Concentrate on using the **range** and **depth** of your vocabulary and your control of different sentence structures to catch and hold the reader's attention.

◎ Language

DESCRIPTIVE WRITING

- When writing prose fiction, create descriptions which bring people, places and events vividly to life.

- Think about the **senses** when writing descriptions, and try to appeal to sight or sound, for example. This scene is taken from *A Kestrel for a Knave* by Barry Hines:

> A thrush ran out from under a rhododendron shrub and started to tug a worm from the soil between the loose asphalt chips. It stood over the worm and tugged vertically, exposing its speckled throat and pointing its beak to the sky. The worm stretched, but held. The thrush lowered its head and backed off, pulling at a more acute angle. The worm still held, so the thrush stepped in and jerked at the slack. The worm ripped out of the ground and the thrush ran away with it, back under the shrubs.

- Because of the precise description of angles and movement, it is easy to visualise this scene.

- This short passage from Susan Hill's *I'm the King of the Castle* shows how you can appeal to the reader's sense of sound as well as sight:

> There was a slight, persistent movement of wind through the yew tree branches, and the elms and oaks of the copse, and a rustling of the high grasses in the field. The moonlight, penetrating a thin place between two trees, caught the stream that ran through its centre, so that, now and then, as the branches stirred, there was a gleam of water.

- Visualising scenes in this kind of detail is a sure way of capturing the reader's interest.
- The use of onomatopoeic words like 'rustling' appeals to the reader's sense of hearing.

- Movement and colour are useful ways of describing people, especially their faces. This can say a great deal about their character. This description of a young woman is from L.P. Hartley's *The Go-Between*:

> Her hair was bright with sunshine, but her face, which was full like her mother's, only pale rose-pink instead of cream, wore a stern, brooding look that her small, curved nose made almost hawk-like. She looked formidable then, almost as formidable as her mother. A moment later she opened her eyes – and her face lit up.

- The use of colour makes the woman sound attractive, but other words such as 'brooding' and 'formidable' and the image of the hawk suggest more menacing qualities.
- The movement described in the last sentence suggests that she has a powerful presence.

■ The art of effective description is to observe details – either in reality or in your imagination – and then to use the most precise words and images you can think of to capture those details.

■ This is an example of a candidate's work from an actual GCSE paper. It is the start of a story called 'The Dare', which was awarded a Grade A:

> On a midsummer afternoon, the sun was like a burning eye looking down at us, making us sweat like pigs. My brother, my friend Peter, his brother Andrew and I were wandering around the streets, our feet lazily following the intricate track of the pavement like a train. It was too hot to do anything but suddenly Peter shouted out, 'Let's play Double Dare.' This was a game we had devised a long time ago and only emerged when days like this pulled it out by the hand. Everyone's face lit up like a lantern and suddenly we were sitting on the floor spinning a bottle and devising dares to carry out before the bottle stopped.

- There is variation of **sentence structures**, conscious choice of **vocabulary** and use of **imagery** to interest the reader, which can be seen in phrases such as 'the sun was like a burning eye looking down at us', 'our feet lazily following the intricate track of the pavement like a train' or 'Everyone's face lit up like a lantern'.
- There is an occasional misjudgement: 'sweat like pigs' is a cruder comparison than any others in the passage. It would have worked better as dialogue, in other words, if one of the characters had said, 'I'm sweating like a pig!'.
- The passages shows awareness of the need for **description**, and some sense of style in achieving it.

WRITING DIALOGUE

■ Narratives are often more lively and interesting if they contain dialogue – the Margaret Atwood story on page 98 consists entirely of dialogue, and the story about the unexpected event on a school trip would certainly need dialogue to bring the main incident to life.

■ Use the opportunity to show your ability to use non-standard English in creating lifelike characters. This is another extract from an examination answer. The candidate, who was awarded a Grade C overall, is writing a story about a teenage girl whose mother walks out on her family. Karen, the daughter who suspects what has happened, is on the phone to her aunt, Denise:

A/A* EXTRA

▸ You need to be able to 'consciously shape and craft language and structure to achieve sophisticated effects'.

▸ Look back at the Margaret Atwood extract on page 98 and see how she uses a traditional structure, with unexpectedly modern language and ideas, to interest and amuse the reader.

▸ The L.P. Hartley extract opposite, which achieves its impact through the careful choice and accumulation of vocabulary, is also a sophisticated piece of writing.

'Hi, Denise, how are you?'

'Fine, thanks. What's up, Karen?'

'Oh, I was just ringing to speak to mum.'

'Your mum, what would she be here for?'

Karen was shocked by this reply. 'Oh. I, I thought she said she was popping in to see you today.'

'No, I've not seen her for ages. Sorry, love.'

'It's OK. Bye.'

- This passage shows a sound ability to write a convincing, but not very demanding, passage of conversation.
- The words sound realistic, using non-standard forms such as 'Hi' and 'Bye' and abbreviations commonly used in speech, but we do not experience a strong sense of two different characters, or of a tense situation, which a better candidate would have been able to suggest.

■ Achieving a balance of description and dialogue while moving the plot forward is very much at the heart of a well-planned story; this balance can often be achieved by describing a small but important incident in detail.

CHECK YOURSELF QUESTIONS

Q1 Rewrite the above conversation between Karen and Denise, including detail to make the aunt sound more concerned and the teenager more confused. At the end, add Karen's reflections after the phone call.

Your answer will not be the same as the one given, but if you have used similar techniques, you will have raised the standard of the passage from Grade C to nearer Grade A.

Q2 You always need to plan the whole story so that you know exactly what is going to happen, who is involved, where it takes place, what the central idea is, and how it is going to be told.

Plan the story of the quiet boy who saves the popular, friendly boy from a perilous position on the castle tower. Under each of the headings ('plot', 'characters', 'setting', 'idea' and 'structure'), jot down brief notes which would help you write the complete story.

Answers are on page 170.

Writing to inform, explain and describe

> ■ You need to be able to recognise certain qualities and use certain techniques when producing informative writing.

KEY EXAM SKILLS

What kind of writing is this?

- This category includes writing which tells someone **how to do something**, or **how something works**, or **what it looks or feels like**.

- It involves describing **actual events**, **places** or **objects**, so that someone can find their way somewhere, learn how to do something, or recognise a feeling. It is not the kind of describing where the intention is to create character or setting in a piece of fiction.

- Writing of this kind is often based on **experiences** and **observations**.

- In an examination, you will often be given some material you can use in your answer, some indication of the audience you are writing for, and some general idea of the purpose of your writing.

- The sorts of writing tasks set within this category could include the following (all are taken from sample GCSE examination papers):

> • You are a member of your school or college council. The council has recently agreed to try to make the school or college more environmentally friendly. Write a letter to your Chair of Governors in which you inform her/him of the council's decision and explain ways in which you would like to see it carried out.
> [This is a task which requires you both to inform and explain. Note that the audience will mean a polite, formal letter.]
>
> • Many poets or novelists write about their earliest memories and how these memories have affected them. Write about a memory and explain how it has affected you.
> [This is a task which requires you mainly to explain, but will also involve some describing. If an audience is not given, assume that you are writing for a sympathetic, intelligent adult.]
>
> • Describe a place at two different times of the year or at two different times of the day. It could be a place that you know very well or one that you have imagined.
> [This is a task which requires you to describe. Again, no audience is given, so assume you are writing for a sympathetic, intelligent adult.]

Early memories can be very vivid.

- It is often difficult for examiners to completely separate informing, explaining and describing. Note which of those words are used in any question, and make sure that you write appropriately for the stated purpose and for any given audience.

◎ Informing

■ This is part of a leaflet published by the Government Information Society Initiative, which informs the public about the uses of information technology, and how they can find out more if they are interested:

So how can I find out more?

There are many different ways you can find out more about IT.

To start, you could become more familiar with some of these technologies.
Ask friends. Try things out yourself.
Don't be afraid or embarrassed.
The 'Information Society' is nothing to be scared about.

Come and take part.

For a handy guide to some everyday IT technologies, take a look at our jargon busters list over the page.

Get the facts for <u>free</u>

Another smart step is to call the free
'IT for All' Information Line on

0800 456 567

Tell us your name and address and we'll send you a copy of our special booklet, *The Guide To How IT Can Help You,* explaining everyday information technologies in plain, simple language. What's more we'll also keep you informed of any 'IT for All' activities in your area. It won't cost you a penny.

Make the most of IT

Some ideas to think about...

Try out a computer

Today's computers are versatile and fun. Try a friend's or visit one of the high street stores. A home computer is one of the best ways to give your family a flying start in IT.

Experience the Internet

It won't take long to get used to using the Internet, and it is fascinating. Ask if your library can give you a demonstration or look out for an Internet Café. There's one in most major towns.

Learn about the basics

A little knowledge goes a long way. Call the 'IT for All' information line and we'll send you our special booklet, *The Guide To How IT Can Help,* as well as keeping you informed of any 'IT for All' activities in your area.

Read all about it!

The national press and television often dedicate features and programmes to IT topics. With an understanding of just a few basic terms they are easy to follow.

- Although it is written in a style appropriate to a leaflet, rather than in continuous prose, it shows some of the approaches you can use in informative writing, including similar presentational techniques (depending on purpose and audience).
- The leaflet:
  - uses straightforward, friendly and welcoming language;
  - uses a reassuring tone;
  - suggests alternative ways of obtaining the information;
  - refers to where more information is available if required;
  - repeats key points.

⚡ A/A* EXTRA

▸ You need to be able to show a 'clear and controlled relationship between successive paragraphs' with 'sustained crafting'.

▸ Even a leaflet which uses a variety of presentational devices needs to guide the reader. Look again at the example opposite and note the use of linking words and phrases such as 'So how', 'Another', 'What's more' and so on.

▸ Practise using conjuncts such as 'however', 'nevertheless', 'on the other hand', 'although' in your own writing.

■ Taking as an example the task on page 105 on making a school or college more 'green', think about:
- the **tone of language**: you are addressing a formal letter to someone you may not know very well, or even at all, and you are suggesting some changes which may be seen as revolutionary! You need to reassure, as well as merely inform;
- suggesting a number of **alternative schemes** or approaches, so that the Chair feels he or she has some choice;
- using **structural devices** such as bullet points or headings to make your suggestions clear and immediate;
- using **repetition** appropriately, to emphasise your reasons for wanting change;
- offering ways in which the Chair could discuss this further with the Council if he or she wishes.

◎ Explaining

PURPOSE AND AUDIENCE

■ Good explanations address **purpose** and **audience**. In other words, why are you writing the explanation, and who is it for?

■ Decide how much your audience needs to know, i.e. why they require the explanation, and what they know about the subject already. This will help you decide on the amount of detail to use, and on the appropriate language level.

■ Compare these two descriptions of the Internet:

1

The Internet (or Net)

The Internet (or Net) is like a huge telephone system linking computers from all over the world. This means that you can make contact with anyone else, anywhere, who is also on the Net. With the right equipment, home computers can connect to the Internet on a normal phone line, often to a local number.

▸

---

2 Come on, 9 million?

The plain fact is, no one really knows just how big the Internet really is. That's because no one really owns the Internet. But several organizations make it their business to periodically try to find out how big the Internet is. The science is far from exact, but these organizations are able to come up with pretty reasonable estimates.

The best known of these Internet bean-counters is Network Wizards, which does a survey every year. In January of 1996, Network Wizards found that the Internet connected 240,000 separate computer networks and that more than 9.4 million separate computers existed on the Internet. When compared with 1995's numbers, the 1996 survey shows that the Internet has more than doubled in size in the past year. Or to put it another way, three new computers were added to the Internet every second.

Truth is, estimates such as Network Wizards are probably low. Consider that three of the largest online services – America Online, CompuServe, and The Microsoft Network – together support more than 10 million users. No one knows exactly how many of these users actually use the Internet. Still, the indisputable point is that the Internet is big – and getting bigger every day. If you find these figures interesting, you can check up on the latest Internet statistics from Network Wizards by accessing its Web site, www.nw.com.

- The first comes from the same leaflet we looked at on page 106.
- It is intended to be an explanation for someone who knows almost nothing about the subject, so it is brief and simply laid out.
- The language is simple, comparing the Internet to something which every reader will understand ('a huge telephone system').
- It gives only basic details; although it tells you how to connect to the Internet and what you can do on it ('make contact with anyone else, anywhere'), it doesn't tell you why you might want to do this.
- The second example is taken from a book entitled *Internet Explorer 3 for Windows 95 for Dummies*.
- The book is obviously not for total dummies, however, as the explanation assumes the reader will understand terms such as 'bean-counters', 'computer networks', 'online services', 'accessing' and 'web site'.

■ One of the most common errors in explanatory writing is to assume that your reader knows and understands all that you do – which is why explanations in instruction manuals for all kinds of equipment (such as how to programme video recorders) are often notoriously difficult to follow.

STRUCTURE

- Think about the **structure** of your writing: what is the best, most logical order in which to present explanations so that your reader does not become muddled or confused.

- Do not throw too much information at your reader at once: technical terms or complicated ideas may need to be **repeated several times**, and **in different ways**, to make sure they are understood.

- You may be asked to explain how something has happened rather than how it works, or what it is (as in the task on page 105 about an early memory and how it has affected you). The way to approach this is still the same. Think about:
  - *who* **you are writing** for, and what they know about you already, if anything;
  - *why* **you are writing**: to explain why an aspect of your personality has been shaped by that early memory;
  - **describing the memory in a logical, straightforward way**: use the best words and grammatical structures you can, but remember this is essentially an introduction to your explanation, not a developed piece of exploratory or imaginative writing;
  - **making your explanation clear** by giving examples of how this early memory affects the way you relate to people, or your interests, or your fears (giving several examples will emphasise the effect on you, as well as ensuring the reader understands the point you are making).

◎ Describing

- Non-fiction descriptions are often intended to **produce an effect** on the reader; descriptions of people or places are seldom totally objective, and the same may be true of the description of an object, especially if someone is trying to sell it.

- Think about the sample exam question at the start of this session, which was to describe a place at two different times of the day or two different times of the year. You might want to convey your strong feeling that the place is miserable in winter, or threatening at night, for example.

- In writing such a description, you would therefore need to:
  - **observe** or **remember** (or imagine) **accurately**, and **in detail** (if imagining, relate as much as possible to real places you know);
  - select what is **important for your purpose** (is it to create a particular atmosphere, or a strong feeling?) and your **audience** (how formal should your writing be? Are your readers likely to sympathise with your point of view?);
  - choose words which describe **precisely** and **accurately**, and remember to vary sentence structures and lengths for effect.

◎ A candidate's work

- This is part of an examination answer in which the task was 'Put together a fact sheet on truancy for parents of teenage children. Explain what causes truancy, describe who typical truants are, and inform parents how they can help prevent truancy.'

- Candidates were provided with some materials to help them, including statistical information.

Fear of French and Petrified of P.E.?

A THIRD OF TEENAGERS TURN TO TRUANCY!!

The Truth behind Truancy

It's time to face up to the facts! Truancy cannot just be ignored, it is alive and well and could be effecting YOUR child. Truancy is becoming serious, with shocking figures that could include your family:

- 1 in 10 fifth formers admitted truanting once a week
- 8% admitted truanting
- ¼ of fifth formers truanted once per month

The figures are real and can't be hidden so it is no use passing the blame – it may be happening near you.

Who Truants – Not Our Family!

I hear you say. This may very well be true but can you be entirely sure? Figures show those most likely to truant school are 16 year old boys and girls followed closely by 15 year old boys then girls. At such a vital age at GCSE level <u>truanting school over a period of 2 years could cost them a qualification for the rest of their life!</u> Is it really worth it? An estimated 200,000 truant during their GCSE year.

- The candidate was awarded a Grade A for the overall examination, and the extract from the fact sheet shows good use of:
  - information (e.g. the statistics);
  - explanation (e.g. the headline which suggests fear of certain lessons);
  - description (e.g. who it is that actually truants).
- The candidate has also thought carefully about maintaining the reader's interest by using:
  - a range of appropriate presentational devices such as headlines and sub-headings;
  - different font sizes and styles;
  - upper- and lower-case letters;
  - underlinings and bullet points.
- The language is direct and often poses questions to make the reader stop and think. The headlines use alliteration to eye-catching effect. The purpose of this leaflet is to make its target audience (concerned parents) gain a better understanding of truancy, and the sample response succeeds in this.

CHECK YOURSELF QUESTIONS

Q1 On the right is an examination answer by a candidate working at borderline C/D level. The task was to write a letter from a school to parents, informing them about a planned trip for pupils, explaining the arrangements and describing the purpose of the activity.

Write such a letter, remembering the qualities this category of writing should display. You may use the example as the basis of your answer if you wish, but try to make your letter much more successful in achieving its purpose!

Answers are on page 171.

Anytown Comprehensive School
Anything Road
Anywhere
Blankshire
XX9 9ZZ

10 June 2002

Trip to Thorpe Park

Dear Parent/Guardian,

We are planning a trip to Thorpe Park on 5 July, and any one is welcome. We shall depart at eight o'clock in the morning from the school gates, and are planning to return at five o'clock.

Thorpe Park opens at ten o'clock, the students shall be free to go where they please within the Park as long as they are in a group of at least three.

Everyone will meet up again at twelve o'clock for lunch, may I advise your child to bring a packed lunch, although food can be bought from the cafe.

The coach shall leave at three o'clock, so everyone should be ready on the coach for quarter-to-three.

Your child can go on any of the rides, but I must reccomend Space Station Zero, a fast and exhilerating ride through moving coloured lightes, made more terrifying by the tilt of the seats; I would also advise your child to bring waterproofs, especially if they are planning a ride on Thunder River.

If your child is interested please fill in the attached form along with £7.00 to cover admission and travelling.

Thank you.

Yours sincerely

Miss Candidate Five

Writing to argue, persuade and advise

KEY EXAM SKILLS

■ You need to be able to recognise certain qualities and use certain techniques when producing persuasive writing.

◎ What kind of writing is this?

■ This category includes writing in which the purpose is to present opinions in ways which make them seem attractive and convincing to the reader. Your intention is to:
  • change the reader's way of thinking if it differs from your own;
  • strengthen the reader's views if they are similar to yours;
  • suggest reasons why it is correct to think in a particular way.

■ The sorts of writing task you might be given within this category could include the following (all are taken from sample GCSE examination papers):

• 'The world would be a better place if television had never been invented.' Write an essay in which you argue either for or against this statement.
[This is a task which asks you to argue, but some persuasion will also be involved. You would have to assume that you were writing for an intelligent adult, as no audience is given.]

• Write an article for a teenage magazine about skin problems. Reassure your readers that they should not be so worried about imperfections in their appearance that they become easy prey for advertisers of cosmetics and other products.
[This is essentially a persuasive task, with some elements of instruction and argument. Note that a specific purpose and audience is given, so that you can use appropriate language and presentation.]

• Write an article for primary-school children in which you explain the dangers of too much sugar in their diet and also give some advice about keeping healthy teeth.
[This task calls for instruction, although some argument and persuasion may well be involved. A specific purpose and audience is again given; candidates were also provided with some reading material on another part of this paper to help them with useful information.]

BRUSH UP your 4

HEALTHY GUMS MEAN HAPPY TEETH

Getting rid of PLAQUE makes sense.

● Your mouth looks better
● Your mouth feels better
● Strong healthy teeth and gums
● Fresh breath

Then you'll
HAVE SOMETHING TO SMILE ABOUT!

An uphill task of persuasion!

■ When writing to argue, persuade or instruct, it helps to have strong feelings on the subject. Sometimes, shocking the reader with a strong viewpoint is an effective and powerful way of opening an argument before going on to persuade or instruct.

- This is part of an advertisement for Amnesty International:

"The men stripped me naked and assaulted me. I begged them to kill me. Instead, they cut off my hands with machetes." – SALLAY GOBA

DON'T LOOK THE OTHER WAY.

- As the start of a piece about Amnesty International's aims, the combination of shocking picture, distressing personal account by the victim and the large black headline which challenges the reader not to ignore it, is undeniably powerful.
- The rest of the Amnesty International advertisement (not shown) takes up more than a page of small print which presents other case histories. They are still upsetting, but are presented in more detail and are linked to political decisions about refugees made by European governments.
- Once the organisation has got your attention, it uses evidence to persuade you that there is a genuine problem, one which you can do something about.

◎ Achieving the best effect

- In this kind of writing, present material **powerfully**, but do not allow strong emotions, or the conviction that your views are right, to weaken the argument: readers may just switch off if you are incoherent, or if they feel they are being preached at.

- To persuade people, you need to **instruct** them as well; in other words, to present them with **evidence** which makes them think about, and perhaps change, their views.

- This is an extract from an examination answer in which the candidate was asked to write a letter to a newspaper, arguing against another letter (from a Mr Glass) which had claimed that drinking and driving is not dangerous:

Mr Glass says that he regularly drives his car when he is over the limit. I don't think that this is anything to be proud about. Although very stupid, he has been a very lucky person not to have had an accident in the 20 years he has been driving. A third of all drivers and motorcyclists who die in UK road accidents have blood alcohol levels above the legal limit.

Mr Glass claims that he feels more alert and alive after he has drunk a few pints, and that his driving improves because of this. Alcohol is a repressant; even small quantities impair reaction times, blur vision and reduce the ability to judge speed and distance. It also gives a false sense of confidence, which explains why he feels a better driver, when in reality he could be swerving all over the road, and being a danger to other drivers. ▶

Another point which Mr Glass has misunderstood is the claim that if you drink with a meal, eating the food will mean you can drink more yet still be safe to drive. Nothing, not food, or coffee or anything can reduce the amount of alcohol in your blood, or the risk of drink driving. Food only delays the absorption of alcohol into your bloodstream, thus delaying the effects of the drink. Waiting half an hour as Mr Glass suggests before driving home is only giving the alcohol time to take effect. It can take 24 hours for your body to get rid of the alcohol you have consumed, meaning that you can still be over the limit driving to work the morning after an evening of drinking.

- The letter is argued forcibly and skilfully, taking points raised by Mr Glass one by one and using evidence to support the writer's case that Mr Glass's views are wrong.
- This is part of an examination performance which was awarded a Grade A overall. The only slight miscalculation in this extract is where the writer calls Mr Glass 'very stupid' – you are unlikely to convert people to your way of thinking if you insult them, so keep cool, whatever the provocation!

◎ Devices and structures

TO SHOCK OR NOT TO SHOCK?

- ■ 'Keeping cool' can be a most effective technique in this category of writing.

- ■ The newspaper article about public executions in Jedda (page 85) ends (after the man was beheaded, his female accomplice was stoned to death by the crowd) like this:

The execution of the man? Well, let us not forget that it was as recently as 1936 that the French held their last public execution. And the beheading was at least humanely and quickly carried out.

But the doing to death of the woman is something which the handful of horrified Europeans in the crowd will not quickly forget.

It took just over an hour before the doctor in attendance, who halted the stoning periodically to feel the victim's pulse, announced her dead.

This double execution took place just the other day.

- Given the subject matter, this is indeed a 'cool' piece of writing, yet it is clearly intended to argue that capital punishment is barbaric, to persuade readers to the author's point of view, and to instruct them in what took place in the world when the article was written.
- There is no gruesome detail of the woman's slow death and no particularly colourful language in the passage ('doing to death' and 'horrified' are the strongest words used): it makes its effect by being purposely detached – note especially the last sentence – and by the short paragraphs which give the reader time to stop frequently and take in just what is being described.

CONSIDERING DIFFERENT POINTS OF VIEW

■ One other important feature shown by the above piece of writing is that, although the author clearly believes that the executions were wrong, he nevertheless puts forward some information which, if not actually supporting the events, does **make the reader think more carefully** about their reaction to them. In pointing out the recent abolition of public executions in France, and the humane speed of the beheading, the author suggests that the Western world may not be blameless in its own involvement with capital punishment.

■ This willingness to see another point of view **strengthens** the argument, since it makes the reader believe that the author is a reasonable person, not a fanatic willing to consider only one viewpoint.

■ When writing to argue or persuade, include some points of view with which you disagree, or acknowledge that a different point of view from your own may have some virtues.

PRESENTATIONAL DEVICES

■ In writing where you are presenting factual evidence, or drawing conclusions from this evidence, any of the following **presentational devices** may also be useful:
  • titles, headings and sub-headings;
  • underlinings and frames;
  • bullet points;
  • graphics, including charts and tables of statistics.

STYLISTIC DEVICES

■ Depending on the approach in a particular piece of writing, i.e. whether shock tactics or gentle persuasion are being used, the whole range of **stylistic devices** might be appropriate. Think about the effective use of:
  • precisely chosen individual words;
  • images;
  • direct appeals;
  • questions, to make your reader think about the views they hold and what they are prepared to do about something;
  • repetition;
  • appropriate endings.

CHECK YOURSELF QUESTIONS

Q1 The following piece of writing is part of an examination answer in which the candidate was asked to write about whether countries should keep nuclear weapons. The whole answer was assessed at just below Grade C.

Rewrite this part of the answer, identifying some of its faults and improving it where you can.

Why does nearly every country in the world compete for nuclear weapons? Nearly every country in the world has nuclear weapons. Those countries with large economies have bigger and better nuclear weapons, which could destroy the whole world in seconds. Other countries have smaller weapons, but these could still do a lot of damage. Today there are a number of groups which are trying to get every country which owns nuclear weapons to dispose of them safely. We have nuclear weapons to protect our country, we then think we are safe from being attacked by another country. All the main countries with large economies are living in fear because they know that one day they may be attacked and that nuclear weapons will be used in the attack. They may also think that the more weapons they have the less chance they have of being attacked. Today, no country is prepared to be the first country to dispose of their weapons, they say that we couldn't survive if we didn't have nuclear weapons. They think they will be attacked by other countries and they won't have any weapons to defend themselves.

Answers are on page 172.

Writing to analyse, review and comment

■ You need to be able to recognise and use certain qualities and techniques when producing analytic writing.

◎ What kind of writing is this?

■ This is probably the most difficult kind of writing required in the GCSE examination. It involves:
  - **analysing**: identifying and describing the particular qualities of something, e.g. a person, a place, an event, a book or an advertisement;
  - **reviewing**: thinking about those qualities and what they tell you about the person, place, event, book or advertisement;
  - **commenting**: putting your ideas into a shape and structure which explains your reaction and why it is significant.

WHEN WILL I WRITE LIKE THIS?

■ Writing of this kind is required:
  - when analysing texts, such as set books for a literature examination or media and non-fiction texts (such as newspapers or advertisements) for an English examination;
  - in personal writing, when reflecting on people, places, events or feelings, such as memories of early childhood or an account of work experience or a foreign holiday.

■ Typical tasks could include the following (both are taken from sample GCSE examination papers):

- Look carefully at the materials from the NSPCC included with this examination paper. They are part of a Christmas appeal. Consider how successful you think this appeal would be in encouraging people to give money.
  [This task will clearly involve analysing, reviewing and commenting.]

- Most people at one time or another are involved in some kind of celebration or festivity. This often includes a ritual or ceremony. In your own words, give an account of any occasion such as this in which you took part, or which you observed. Comment on why it was memorable.
  [This task is directed towards commenting, but will involve some analysis and review.]

Purpose and audience

■ These are key words for writing effectively in this category. For example, when writing to entertain a group of young children, describing and entertaining would be more important than analysing, reviewing and commenting, whereas for a more mature audience, the purpose of writing is to introduce general ideas, so the proportion of analysis, review and comment will be much greater.

Writing about a place

■ This extract is from a column in *The Guardian*:

London, my London

Sebastian Faulks

It is 20 years ago to the day that I arrived in London for a job interview in Camden Town. Twenty summers with the length of 20 long winters; and still it seems to me that London is not really appreciated either by the rest of the country or by the phlegmatic people who live there.

It is a wonderful city, diverse, un-pushy, a bit tawdry, but a serious place to live, with the vast reserves of historical character and contemporary activity. The rest of England, with the exception of parts of Cornwall and the Yorkshire Moors, is a suburb.

In this country there has been no flight from the countryside, as in France, because the towns in England have come to meet the country. The two have joined sticky hands around the in-filled lanes, the street-lit roads and green-site superstores. Compared with Montana, the Marche or the Auvergne, the English countryside is a tarmac non-event. But compared with New York, Rome or Paris, London is unashamed.

- The author identifies and describes features of London which he likes – 'vast reserves of historical character and contemporary activity' – and features of the rest of England which he does not like: 'with the exception of parts of Cornwall and the Yorkshire Moors, [it] is a suburb.' In other words, he analyses his feelings about London.
- He thinks about those qualities and what they tell him about London: 'It is a wonderful city, diverse, un-pushy, a bit tawdry, but a serious place to live ...'. In other words, he reviews his feelings about London.
- He then puts his ideas into a shape and structure which explains his reaction to London and why it is significant: 'still it seems to me that London is not really appreciated either by the rest of the country or by the phlegmatic people who live there'. In other words, he comments on his feelings about London.
- Some of this article is information and description, and part of its purpose is to persuade you of the virtues of London, but for the most part it consists of analysis, review and comment.
- Reflective writing needs vocabulary which can precisely describe the feelings and reactions of the writer; note the use here of words such as 'phlegmatic', 'diverse', 'un-pushy', 'tawdry', 'unashamed'.
- Two striking images are used: the idea of the town and the countryside having 'joined sticky hands' and the countryside being 'a tarmac non-event'. These stylistic features give the article a sense of accurate observation (the choice of vocabulary) and individuality (the original images), which are qualities you want to achieve in this category of writing.

◎ Writing about a concept or idea

■ This extract is from a Grade-A examination answer by a candidate writing about the intrusion of the press into the private lives of rich and famous people, and the proposal that there should be restrictions on newspapers:

To have your private life splashed across the front pages of national newspapers must be at best humiliating, but it is a risk those in the public eye must take. If they are unprepared to accept this aspect of their position, they should not occupy it. The Royal Family and the government are the representatives of our country, so they are naturally expected to behave responsibly. This is not an unjust expectation and those who do not live up to it must suffer the consequences. However, I think that the issue goes far beyond the invasion of privacy of a handful of people. The public has a right to know what is going on, and the proposed curbs would cut information that is revealed down to a minimum. A free press is what keeps a country as a democracy – otherwise the papers become propaganda and the government a dictatorship, because no one is allowed to question their actions.

In the end, it comes down to this: no government has the right to act as God, to say what we should or shouldn't read or indeed, what we should or shouldn't write. As the 'Daily Mirror' says, 'The freedom of the press is ... the inalienable right of every citizen to speak his mind in public without fear of penalty, prosecution or persecution.'

- The analysis of the situation is in the first sentence of each of the first two paragraphs. This shows the candidate has thought carefully about the structure of the answer, and is setting out the main issues at the beginning of each section, after which they are reviewed and commented upon.
- Review is in the third sentence of the first paragraph ('The Royal Family and the government ...') and the third sentence of the second paragraph ('A free press ...').
- The rest of the extract can be described as comment, although it can be a false exercise to try and distinguish absolutely these three aspects of the writing category – the last sentence of the second paragraph, for example, ('A free press ...') is arguably analysis, review and comment all at the same time.
- This answer uses an appropriate style of writing (impersonal, but still engaged – 'However, I think that ...') and a coherent structure.

◎ Writing about emotion

- Analysing, reviewing and commenting on emotions is challenging, but is a useful skill to develop not only in writing about yourself, but in writing fiction, when you may wish to open up the thoughts and feelings of a character in a story, for example.

- Richard Hillary, a fighter pilot in the Second World War, wrote an account of his experiences and feelings, *The Last Enemy*, from which the following extract is taken. He has just killed his first enemy pilot:

My first emotion was one of satisfaction, satisfaction at a job adequately done, at the final logical conclusion of months of specialised training. And then I had a feeling of the essential rightness of it all. He was dead and I was alive; it could so easily have been the other way round; and that would somehow have been right too. I realised in that moment just how lucky a fighter pilot is. He has none of the personalised emotions of the soldier, handed a rifle and bayonet and told to charge. He does not even have to share the dangerous emotion of the bomber pilot who night after night must experience that childhood longing for smashing things. The fighter pilot's emotions are those of the duellist – cool, precise, impersonal. He is privileged to kill well. For if one must either kill or be killed, as now one must, it should, I feel, be done with dignity. Death should be given the setting it deserves; it should never be a pettiness; and for the fighter pilot it never can be.

- Analysis: the author identifies and describe his feelings of satisfaction, relief and 'rightness'.
- Review: he thinks about the situation, and why he has those feelings.
- Comment: the last sentence sums up Richard Hillary's reaction to the situation.

? CHECK YOURSELF QUESTIONS

Q1 Answer this GCSE examination question. Allow yourself about 45 minutes and compare what you have written with the model answer and comments on page 173. Remember that your purpose is to analyse, review and comment on the success of the project.

Your school has been running a very successful project called 'Improving our School'. As one of those involved, you have been asked to write an article about this project for the school magazine. You have made the notes shown here.

Answers are on page 173.

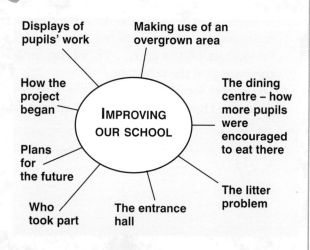

EXAM PRACTICE

AQA Specification A – Paper 1

Section A: Reading (Non-literary and media texts)

In this part, you are asked to follow an argument, select material appropriate to purpose and tell the difference between fact and opinion. This means you should respond to the leaflet as a written text.

1 Give examples of two facts and two opinions in the leaflet, 'Dads & Sons' (see pages 122–125). (3 marks)

2 The leaflet indicates various benefits from closer involvement of fathers in their sons' education. What are they? (6 marks)

3 How does the leaflet use language which is likely to make fathers want to take its advice? (6 marks)

In this part, you should respond to the leaflet as a visual media text.

4 How does the design of the leaflet suit its purpose? (6 marks)

5 How does the design of the leaflet suit its intended audience? (6 marks)

Total: 27 marks

WORD UP!

He's way too old for bedtime stories, but there's lots of other stuff you could try to help him stay on top of reading and writing – without him thinking you're interfering in his life!

TIPS

STARTER FOR 10

Watch TV quiz shows together and see how many questions you can get right. Sit with the encyclopaedia and get him to look up the answers while the contestants are scratching their heads. Or suggest he puts together his own quiz show with parents and/or brothers or sisters as contestants, using a popular game show format, like ITV's Who Wants To Be A Millionaire? He could research questions in the encyclopaedia, in the Guinness Book of Records or on the internet. It's all good practice for looking things up and putting information together in clear, concise, bite-sized chunks.

TOP OF THE FORM

Get him to fill in forms himself – whether it's to join a club, subscribe to a magazine or to register online – it'll help him with all those forms he'll have to complete later on in life.

LOST THE PLOT?

Have a discussion about a book or favourite magazine he's reading. If it's a novel, ask him to talk about how the plot has been developed. What about the characters: do they seem real, the sort of people he might actually meet or know and could he imagine them in other situations outside the story? Talk to him about how he would change the plot or the ending if he doesn't like it.

READING CAMPAIGN

DO YOU KNOW A CHAMPION?

The National Reading Campaign wants to hear about dads, grandads and brothers who encourage others to read. Visit www.literacytrust.org.uk/ campaign/champions.html for details.

BOOKMARK THESE!

These sites have lots of tips and advice plus reading lists of books:
www.dfes.gov.uk/parents
www.rif.org.uk
www.booktrust.org.uk
www.boox.org.uk
www.fathersdirect.com

● CURRICULUM ●

WHAT'S HE UP TO?

By the age of 14, most pupils are reading a whole range of books, plays and poems, including:

❶ at least one play by Shakespeare
❷ novels and poetry from different times, including writers working at the moment
❸ plays, poems and fiction by writers from different cultures
❹ non-fiction writing eg, diaries, travel writing and science writing.

There's more detailed information on the whole curriculum in The Learning Journey: a parent's guide to the secondary school curriculum. You can order your free copy by telephoning 08000 96 66 26 or download it from the web at: www.dfes.gov.uk/parents

NIALL QUINN
SUNDERLAND FC

"Kids can so easily pick up on what you say and the way you feel. I believe that if I'm positive and optimistic around my son then he'll develop the confidence and self-belief he needs to take him through his important teenage years. When my son is the right age, I would like to show him how I deal with difficult issues and encourage him to enjoy taking on new challenges."

To get details of Dads & Sons activities happening near you, visit the website:

www.dfes.gov.uk/ dadsandsons

COUNT ON ME!

You don't have to be a maths genius to help him improve the maths he is learning at school every day. Here are ways you can play a part.

TIPS

CHANGING ROOMS

A spot of DIY offers lots of opportunities to test your son's number skills, without it feeling like extra homework. And if you're not doing any right now, you could always pretend you are for the purposes of this. Get him to measure up a wall to be tiled and work out the surface area in square metres and how many tiles of a particular size he'll need. You can vary this for painting (how many tins?) or wallpapering (how many rolls?).

> Times, figures and statistics have always been an important part of my life, both as an international athlete and now as Race Director of The Flora London Marathon. When you're watching the race in April, why not sit with your son and convert the 26.2 mile course into kilometres or work out the average time per mile of the race leaders?

DAVID BEDFORD
CHAMPION ATHLETE

TWO OF NO 23

MENU
TAKEAWAY
1. fried rice
2. egg fried rice
3. prawn crackers
4. egg foo yung
5. chop suey
6. chow mein
7. peking duck
8. sweet & sour
9. young chow
10. beef chop suey
11. roast duck
12. king prawn

When you order a takeaway, tell your son what you've got to spend and get him to work out if there's enough to cater for everybody's different tastes in the family.

£54.76, PLEASE

As you go round the supermarket, ask your son to work out the running total of the weekly shop in his head: he can round the prices up or down to make the sum more manageable. Check it against the till receipt: was he far off? He can also work out the exact savings of every bulk purchase (the price of eight toilet rolls compared with two, for instance), or items bought in bigger sizes (such as fizzy drinks). Collect the receipts for the month, then get him to estimate your annual food bill.

BOOKMARK THESE!

There are lots of ideas for things to do and maths games to play on the website:
www.counton.org.uk
www.learn.co.uk
www.bbc.co.uk/schools
and for more maths links check out the parents' website: www.parents.dfes.gov.uk

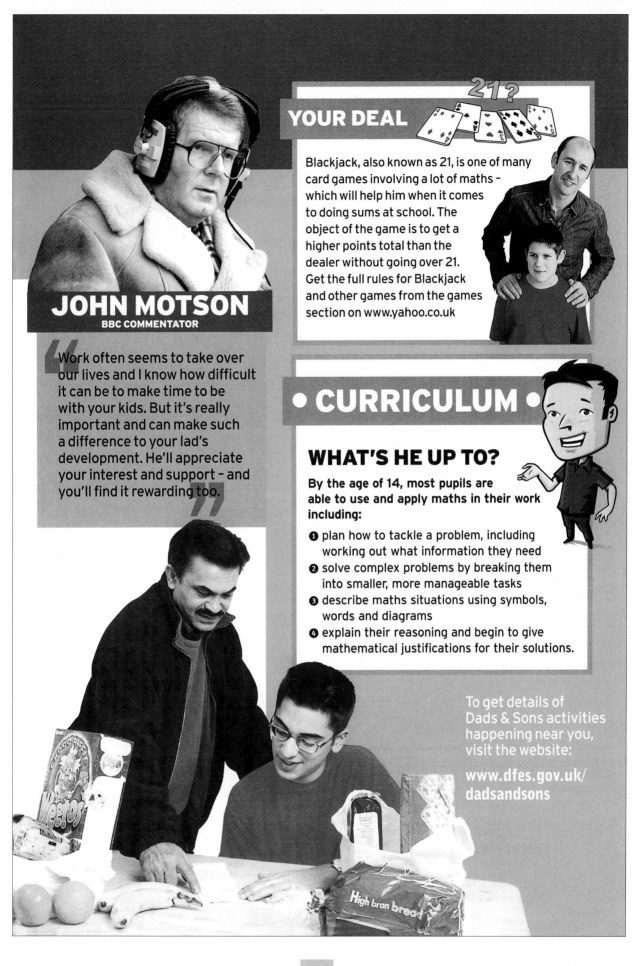

YOUR DEAL 21?

Blackjack, also known as 21, is one of many card games involving a lot of maths - which will help him when it comes to doing sums at school. The object of the game is to get a higher points total than the dealer without going over 21. Get the full rules for Blackjack and other games from the games section on www.yahoo.co.uk

JOHN MOTSON
BBC COMMENTATOR

"Work often seems to take over our lives and I know how difficult it can be to make time to be with your kids. But it's really important and can make such a difference to your lad's development. He'll appreciate your interest and support - and you'll find it rewarding too."

• CURRICULUM •

WHAT'S HE UP TO?

By the age of 14, most pupils are able to use and apply maths in their work including:

❶ plan how to tackle a problem, including working out what information they need
❷ solve complex problems by breaking them into smaller, more manageable tasks
❸ describe maths situations using symbols, words and diagrams
❹ explain their reasoning and begin to give mathematical justifications for their solutions.

To get details of Dads & Sons activities happening near you, visit the website:

www.dfes.gov.uk/dadsandsons

Answer one question in this section. You may use some of the information from Section A if you want to, but you do not have to. If you use any of the information, do not simply copy it.

Remember to:
- spend five minutes planning your material;
- write at least one side in your answer book;
- spend five minutes checking:
  - your paragraphing;
  - your punctuation;
  - your spelling.

1 Write a letter to your local newspaper which argues that teenagers need role models who are not just pop or sports stars.
   Remember to:
   • use language and ideas that will appeal to adult readers;
   • organise your letter into coherent paragraphs.

   (27 marks)

2 Write a feature for a teenage magazine which persuades young people to take their education more seriously.
   Remember to:
   • use language and ideas which will appeal to a teenage audience;
   • use real-life examples;
   • show the benefits and disadvantages of different choices.

   (27 marks)

3 Write some advice for members of a parenting class about how they can support their children in their schoolwork without being bossy or patronising.
   Remember to:
   • use language that will make your readers want to take your advice;
   • be practical about what can be done;
   • point out the dangers of being bossy or patronising.

   (27 marks)

4 Write a letter to a friend who is keen to leave school early, arguing that it is better to stay on, and persuading him/her that he/she will be able to cope with another two years in education.
   Remember to:
   • use different language for **arguing** and **persuading**;
   • use different methods of argument and persuasion.

   (27 marks)

(Sample answers and Examiner's comments are given for Question 4 only.)

Section A: Reading (Poems from different cultures)

Island Man
(for a Caribbean island man in London who still wakes up to the sound of the sea)

Morning
and island man wakes up
to the sound of blue surf
in his head
the steady breaking and wombing

wild seabirds
and fishermen pushing out to sea
the sun surfacing defiantly
from the east
of his small emerald island
he always comes back   groggily, groggily

Comes back to sands
of grey metallic soar
                to surge of wheels
to dull North Circular roar

muffling muffling
his crumpled pillow waves
island man heaves himself

Another London day

Grace Nichols

Night of the Scorpion

I remember the night my mother
was stung by a scorpion. Ten hours
of steady rain had driven him
to crawl beneath a sack of rice.
Parting with his poison – flash
of diabolic tail in the dark room –
he risked the rain again.
The peasants came like swarms of flies
and buzzed the name of God a hundred times
to paralyse the Evil One.
With candles and with lanterns
throwing giant scorpion shadows
on the mud-baked walls
they searched for him: he was not found.
They clicked their tongues.
With every movement that the scorpion made
his poison moved in Mother's blood, they said.
May he sit still, they said.
May the sins of your previous birth
be burned away tonight, they said.
May your suffering decrease
the misfortunes of your next birth, they said.
May the sum of evil
balanced in this unreal world
against the sum of good
become diminished by your pain.
May the poison purify your flesh
of desire, and your spirit of ambition,
they said, and they sat around
on the floor with my mother in the centre,
the peace of understanding on each face.
More candles, more lanterns, more neighbours,
more insects, and the endless rain.
My mother twisted through and through,
groaning on a mat.
My father, sceptic, rationalist,
trying every curse and blessing,
powder, mixture, herb and hybrid.
He even poured a little paraffin
upon the bitten toe and put a match to it.
I watched the flame feeding on my mother.
I watched the holy man perform his rites
to tame the poison with an incantation.
After twenty hours
it lost its sting.

My mother only said
Thank God the scorpion picked on me
and spared my children.

Nissim Ezekiel

Presents from my Aunts in Pakistan

They sent me a salwar kameez
              peacock-blue,
                        and another
        glistening like an orange split open,
embossed slippers, gold and black
              points curling.
        Candy-striped glass bangles
              snapped, drew blood.
        Like at school, fashions changed
              in Pakistan –
the salwar bottoms were broad and stiff,
              then narrow.
My aunts chose an apple-green sari,
        silver-bordered
              for my teens.

I tried each satin-silken top –
        was alien in the sitting-room.
I could never be as lovely
              as those clothes –
        I longed
for denim and corduroy.
        My costume clung to me
              and I was aflame,
I couldn't rise up out of its fire,
        half-English
              unlike Aunt Jamila.

I wanted my parents' camel-skin lamp –
        switching it on in my bedroom,
to consider the cruelty
              and the transformation
from camel to shade,
        marvel at the colours
              like stained glass.

My mother cherished her jewellery –
        Indian gold, dangling, filigree.
              But it was stolen from our car.
The presents were radiant in my wardrobe.
        My aunts requested cardigans
              from Marks and Spencers.

My salwar kameez
        didn't impress the schoolfriend
who sat on my bed, asked to see
        my weekend clothes.
But often I admired the mirror-work,
        tried to glimpse myself
              in the miniature
glass circles, recall the story
        how the three of us
              sailed to England.
Prickly heat had me screaming on the way.
        I ended up in a cot
in my English grandmother's dining-room,
        found myself alone,
              playing with a tin boat.

I pictured my birthplace
        from fifties' photographs.
              When I was older
there was a conflict, a fractured land
        throbbing through newsprint.
Sometimes I saw Lahore –
        my aunts in shaded rooms,
screened from male visitors,
        sorting presents,
              wrapping them in tissue.

Or there were beggars, sweeper-girls
        and I was there –
              of no fixed nationality,
staring through the fretwork
        at the Shalimar Gardens.

Moniza Alvi

1 Compare the ways in which contrast or conflict is presented in *Island Man* with the way it is presented in either *Night of the Scorpion* or *Presents from my Aunts in Pakistan*.

   Write about:
   • the kinds of conflict in the poems;
   • what the poets have to say about the conflicts;
   • how language is used to present situations and ideas.

2 Compare *Search for my Tongue* with any other poem in the Different Cultures selection, showing how the poets bring out attitudes, ideas and feelings about their culture or cultures.

   Write about:
   • attitudes, ideas and feelings in the poems;
   • what you think are the poets' own attitudes, ideas and feelings;
   • ways in which they use form and language to convey attitudes, ideas and feelings.

(Sample answers and Examiner's comments are given for Question 1 only.)

Section B: Writing (to inform, explain or describe)

Remember to:
* spend five minutes planning your material;
* write at least one side in your answer book;
* spend five minutes checking:
  – your paragraphing;
  – your punctuation;
  – your spelling.

1 Write a letter to a new local supermarket **informing** them why you will not be a customer when it opens.

2 Write a letter to your local council to **explain** why many young people are not interested in elections or politics.

3 Write a **description** of your bedroom as you see it and as your mother/father/guardian sees it.

4 Write an article for a family magazine **describing** what it is like to be a sixteen-year-old these days, and **explaining** how parents and other adults can do more to make life better for youngsters.

AQA answers and comments

PAPER 1, SECTION A

Q1 Two facts are 'By the age of 14, most pupils are reading … at least one play by Shakespeare, etc.' and 'There's more detailed information on the whole curriculum in *The Learning Journey* …'

Two opinions are '… if I'm positive and optimistic around my son, then he'll develop the confidence and self-belief he needs' and 'He'll appreciate your interest and support – and you'll find it rewarding too'.

Examiner's comments Three marks out of a possible three. Effective choices. The question didn't need reasons. There's no need to spend a lot of time on this, as it's only worth three marks.

Q2 The benefits of fathers working with sons are that:
- they will get on better together, watching TV as well as working;
- the son will do better at school;
- the father will feel better as a parent because he has made a difference;
- they could get mentioned in the National Reading Campaign.

Examiner's comments Four marks out of a possible six. It's OK to write bullet points because it's reading, not writing, that's assessed here. The student could also have pointed out that fathers may also improve their own education.

Q3 It uses words which are informal and not 'official', such as 'stuff', 'way too old' and 'Lost the plot?'. There are phrases which remind readers of TV and hobbies like 'Starter for 10', 'Top of the Form' and 'Your deal'. These connect learning with recreational activities which are fun. Tips are presented in short sentences starting with an active verb like 'Sit' or 'Watch'.

Examiner's comments Four marks out of a possible six. This gives details of words, phrases and sentences. The student could also refer to the catchy adaptation of 'Wise up!' in 'Word up!' and the frequent use of questions like 'Do you know a champion?' and 'What's he up to?'

Q4 **Purpose**
The leaflet is designed for home delivery or to be picked up in shops or pubs or places where men go. It's compact, doesn't seem like government instruction, even though there are excerpts from the curriculum. The paragraph sections are short and not threateningly long. It's eye-catching, like a teenage magazine, so it could be picked up casually and put in a pocket. It has a sports theme because of Niall Quinn and David Bedford, so it could be about enjoying things men and boys like. The page is broken up into magazine-style parts, so it doesn't seem like official information. It uses cartoon-style drawings to make it feel informal, and the pictures of a Dad and his son wearing casual clothes don't make it seem for people who are posh. The photos show dads and sons of different races so it makes it seem that it's for everyone.

Examiner's comments Six marks out of a possible six. This points out the way it avoids seeming like government information or instruction. It also shows how it is designed to be attractive as a free item to be picked up in a store.

Q5 **Audience**
The intended audience is fathers and their sons. The pictures of dads and sons look attractive. The leaflet uses familiar, non-threatening language. It sounds like someone offering friendly advice, e.g. there are examples of words chosen to suit males, drawn from football and other 'macho' activities.

The icons and logos represent things of interest to men and boys.

The colours are bold, not soft and sentimental – masculine colours.

Examiner's comments Three marks out of a possible six. This points out the male appeal of sports, but it could be more detailed, referring to David Bedford and Niall Quinn, and to athletics as well as football. The use of question marks and exclamation marks in the headings are also worth a mention.

PAPER 1, SECTION B, QUESTION 4

Grade C response

Dear Mike,

I've thought about what you told me last night about leaving school and I've decided to write out a few points for you to consider.

Firstly, if you leave now, you'll be wasting the work you've already put in. It's been a bit of a slog so far, so you may as well carry on to make the effort worthwhile.

Secondly, you'll be missing out on the laughs we all have as a group at school. Just think, no more winding up Skelton and no more of Wally's jokes!

Thirdly, and most importantly, you'll regret it later in life when you wonder how well you could have done if you'd tried. Don't waste your potential.

I know it can seem attractive to start earning some money and get exam work out of your life, but there's a lifetime of that ahead of you. Are you ready to join the rat-race yet? Think it over. Give me a bell. Your old mate is going to hack it for the rest of the time and it'll be easier for both of us if we hack it together.

Examiner's comments
Communication and organisation
There is clear identification of purpose and audience. There are several strategies used in the argument – stressing the positive, warning of possible consequences and maintaining friendship. The candidate varies the paragraph openings and establishes a simple, rational and coherent sequence in ordering them numerically. It has development and it prioritises the strongest point. There is confident use of rhetorical questions and some discursive markers used to enhance the appeal, e.g. 'if', 'so', 'Most importantly' and 'can seem'.

Sentence structures, spelling and punctuation
There is a variety of sentence structures. There is some persuasion linked to the argument paragraphs, and the persuasion is developed at the end with a familiar tone, e.g. 'slog', 'you'll', 'hack' and 'give me a bell' to avoid a sense of lecturing.

Spelling is accurate, and punctuation clarifies meaning and purpose. Apostrophes of possession ('Wally's') and of omission ('it's', 'don't', 'you'll') are secure.
In-sentence punctuation is effective, e.g. parenthetic commas to separate clauses in a sentence.

Grade A/A* response

Dear Jennie,

I've just heard from Carrie that you're thinking of leaving to get a job. I know things have been bad recently, and school gets all of us down at some time or another, but don't do anything rash until you've thought it over and talked it through. I'm available if you need an ear.

The important thing to cling on to is that it's only another year. You've already put in the five years up to GCSE and you've done pretty well, so it would be a shame to waste the effort you've already put in.

It would also be a shame to miss out on the social life. Even if school gets you down sometimes, remember that it's not all work and misery. Think of those lunch-time gossip sessions and the joy of watching the posers in the common room!

Another thing to remember is that you're not the first to feel this way. Other people have gone through similar feelings and survived. My Mum says she wanted to do the same, but stuck at it, and now she's grateful because her qualifications mean she can do something better than sitting at a cash till.

Most importantly, you don't want to do something now that you'll regret in later life. You've got a good brain and you can do well. Qualifications aren't everything, but they go a long way. Do you want to be flicking through the 'Unskilled' sections of the Job pages when the rest of us are brain surgeons and top lawyers? Are you sure that the big, bad world is best?

Ultimately, the choice is yours and I'll back you in whatever you do, as long as you're sure it's right for you. Ring me soon or sooner. As Del Boy says, 'You know it makes sense', and if I can get you back on track, I'll be doing myself a favour, too, because I don't want to see you disappear over the horizon after all we've been through together.

This response has all of the features of accuracy of the Grade C response, but has a more sophisticated vocabulary ('rash', 'misery', 'Ultimately') and more controlled complex sentences. The main difference in achievement is that this response uses a wider range of strategies, e.g. 'Think of those gossip sessions … posers' and 'Do you want …' and a more developed use of example, e.g. 'My Mum …'.

Communication and organisation
Form, content and style are consistently matched to purpose and audience, showing subtlety and ability to adapt tone to manipulate the reader. There are varied paragraph starts which establish fluent links with and developments from previous paragraphs. This writing shows conscious crafting. There are several argument strategies, including warning, reference to other people's experience and using potential. The persuasive devices are the appeals to friendship, understanding and sympathy, warning of disappointment, a touch of humour and the rhetorical questions. There is some persuasion linked with paragraphs of argument and a stronger persuasive appeal in the last paragraph.

Sentence structures, spelling and punctuation
Sentence structures are varied and well controlled. Spelling is highly accurate, and there is a range of punctuation used to enhance meaning and purpose.

PAPER 2, SECTION A, QUESTION 1

Grade C response

I have chosen to compare the way *Island Man* presents conflict compared with *Night of the Scorpion*.

In *Island Man*, the conflict is between the place the Man remembers and the place he lives in now. The place he remembers is full of colour and pleasant noises ('surf' and 'seabirds') and the place he lives now (London) is grey and unpleasant and full of traffic noise.

He remembers the fishermen, the sun and the 'emerald' island, which suggests colour and something precious, then he feels a conflict because what is really around him is 'grey' and 'metallic' and 'dull'.

The conflict is he really likes the place he remembers and it is still nice in his head, but he has to live in London because it is where he works.

In *Night of the Scorpion*, there is only one culture presented, but there is a conflict in that culture between the old faith of the villagers and the more disbelieving attitude of the man.

Examiner's comments This answer has effective use of supporting detail and an understanding of feelings and attitudes. There is some cross reference to show similarity and difference.

More attention to authorial techniques and purposes would raise the grade.

Grade A/A* response

Both *Island Man* and *Presents from my Aunts in Pakistan* show how a writer can feel torn between two cultures. This is because the poet in each case feels part of both cultures, but for different reasons.

In *Island Man*, the memory of the exotic place he remembers still lingers in his memory, especially when he is asleep. It's only when he wakes up to the reality of a London morning that he realises that he's not back in the West Indies with its colourful scenery, its native activities (fishing) and the sound of the surf. He's brought back to reality by hearing the traffic roar outside in the grey British morning as London starts its day. In a way, the poet presents this as sad because the London day seems colourless, dull, mechanical and unattractive in comparison, but it's also possible that the poet is saying that this is a healthy conflict because there is still something of the old culture surviving, and this is enough to help him to put up with the less attractive life he leads now.

In *Presents from my Aunts*, the writer is also pulled two ways. She enjoys the Western freedom symbolised by denim and trendy clothes, but she also likes the exotic richness of the fabrics which symbolise the older culture, far away. This conflict is shown to be more than a teenager's conflict because the aunts themselves, although trying to keep her familiar with the clothes of her old culture, also like to buy Marks and Spencer's clothes for themselves.

The writer juxtaposes West and East, young and old, to show how someone can enjoy parts of different cultures, being of 'no fixed nationality'.

Examiner's comments This answer has its references integrated with argument and shows empathy with the writers' ideas and attitudes, as well as exploration of meaning. There is also analysis of the variety of the writers' techniques in use of structure, symbolism and contrast.

PAPER 2, SECTION B, QUESTION 1
Grade C response

Dear Sirs

This is to inform you that I shall not be a customer of yours when your new store opens on July 15th.

I have looked at your advertising publicity about the benefits of the new store and do not think I can gain anything from a new store.

When it was first proposed to close the old hospital buildings and sell the site, there was a petition going round asking for a multiplex cinema which I signed because I did not think there was a need for a third supermarket in the town.

Also, I shall use the local shops which still offer personal service. I shall not be tempted by the opening offers which are trying to buy me as a customer.

Examiner's comments
Communication and organisation
Sense of purpose is stronger than sense of audience, which is often a feature of this kind of writing. Informative writing expresses facts. This response uses emphatic sentence starters, such as 'I shall' and 'I have' to give clear information about what is intended and why. There is no embellishment in description or emotional language because the purpose is to communicate information about something already done efficiently and directly. Informative writing does not need to argue or persuade.

Sentence structures, spelling and punctuation
Sentence forms match the purpose of information. The writing is secure in spelling, though the range of vocabulary is limited.

Grade A/A* response

Dear Sirs,

When you open your doors to the new superstore on July 25, I will not be there. Nor shall I ever set foot in your store.

Because I believe that communities like ours should preserve their own individual character, I do not want to see another multinational megastore in the town. I prefer the pleasure of shopping in a number of outlets with their own character and ambiance.

On a more serious note, I do not want to see trade taken away from small local businesses, run by people who live here and care for this town. Supermarkets tend to dominate the local economy, and this is unhealthy, partly because they have the power to exploit third-world countries for cheap labour to undercut local shops and partly because their financial muscle allows them to bring in vegetables and fruit from abroad when it is out of season. This increases the pollution and consumes valuable resources, as well as breaking down the idea of seasonal variety in our eating.

So, for personal, economic and social reasons, I shall not be a customer of yours. Even your introductory offers, raffles and free parking will not induce me to abandon my principles or my loyalties.

Examiner's comments
Communication and organisation
This response shows clear and confident control of purpose and awareness of audience, including reference to what the supermarket promoters may say to attract custom. The response is well organised, with paragraphs which have varied beginnings and links between them. Vocabulary is well chosen to emphasise the writer's personal preferences in the explanation – 'multinational megastore', 'ambiance', 'exploit' and 'financial muscle' – and explains attitude as well as reason.

Sentence structures, spelling and punctuation
There is variety in the openings of sentences, and sentences are crafted to develop links between intention and the ideas which lead to intention, e.g. 'Because I believe ...' and 'So, for personal, economic ...' Spelling of complex words is highly accurate, e.g. 'muscle', 'resources', 'principles'.
    In-sentence punctuation, especially commas, shows crafting to enhance purpose and meaning.

Grade C response

Dear Sirs,

I am writing to explain why young people today don't show much interest in politics. There are lots of reasons, but I'll give you the main ones which are not just my reasons, but what most of my friends think.

Firstly, they aren't interested because politics are always about things that don't interest young people, for example new roads and house extensions.

Secondly, it's because the politics are about things that don't affect today – they're always set in the future. Young people want to know about what's happening now.

The third reason is that the language is like a foreign language and this is not how young people speak.

Lastly, and most importantly, young people don't get interested in politics because when they really want something done, like having a leisure centre with a skateboard park, a fun pool and a dirt track, it's less important than other things like supermarkets and car parks.

If you want young people to take an interest in politics, politicians should take an interest in young people.

Examiner's comments
Communication and organisation
There is a clear sense of audience and purpose in the opening statement. The candidate uses simple Standard English and claims to speak not just personally, but for others, too. The letter is organised in paragraphs that begin with different phrases in order to provide variety and sustain the reader's interest. The paragraphs show simple ordering of ideas ('Firstly', 'Secondly', 'The third reason', 'Lastly') and some prioritising of importance, as well as summarising at the end. Explanation is made clear by the use of 'because' and 'reason why'. There is a range of reasons and a conclusion.

Sentence structures, spelling and punctuation
There is variety in sentence length, e.g. 'Young people want to know ...' and 'Lastly, and most importantly, ...'. Spelling and punctuation are accurate.

Grade A/A* response

Dear Sirs,

It seems that some politicians have decided that young people should take more interest in politics. I'm writing as a young person to say why I don't share this opinion.

At the age of sixteen, I have enough to worry about with my exams and future career choices. I don't have emotional or intellectual space to worry about other issues in my community.

Another reason why I don't take any interest in politics is because I don't really know enough to have political opinions. I think it's better to leave these things to people who are confident that they do know. I also think that people who are paid to make political decisions are the ones who should take them, not amateurs like me.

If I have to be honest, I should also add that I don't see how politics can solve some of the problems that worry me most, like the ozone layer or global warming. Taking an interest in planning applications or who sits on the highways committee doesn't seem to tackle what's most worrying on the planet at the moment.

These are my own views, but I think they may be typical of other people my age. My generation has become rather cynical about politics because we hear politicians always opposing each other and never saying they have been wrong themselves. Also, there have been so many examples of politicians doing things to get votes rather than do what's right.

I hope this helps you to understand that we are not interested in politics because we have so much else to be interested in, and because politics does not seem to offer answers to the problems that worry us.

Examiner's comments
Communication and organisation
Purpose and audience are well served by the choice of sophisticated Standard English and a tone which avoids assertion. Several reasons are given, and the response is organised in paragraphs which have varied starts and links between them. Vocabulary is well chosen to make ideas and attitudes clear. There is a developed and convincing account of why the candidate's views are typical of other people's views. The conclusion provides a crafted summary in a non-threatening manner.

PAPER 2, SECTION B, QUESTION 3

Grade C response

What a nice room. Its got everything I need in it – television, computer and my wardrobe full of ace clothes. I can relax in here and shut the world out. Its got all my favorite posters on the walls – Britney, Becks and Spiderman and photographs of me with my mates last year on Ibiza.

My room may not be the tidiest room on the planet, but its mine, and I like it the way it is. There may be heaps of things flung on the chair and in the corner but where it matters in my wardrobe and on my CD shelf everything is neat and where it should be.

What a tip! When is he going to clear away all these things. There are mugs on the windowsill with green mold in them from weeks ago and he's left some toast crusts on a plate under the bed. I don't know what he see's in these pop stars. Theres his computer over there with it's console that he uses when he should be doing homework and the television that comes on in the morning and as soon as he gets home at night. And look at his wardrobe. Does he ever wear anything other than T shirts?

Grade A/A* response

Open the door to my room and you'll be confronted with an Aladdin's cave, a grotto of delight, a mini-palace of pleasure and a Parent No-Go zone.

If you're not a parent and you pass the portal to enter the grotto, you'll catch your breath at the tasteful array of necessary accoutrements, from the 100-watt Megabass speakers at the window side, to the Intel-Inside cyber-station in the corner which links me with the global community and the bookcase/CD storage racks along the wall beside my bed. Every Stephen King and every Led Zeppelin you've heard of can be found in this cultural archive proclaiming the occupant's exquisite literary and musical taste.

And speaking of taste, note the special comfort facility in the bedside cabinet, where Jaffa cakes, mini-Jamaica cakes and (appallingly named) Ginger Nuts are stored for nutritious and delicious relief when famine threatens or when crumbling self-esteem calls for emergency measures.

Words fail me when I make my unofficial (and unadmitted) Health and Safety check on the war zone called my son's bedroom. Objects impelled by their own kinetic forces tangle, tumble and trail over furniture and floor in unlikely combinations. How else can a single trainer containing an apple core end up on a chair under a pile of magazines and a plate of biscuits covered by a Led Zeppelin T-shirt calling out for a wash?

How he manages to live in a state like this, I don't know. Try to find a school textbook on the shelves and you'll have no luck. And under the bed, where the Hoover nozzle never goes, is another story. Socks and underclothes gather there in fabric solidarity, fearing the washer, awaiting the call to be re-used when the clean clothes drawer proves empty again.

distinction between the two observers and some reference to the potential differences between the observers.

The whole response is organised into paragraphs which use a range of starting phrases, some of which make links between paragraphs. Vocabulary is well chosen to sustain interest and create a sense of unique detail: 'portal', 'grotto', 'palace' and 'cultural archive' all convey an image and an attitude to the place. There is some word choice to create enjoyable exaggeration, such as 'famine' and 'impelled by their own kinetic forces', and there is also the use of figurative language where the clothes 'gather' in 'solidarity', 'fearing' the washer. Humour is introduced with the reference to '(appallingly named) Ginger Nuts'.

Sentence structures, spelling and punctuation
There is a range of sentence structures, and spelling is highly accurate, including complex words, e.g. 'accoutrements', 'archive', 'exquisite', 'nutritious' and 'impelled'. There is effective use of parenthesis to enhance purpose and meaning.

PAPER 2, SECTION B, QUESTION 4

Grade C response

If you think of exams and spots and boy/girl problems, it's obvious that it's tough being a teenager. Just because you've turned 16 it doesn't mean you've sorted out these things in your life. These days are supposed to be the best in your life, but doing GCSEs and having to decide about staying on or getting a job don't make life easy.

Most sixteen year olds are old enough to want to go to pubs and clubs and have a car, but the law says they're too young and they don't have enough money for these things. It's like seeing stuff in a shop window but not being able to buy.

Another thing that makes it hard to be a sixteen year old is the way older people treat you. On the one hand they're telling you to act sensibly because you're supposed to be mature, then they tell you you're not eating enough vegetables or you're staying in bed too late as if you're a baby.

What adults can do to help teenagers have a better life is understand that they're under more pressure these days and they don't need extra stress by being told to keep their rooms tidy etc.

Another thing they can do is show some respect for teenagers who have GCSEs which take up their time in coursework and exams, and teachers who always think that their own homework is more important than anyone else's. Teachers can help too by realising that teenagers need a social life and if their weekend is full of schoolwork they're not going to relax and enjoy themselves, and get all stressed and dull.

Examiner's comments
Communication and organisation
This response shows language adapted for audience and purpose, being mainly Standard English with some personal address, and referring to a suitable range of people responsible for adults. There is awareness of the difference between description and explanation: description is helped by the comparison with looking at a shop window, and explanation is helped by phrases such as 'On the one hand' and 'can do' and 'don't need'. It is organised in paragraphs with varied beginnings to sustain the reader's interest.

Sentence structures, spelling and punctuation
Sentences are structured accurately and with some variety. Spelling is secure, and on the whole there is accurate sentence punctuation, though there is limited use of the whole range of punctuation. Apostrophes are accurately used.

Grade A/A* response

Pressure, anxiety, stress, insecurity, relationships, money, the future, global warming, Al Qaida and writing English exams … Need I go on? These are just a few of the things that make it a time of tension for teenagers. It's bad enough having gone through rapid growth spurts for a few years, as well as SATs and getting shoved around by older pupils. Just when you thought you'd got over the last few challenges, along comes more of the same, only worse.

When I look at my friends, I see people crumbling under the stress of exams and career choices. I look at their faces and I see misery, gloom and grief where I should see joy, confidence and optimism. When we ring each other in the evening, it's not to discuss all-night parties or weekend binges as our parents seem to think – it's to check on the latest deadline, console each other after a bad day at school or swap notes on the next practice exam.

Admittedly, you can see some sixteen-year-olds who are cheerful and happy, but don't be fooled by their own delusion. They're the ones who've decided that the best in life is getting a job stacking shelves or getting engaged or getting a motor scooter on HP. But they're only putting off the moment when they discover that these aren't the answer to Life's Great Questions.

Given all this as the reality, it's time adults – parents and teachers especially – wised up and started to show some grasp of what it's like to be sixteen these days. Understand that from Key Stage 2 SATs, these poor people have been part of the national statistics, driven harder and harder to succeed to prove the Government's policies right. They're the ones who've been targeted by merchandisers and advertising, made to feel like fashion outcasts if they haven't got the latest Nike air trainers, or are underweight or overweight or don't have the right CDs.

Above all, adults should understand that this generation of sixteen-year-olds has had some of its childhood irresponsibility stolen from it and faces a future more alarming than its parents faced.

Criticism is always easy. Understanding is less easy. Sympathy is even harder. But if someone is to make the world a better place, it's likely to be someone from today's generation of sixteen-year-olds, faced with problems they didn't create.

So, have a little respect for your youngsters, all you teachers and parents. You may need to rely on us sooner than you think.

Examiner's comments

Communication and organisation
This response shows a strong sense of audience and purpose. The beginning engages the reader's interest by listing causes of stress, with a humorous reference to writing in English as one of them. The response is well matched to purpose and audience, with some rhetorical address in 'Need I go on?' and in the conclusion, and there is acknowledgement of adults' opinions in the reference to what they think teenagers talk about on the phone. The writing mingles advice with explanation, shows a good range of vocabulary and sentence structures.

The whole response is well organised in paragraphs to enhance meaning, rather than being mechanically paragraphed, with paragraph beginnings conveying linkage and development, such as 'Admittedly', 'Given all this' and 'Above all'. The response shows sensitivity to the reader by varying the mode of address and appeal – for example, recommending, warning and engaging sympathy.

Description is well distinguished from explanation. Description uses detail, exaggeration and emotive appeal in reference to 'fashion outcasts' and the various worries that oppress teenagers. Explanation is marked by the use of imperatives 'Understand' and 'Have a little'.

Sentence structures, spelling and punctuation
In the last but one paragraph, there is conscious crafting of three short sentences for effect, making a point about criticism, understanding and sympathy. Spelling and punctuation are highly accurate.

EXAM PRACTICE

Section A

The tasks in this section are based on two passages: *Parent of a Teenager?*, which is taken from a website, and a newspaper article *Teenagers don't do as they're told*. Read both passages carefully before you answer the tasks.

Task 1: Non-fiction text

This leaflet aims to inform parents about problems which may arise when living with teenage children. Read it carefully and then state:

a) what the leaflet tells you about the conflicts which can arise between parents and teenagers and the reasons why these conflicts arise;

b) what the writer thinks parents' responsibilities to their children should be and what they can do to assist them with their problems.

(20 marks)

Parent of a Teenager? Read This

TESTING THE WATERS

Suddenly your once-charming child is slamming doors and telling you to 'get off my back!' The teenage years have arrived. 'Hormones' and peer pressure reign supreme.

Adolescence can be a frustrating time – bodies changing, insecurity, bravado. One minute they're 14 going on 30, the next they are three. But before you swap your teenagers for pet turtles, read on.

PARENTS ARE IMPORTANT

The good news is that parents are extremely important to their teenage children. In fact, young people are influenced by parents – what we do and say makes a difference to how they act. For example, research shows that teenagers are seven times less likely to smoke if their parents disapprove strongly.

Our teenagers need us – we give them standards, limits, security, consistency and love. When they get into difficulties, as most young people do at some time or other, we are there to bail them out, dust them off and let them try again. They'll make mistakes and learn from them.

PARENTS CAN HELP

The bottom line is that we are parents with rights and responsibilities for our children. We must follow our intuition and use common sense to keep our children safe, regardless of what anyone else tells us. Parents seeking advice are sometimes told that their teenagers are now 'grown up' and that parents can do nothing. This isn't true. Start with a few basic steps. Try to:

- find a quiet time to talk with teenagers about how things are going – not after a row or as they are going out, or it won't work. Sit down together; give them a chance to talk. Don't make it formal – this isn't the Spanish Inquisition. Do listen. It is worth the effort to find out their viewpoints and concerns.
- encourage your teenager to talk to other trusted adults, such as teachers, aunts, uncles, grandparents or family friends.

- sometimes kids just don't want to discuss things with parents! That's normal.
- notice when they do something right.
- ensure that they know how to keep safe. Teenagers take risks and think they are invincible, but we know they're not. Suggest that they:

  1 know what to do if they miss their lift home. Tell them to ring you (or a friend or neighbour) no matter what the hour and you will arrange for them to get home safely. Better that than walk home in the dark;
  2 know the number of a friend or a local taxi service as a back-up
  3 carry change for the phone and a phone card or a phone charge card – these are programmed for your number only, but watch out for the bills!
  4 come home with friends at night – never alone. Take a route that is likely to be busy, not isolated;
  5 ring if they are going to be late;
  6 arrange a secret code with you so they can ring if they need help. For example, they call and say 'Has Lisa rung?' That is your cue to ring back in a few minutes and arrange to collect them;
  7 sit on the lower deck of double-decker buses late at night or near the guard on the underground;
  8 never, never get in a car with a driver who is drunk;
  9 never, never hitchhike.

- stand up as a parent and don't be afraid to say No. Let your child use you as an excuse to keep out of trouble; 'My (terrible) parents won't let me' will elicit sympathy from friends and a secret sigh of relief from your child in dangerous situations. Keep your standards – help them set their limits.

- remind yourself that when they blunder, it's probably not your fault. Teenagers will explore, make mistakes and gain their independence. Just think of all the mistakes we made!
- remember that your teenager still loves and needs you, but might not be able to show it just now. Don't take things personally. It is a phase. It does get better!
- show an interest in what they do, but don't try to be their best friend – give them space and privacy as long as they aren't being self-destructive.
- be tolerant. Teenage humour seems to include burping loudly, passing wind, screeching in public, telling horribly sick jokes all while listening to a personal stereo. Charming! Try to ignore small things – they'll outgrow most. Save your energy for issues which really matter.
- be understanding and supportive when they feel isolated from the 'in crowd'. It is difficult to be different if they have other interests or if everyone else is smoking or taking drugs.
- explain in advance the consequences which will follow if they do something wrong. Then follow through.
- be flexible. Let's say a teenager comes home drunk and is sick all night. Maybe the consequences of this are a better lesson than anything you could do!
- use humour as much as possible – it will save your sanity. (Burp back at them!)
- find time to eat around the table and to celebrate special occasions as a family. Teenagers will get to know adults on a more equal level. Don't make them talk if they don't want to – they'll listen and learn.
- don't be fooled by the 'everyone else does it' ploy – they probably don't!
- talk about the dangers of unchaperoned parties – gatecrashing is a big problem and can lead to a trashed house or flat. If teenagers get caught up in this they could use the code (above) to ring you;
- keep up to date about things like drugs. Know how to treat an overdose, just in case.
- get advice and support from family, friends, GP, teachers and anyone else who might help. Being a parent does not mean we have to do everything on our own.

WHEN TO TAKE STRONGER ACTION

Some teenagers sail through these years with no difficulties; others cannot handle what's happening and need our intervention. We may be the only ones who care enough to do this. Watch out for warning signs or completely inappropriate behaviour. Take action if they:

- become very secretive beyond a normal need for privacy – could indicate drug or alcohol abuse;
- are always depressed. Everyone gets depressed now and again, but consistent depression needs help;
- suddenly change their school performance – could be caused by bullying or a 'bad' crowd;
- are extremely hostile and violent;
- are abusing alcohol, gambling, taking drugs;
- stay out all night, constantly run away, truant or refuse to go to school;
- are under the age of 16 and having a sexual relationship with an older person.

WHAT TO DO FIRST

- Find out what is causing the problem. Ask direct questions and tell them you want to understand and help. Don't overreact yet – it may be a one-off.
- Be clear about your standards – show that you disapprove of inappropriate behaviour.
- Seek help from your GP – there may be a physical cause or you may request a counselling referral.
- Contact the school or Help Organisations listed below.
- You will usually be able to sort things out by stepping in and taking a strong stand as a parent. Your teenager will be relieved, though he or she might not show it.

MORE SERIOUS?

If the problem seems to be very serious and you feel out of your depth, then you do have some other options:

- Be decisive, take charge and find help.
- Contact the Child and Family Consultation Service, either directly or through your GP, social services, the school.
- Contact the police, social services or your Local Education Authority – see local directory.
- Seek legal advice. You can resort to the courts, but this is rarely necessary.

REMEMBER

- Parents are legally responsible for their children until they reach the age of 18.
- Parents cannot fix everything. We can support our children, but sometimes they need to experience the consequences of their actions.
- Most teenagers experiment. They get drunk, come in late, try smoking and do dumb things. Many of us did the same, had some fun, took a few risks … and learned. That's why we can give good advice, but in the long run, it is the example we set and our ability to communicate that will most help our children.
- Tell your teenagers often that you love them and are proud of them – they may seem to shrug it off, but they need to know it now more than ever. We need to boost their self-esteem, not tear them down. They may appear outwardly to be confident, but inside they still need our approval and love.

HELP AND ADVICE FOR PARENTS

Parentline Plus	0808 800 2222
Gamblers Anonymous	020 7384 3040
Alcoholics Anonymous	01904 644026
The National Drugs Helpline	0800 776600
Samaritans	08457 909090
Youth Access	020 8772 9900
Children's Legal Centre	01206 873820
Advisory Council for Education	020 7354 8321
Education Otherwise	0891 518303
Quitline (smoking)	0800 002200

FREE BOOKLETS

For free booklets about child protection, bullying or child abuse, send a large SAE to:

Kidscape, 2 Grosvenor Gardens, London SW1W 0DH, tel.: 020 7730 3300 www.kidscape.org.uk

Look closely at and comment on the ways in which information, opinions and beliefs are presented in this article. Explain what you think the writer's purpose is in writing the article, and how successful you think she has been in achieving it.

(20 marks)

Teenagers don't do as they're told

But only a judge could be shocked by that revelation, writes **Maureen Freely**

Teenagers like this – targeted by raging hormones and insidious marketing messages – aren't likely to listen to sweetly reasoned arguments.
Getty Images

SHE OUGHT TO have seen it coming.

According to her daughters' head teacher, every other possible avenue had been explored. The educational authorities got in touch with her the moment they knew the girls were not turning up at school. She'd later had warnings from the police. She'd even been asked to go to magistrate's court. But no matter how hard the various arms of the law tried to scare her, they were not able to get Patricia Amos to use the same tactics on her daughters. Fifteen-year-old Emma and 13-year-old Jackie just carried on truanting. They were as surprised as everyone else when an Oxford judge blamed this on their mother, and sent her to Holloway for 60 days for 'failing to ensure' her children attended school.

The judge and his friends are hoping that a stint in prison will teach her a lesson. Somewhere inside Holloway, she'll find the road to Damascus. She'll come out renewed and energised, and determined to show those two girls who's boss. It is, of course, an exemplary sentence. She's serving it so that the rest of us can learn from her misfortune. But say we all woke tomorrow to find ourselves converted. Say we decided that from now on, our teenagers were going to Behave Or Else. How many teenagers would pay attention? Of those who did, how many would laugh? And how many parents would laugh with them?

If they do find this sentence risible, it's not because they subscribe to the forces of darkness, and pray every night that their teenagers turn into drug-taking car-jackers. At the end of the day, I'd say most British parents have roughly the same aspirations for their children as that Oxford judge. The problem is that we just don't wield the kind of authority he thinks we do. This is partly due to changes in the way we discipline, or some might say fail to discipline, our children. The main eroding agents come from the outside, and they cause most parents terrible grief. Most fight them, at least for a while. Most lose.

When children are little, you can fool yourself that you are the one shaping their characters. But by the time they reach double digits, forget it. The fairy tale is over. From here on in, you are in competition with a thousand other influences, 900 of them profit-oriented, and market-driven, and pernicious.

It's hard to know what's worse – finding out that you're not a god any more or finding out that the new god is Britney Spears. I'm sure my own parents felt similarly threatened by the Beatles. But the consumerisation of teens was only just beginning then, and children weren't teenagers until they turned 13. Now you can buy teenage-type clothes and accessories from the time your child is two-and-a-half. You can always say no, of course. But it is one thing to tell an eight-year-old wannabe that you don't think she's quite old enough for high-heeled jellies and a padded bra. It's quite another to expect a shy and anxious 14-year-old boy to wear trainers that make all his classmates laugh at him.

[continued on next page]

You might think it's terrible that teenagers take peer pressure so seriously, and even worse that multi-billion-pound industries are able to manipulate this force with such ease. But if the Government is unwilling to make laws to stop them, there's not much you can do. While we're on the subject of the law, it's good to remember that it's not always there to back you up.

At 16, a child is no longer a child, but a young person. He can leave school, take up employment, seek medical treatment or indeed leave home without seeking your permission. But by and large, parents continue to have the same legal and financial responsibilities as before. The only difference is that their children only have to listen to them if they want to.

As someone who has already seen two children through adolescence, I don't think this is necessarily a bad thing. I wouldn't want any child of mine to obey me if they thought I was very wrong.

And neither would I want them to do anything, right or wrong, just because they feared me. Especially when a child has grown into a teenager, they need parents they trust and respect. The adults teenagers most look up to are the ones who return the compliment. Being a teenager and bringing up teenagers is universally difficult. Of the 225,000 calls that Parentline Plus received from parents and other carers last year, 45 per cent concerned teenagers. When things go wrong, they've found, the reasons are complex. And wherever attempts to redress those problems work, it is because great attention has been given to context. If you want a working definition of attention-to-context, it's what the Oxford judge didn't do before he sent Patricia Amos off to Holloway without let-

ting her make arrangements for the care of her daughters.

In most recent studies of parents with teenagers, the recurring themes are frustration, isolation, powerlessness, lack of social support, and the low social status their work has. In studies that invite adolescents to speak for themselves, the same themes return. They complain about their lack of power and their low standing in the adult world. They are particularly distressed by the demonisation of teenagers in the media.

The common refrains are: why do they hate us so much? Why do adults cross the road when they see us coming? Why are my parents the only ones who seem to like me? If my parents are cruel to me, why is it so hard to find help? Why do we have so little say about how our schools are run? Why is there nothing for us to do after school?

Section B

Task 3: Writing to Inform, Explain, Describe.

Describe an occasion or occasions when a conflict with your parents might have arisen, but was avoided. Explain how this happened and what you learnt from the experience.

(20 marks)

Write 350–450 words.
Leave enough time to check through and correct what you have written.

OCR answers and comments

TASK 1A

Grade C response

When the teenage years start, hormones and peer pressure become important. It is a difficult time for parents who sometimes feel that there is nothing they can do. Most problems come from teenagers behaving badly such as embarrassing their parents by burping loudly and telling sick jokes. Teenagers do not discuss things with their parents and don't listen to what they're told. They get drunk and have wild parties which result in a trashed house or flat. Parents get angry about such behaviour.

Sometimes teenagers get involved in taking drugs or drinking too much. They may be bullied by a 'bad' crowd and refuse to go to school. At the age of 16 they may be having a sexual relationship with somebody older. There are several reasons why they behave like this. They are suffering from raging hormones and they are over confident and don't notice risks. Not all teenagers have these problems, however, some sail through these years without difficulties.

Grade A/A* response

Hormonal changes which affect teenagers lead to temper tantrums, depression, an inhibited approach to showing feelings for their families and a desire to keep themselves to themselves.

Aggressive behaviour also manifests itself. In order to assert their independence, teenagers often become over-confident and refuse to listen to or confide in their parents. Another result of this wish to assert themselves is that teenagers stay out late at night and take unnecessary risks associated with alcohol, drugs and under-age sex. They do not wish to lose face among their friends (either from insecurity or, perhaps, from the fear of being bullied) and this can lead to truanting from school and generally offensive and anti-social behaviour.

Examiner's comments

- Both parts of this task require reading for information and selecting material appropriate to the purpose. Some of the points made in the leaflet are made indirectly by inference and are not directly stated. The ability to identify these points, in addition to the more obvious ones, is a feature of answers achieving a top grade.
- The Grade C answer shows a sound understanding of the main points contained in the passage, but the inferential points are not always identified.
- The organisation and structure are rather loose. The way in which the answer is ordered tends to be over-dependent on the order of the original passage.
- There is a clear attempt to be concise, but it is not always sustained and there is some repetition and irrelevance. The answer uses the candidate's own words, but there is some selective lifting.
- The Grade A answer clearly demonstrates the ability to select and focus on material which is directly relevant to the task.
- There is a very good range of points included, and they are extremely well organised and structured. The candidate has decided to arrange the material by identifying the causes and relating the different problems to each cause which has been identified. As a result of doing this, it is apparent that the candidate has a complete understanding of the material and is well able to select points relating to the task.
- There is a consistent and successful attempt to be concise and to synthesise points. The candidate has used her own words throughout the answer, and the inferential points have been fully explained.

TASK 1B

Grade C response

Parents are important to their teenage children because they influence them. Research shows that teenagers are less likely to smoke if their parents disapprove. Parents can help their teenage children by talking to them about how things are going but not after you've had a row. They can encourage teenagers to talk to other people in the family like aunts and grandparents. Parents can tell teenagers how to stay safe and help if they miss their lift home. They can let their children use them as an excuse to keep out of trouble as the teenager can say that their horrible parents won't let them do something. Parents should be interested in what their children do but shouldn't try to be their best friends. It's a good idea to allow a teenager to come home drunk and be sick all night as it will teach them a lesson. Also parents need to know what to do if their child overdoses on drugs. If there's a real problem parents should get in touch with the school or the Child and Family Consultation Service or even social services.

Grade A/A* response

The main responsibilities of parents are to understand and support their teenagers by being consistent in their attitudes, and by making their principles clear. Parents should be prepared to listen to their teenager's viewpoint and to establish a relationship where mature and informal discussion is possible, with the child being secure in the parents' love and their interest in his/her life.

A sense of humour is a great advantage for parents, as is an acceptance that sometimes the child will be happier talking to another adult instead of them. Rather than overreacting to their children's behaviour, parents should accept that teenagers learn from their mistakes; similarly, parents should give praise whenever possible to help boost children's confidence.

Parents should be aware of issues relating to drugs and other aspects of teenage culture, so that they can offer practical advice. They should realise the problem of peer pressure and allow their child to use them as a reason for keeping out of trouble.

Finally, parents should provide both emotional and material security and be prepared to take decisive action if serious problems arise.

Examiner's comments
- *The Grade C response shows a sound understanding of the main responsibilities, but does not clearly link the relationship between these and the ways in which parents can assist. This results in the answer being loosely structured, and it appears more like a list than a cohesive whole. Perhaps if the candidate had thought more about organising the points into paragraphs, this might have been avoided.*
- *Inferential points may have been understood, but this understanding has not been clearly communicated.*
- *The wording of the task (should be) emphasises*

that some of the points are inferential, and the Grade A response selects appropriate material and organises it logically and coherently with good use of paragraphing.
- *The Grade A response identifies that there is a distinction between the practical, more general things which can be done to support teenagers (such as provide emotional/material security) and the more general, less quantifiable points, such as giving praise and using humour, which are subsidiary to it.*

Task 2
Grade C response

Maureen tells us about Patricia Amos who was sent to prison because she didn't stop her two daughters playing truant. She'd had lots of warnings from the education authorities but they didn't do any good. Maureen Freely thinks that the judge was wrong to put her in prison because she says that parents don't wield the kind of authority the judge thinks they do. She is writing the article to make us question the judge's decision and to make us aware of the difficulties which parents and teenagers have to face.

Maureen is a parent herself. She has had two children who she has seen through adolescence and understands how teenagers think. She realises it's important that teenagers trust and respect their parents and doesn't want them to do things just because they're afraid of them. This is sensible and shows her understanding of her children. She also knows something about the problems which teenagers face. As children grow up and start to be influenced by pop singers like Britney Spears. She also understands about how, once they become teenagers, children need to buy particular clothes and brand labels so that they are not laughed at by their friends. She calls this 'the consumerisation of teens'.

The writer thinks that the judge in Oxford and his friends are not aware of these problems which parents and children have to put up with. She thinks that the sentence won't have any effect and calls it 'risible'. She has strong opinions and expresses them in powerful language. She talks about teenagers 'subscribing to the forces of darkness' and turning into 'drug-taking car-jackers'. This suggests that some people like the Oxford judge see them as being evil beings. She also says that society is to blame for teenagers' behaviour and talks about 'eroding agents' which is another interesting expression.

At the end of the article she puts over her views about the difficult lives teenagers have again and uses the word 'demonisation' to describe what's happened to them. She thinks that they're unfairly treated as they say 'Why do we have so little say about how our schools are run?'

Overall, the writer has written the article to make us aware how unfair life is for parents and teenagers and a lot of what she says is true and makes you think. I think she's been very successful in what she sets out to do.

Grade A/A* response

Maureen Freely has written this article to draw her readers' attention to a recent court case in which a mother was imprisoned for two months for 'failing to ensure that her children attended school'. The writer uses this incident both as an opportunity to be critical of the system which allowed this situation to occur and also to focus attention on the problems parents of teenagers face and to sympathise with parents in a difficult position.

Although the facts of the case are indisputable – the length of the mother's sentence and the reason for it can easily be confirmed by reference to court records – the writer's approach to reporting the issue is very much influenced by her own beliefs and attitudes.

The reader's attention is immediately captured by the headline 'Teenagers don't do as they're told', which appeals because it is a truism and therefore is likely to be of interest to most parents and children. However, it also takes the focus away from the mother by emphasising the all-too-common failure of children in general and is a means by which the readers are encouraged to sympathise with the mother's fate and to question the judgement of the court. This attitude is reinforced by the eye-catching photograph and the use of emotive language in the caption accompanying it. Teenagers are victims of 'raging hormones and insidious marketing messages'; they're not likely to listen to 'sweetly reasoned arguments'. The message is that teenagers shouldn't be blamed, nor can parents do much about the situation; the clear implication is that the system we live under is to blame.

Already, the reader has been predisposed to be critical of the establishment and in particular of the legal system which supports it. The insensitive lack of concern bureaucracy has for the lives of ordinary people is effectively conveyed through the impersonal

tone of the simple sentences in which events leading up to Patricia Amos's trial are described. By initially using the pronoun 'she' rather than giving her name, the writer conveys the way that individuals become depersonalised before the Law.

Through the way the writer refers to the judge and his friends hoping that this experience will teach Patricia Amos a lesson and by using terms such as 'finding the road to Damascus' and 'showing who's boss', we receive an impression of the patronising attitude which is attributed to the judge and the social group which he represents. This is effective, but we have been manipulated by the writer into thinking this, rather than a fact which can be objectively verified.

As the article progresses, the writer becomes increasingly more critical of the system which imprisoned Patricia Amos and sets up a 'them and us' situation in which 'they' are the out-of-touch people in authority and 'we' are the ordinary people, parents and their children, struggling to cope in a world which is ruled by commercial forces which create problems of peer pressure among children which, in turn, create conflict with parents. This is conveyed through the example of 14-year-old boys being ridiculed because of their trainers.

In conclusion, the writer uses the Patricia Amos incident to criticise authority figures who are out of touch with ordinary people and the difficulties in their lives; she conveys this through forceful emotive language – 'risible', 'frustration, isolation and powerlessness' – and by the powerful rhetorical questions – 'Why do they hate us so much?' etc. – with which she ends the article. The reader is left with a strong sense of sympathy for parents and children in a world which does not always appreciate their problems.

Examiner's comments

- For this task, candidates are asked to identify the writer's opinions and beliefs and to analyse the ways in which she attempts to make her readers share them.
- The Grade C answer shows a sound understanding of the writer's argument, although comments on it are lacking in incisiveness and there is a tendency to *describe* points made in the original rather than to *comment* on them.
- There is some evidence that the differences between fact and opinion have been understood.

- Comments are supported by textual references and quotations, but these have not been fully explained or analysed.
- Overall, the candidate has attempted to answer 'how' the writer makes her points rather than merely describing 'what' she says. The candidate has also tried to comment on the writer's use of language, but the comments are usually undeveloped.
- The Grade A response adopts a consistently analytical approach. The candidate clearly identifies and distinguishes between statements which are fact and statements which are opinion and has a good understanding of the writer's purpose and the ability to explain this clearly to the reader.
- Comments are supported by appropriate quotations and reference.
- The candidate has fully evaluated the effectiveness of the writer's argument and the means by which it is conveyed. There is a particularly perceptive appreciation of the writer's use of language. This has been fully supported by quotation and reference and the effects achieved are fully explained to the reader.

TASK 3

Grade C response

A couple of weeks ago I went into town with some mates from school. It was a Saterday night and we thought we'd go for a few beers in the pub and then go on to a club.

We didn't do this sort of thing very often and normally we're quite well behaved. I didn't tell my parents what we were going to do, they don't mind me going out on a Saturday but they get a bit of an attitude if I come home late and wake them up. If I do that, my dad usualy goes mental and shouts at me and then grounds me for a couple of weeks although in most cases when this happens my mum feels sorry for me and talks him out of it and I get repreived after a couple of days.

Anyway, on this particular night I caught the bus into town. It was the end of the month and I'd just been paid from my part-time job in the local supermarket so I had quite a lot of money with me. I met my friends at our usual meeting place and we went into one of the big pubs in the town centre. Luckily we all had some fake ID cards so we were able to get past the bouncers at the door.

We enjoyed ourselves in the pub, we had some beers and some mixers, we played several games of pool and even joined in with the karaoke evening which was taking place. I think I saw one of my dad's friends on the other side of the bar but I don't think he saw me and I don't think he'd have told my dad anyway.

When we left the pub at about eleven o'clock, I was feeling a bit light-headed but was able to walk in a straight line. We stopped at a late night burger bar for double cheeseburger and french fries and then thought we'd try to get into one of the towns clubs. Again, we flashed our fake ID at the doormen, payed our money and walked in confidently. I'd not been to this club before, it was quite a sophisticated place, so I decided to drink cocktails. I don't know what was in them but they tasted nice and I had two or three before I started to feel very funny in the head. The next thing I knew I was sitting on the pavement outside of the club with a couple of my friends next to me. They weren't as drunk as me and one of them used his mobile to call for a taxi. Somehow it got me home.

I payed the taxi driver and staggered up to the front door. I was feeling very sick and wobbly and couldn't find my key. I think my father must have heard me as he opened the door as I stood there swaying. I fell through the door and collapsed on the carpet. 'I'm in big trouble' I thought. Strangely, my father didn't shout at me but started to rock with laughter. He called my mum and she stared to laugh too. They helped me up to bed and told me to sleep on my side in case I was sick. I wasn't sick until next morning and I spent all day with a stinking headache. Surprisingly, there was no telling off and my parents still didn't shout at me. Instead all my Dad said was 'I hope you've learnt your lesson'. I certainly had, I've learnt not to go drinking like that again and I've also learnt that there's another side to my parents.

Grade A/A* response

I suppose that I'm lucky with my parents. I've always assumed that I've got them very well trained and that they'll do what I want. After all, they've had their life and as they are responsible for my being in the world, it's their duty to accommodate my wishes and do what they can for me.

Now that you've read that paragraph, you're most probably thinking what a self-centred and arrogant person I must be. Well, a couple of years ago, you would have been right. I did think like this – or something like this, as I may have exaggerated a little bit, for effect. However, something happened which made me question my attitudes and it's something for which I am immensely grateful.

I come from a conventional middle-class background. I'm sixteen years old, both my parents are teachers in full employment, and we live as a family with my younger brother in a comfortable house in a quiet part of the town. My parents have never really restricted my behaviour; they work on the assumption that I am a rational human being who understands responsibility and that if a problem arises we can find time to sit down and talk things through in a civilised way. This approach seemed to work; I was successful at school and apart from the usual foolish things that people do in lessons, I was never in any serious trouble. I had no worries; the world was mine and I was at the centre of it.

It was as I was approaching the end of Year 9 that the problem arose. I was quite a popular person at school but, like a lot of teenagers, was not as socially confident inside as I may have appeared to be on the surface. I had a group of close friends whom I had known since junior school, and most of them came from a similar background to mine. My parents were happy for me to be with my friends after school and at weekends, and we spent quite a lot of time in sleepovers at each other's houses. We had a lot of fun, but there was a growing rebellious streak within me which led to my becoming dissatisfied with what I had. My friends were fun and responsible, but they were also a little boring. I wanted adventure and excitement, which they didn't seem to offer.

There was, of course, another group at school who were less respectable than my friends. They smoked and spent evenings and weekends 'hanging out' in the town centre. As far as I know, they didn't spend their time in sleepovers safe in each others' houses but, instead, went back their own homes, but very late at night. I wanted to live this type of life, but I knew that my parents wouldn't allow me to. This was my dilemma; as I said, I was self-centred and assumed that the world revolved around me. My parents had always been understanding but, then, I'd not really put them to the test. Apart from a few tantrums when I was in junior school, we'd never been in conflict with each

other. I knew that if I were to be accepted by this other group, my parents would never allow me to go out with them in the evenings and come home after midnight. If I were to do so, it would produce a conflict and if I lost this conflict, my egocentricity would suffer.

To cut a long story short, by encouraging my parents to buy me the right type of branded clothing, I became accepted by the group I wanted to be part of. Saturday night came, and they invited me to join them in the town centre. I lied to my parents and told them that I was going to spend the night at the house of one of my respectable friends. I prayed that my parents wouldn't phone up to check, but they never had in the past. Nervously, but full of excitement, I met up with my new friends in town. To start with, we had a good time – I didn't really like smoking, but I pretended I did – but as the evening wore on, I began to get worried. Increasingly, they became involved in minor acts of vandalism – snapping aerials off parked cars and such like activities. I felt this was wrong and I was scared. I didn't know what to do. It was getting late, and I realised that my excuse for being out was not fully thought through. In the end, I risked losing face; I made some not entirely convincing comment to my friends that I needed to go home as I wasn't feeling well. I don't think they were too concerned, as I most probably hadn't been much fun. I ran down the road and, fortunately, caught a bus which took me home.

When I walked through the front door I found my parents watching television. I couldn't continue with my lie any longer. Something made me confess to them exactly what I had been doing. This looked as if it was going to be the moment of conflict I had been dreading … but it wasn't. They listened thoughtfully to what I told them; they clearly did not approve, but I think they appreciated my honesty; as my father said to me later, it was a sign that I was growing up. Rather than shouting at me, they realised that my evening had taught me a lesson. My parents didn't let me go out with those friends again (not that I wanted to), but told me that if they ever bothered me I was to put the blame on them and say that I wasn't allowed out – it's what you'd expect from schoolteachers, after all.

I learned a lot from this experience; I learned that my parents cared for me and valued me as a human being. I learned that they were human beings and wise ones too, and I realised that it might be a good idea to accept them as part of my world. As I said, I'm lucky with my parents.

Examiner's comments

- The Grade C essay is relevant to the topic, but is a little unbalanced in structure: what the candidate learnt from the experience is rather crammed into the final paragraph.
- The basic approach is more narrative than the Grade A essay, and there is not the personal reflection of the other candidate.
- Nevertheless, this essay is not without merit. The story is told simply and clearly; there are some not-fully-appropriate colloquialisms ('goes mental'), but overall the personality of the candidate emerges. In places, the story is quite amusing, but the candidate is not skilful enough for the reader to be sure whether this humour is deliberate or not.
- The essay is divided into paragraphs which help to structure the content. There is less of a range of sentence types than in the Grade A essay – many sentences follow the same pattern by beginning with pronoun followed by verb which gives a certain feeling of monotony – and there are more errors of spelling (which are sometimes inconsistent – 'Saterday/Saturday') and punctuation. In particular, the candidate's use of full stops to separate sentences is not always fully secure.
- Overall, however, there is sufficient clarity, interest and control of expression and subject matter for this essay to be graded at C; with a little careful revision it could be improved considerably.
- There is a similarity in content between these two essays, and both are perfectly acceptable responses to the topic. However, the Grade A essay presents the material in a more detailed and structured way. There is clear evidence that the candidate is in control of the content and sets out to interest and entertain the reader.

- There is a conscious attempt in the Grade A essay to write with style (notice, for example, the way in which the opening sentence is repeated for effect at the end), and the tone is informal without being over-colloquial. The vocabulary is well suited to the purpose. There are no pyrotechnics – this is an informative essay, after all – but the candidate knows and uses a word like 'egocentricity' correctly when it is appropriate to do so.
- The account of the experience is conveyed clearly and with a consistent ironically self-critical tone which reinforces the candidate's awareness of what has been learnt from the episode.
- Technically, the essay is very correctly expressed. There are no major errors of spelling, expression or punctuation. Paragraphing is used in a positive way to structure ideas and to guide the reader.
- The candidate uses a range of sentence structures to give variety and interest to the account and is also confident enough to use a non-sentence for effect 'To cut a long story short'. The candidate is confident in handling complex sentence structures and also in correctly using the more sophisticated punctuation devices such as semi-colons and dashes.
- Overall, this is a sophisticated piece of written expression containing interesting and convincing content which is fully relevant to the topic and expressed with confidence and flair. We could hardly expect more from any candidate under examination conditions.

Warning to teenagers as mobile phone thefts soar

Robberies hit 25,000 a year with youngsters most likely mugging victims

Mobile phones are a popular target for thieves, with many young victims attacked violently

By Matthew Hickley
Home Affairs Reporter

TEENAGERS are being urged not to use mobile phones in public in a bid to cut the soaring number of muggings.

The violent theft of handsets has become one of the fastest-growing crimes, with youngsters the main victims.

There were an estimated 25,000 such robberies last year, up from 5,000 three years ago. Last week a girl of 19 was shot in the head in an East London street by an attacker who stole her phone.

A study which reveals the scale of the problem will be unveiled by the Home Office today.

The report, covering four inner London boroughs, is expected to show that teenagers are by far the most likely victims, while the

Crime reduction minister John Denham will launch the report at a London school, hoping to persuade pupils to take basic precautions against phone snatchers. A Home Office spokesman said: 'Schoolchildren, particularly teenagers, are statistically most likely to become victims. Our advice is to avoid using phones in

'Some are sold abroad'

Police say that about half of those mugged for their mobile phones are under 20, with a quarter aged 14 to 17. More than half of all robberies involve the theft of a mobile phone.

The Metropolitan Police, which provided the data for today's report, admit the problem is growing and more research is needed.

'We know quite a lot about who the victims are and the pattern of majority of phones are snatched in opportunist muggings in public places.

With 40 million Britons now using mobiles, ministers believe the huge rise in thefts is largely responsible for pushing up figures for violent crime in England and Wales.

While overall recorded crime fell by 2.5 per cent last year, violent offences increased by 4.3 per cent. Mobile phone muggings, many committed by teenagers, are thought to account for a large part of the rise. Last year in London, such robberies rose by a third in just six months.

public, and especially to avoid showing them off ostentatiously.

'Some thefts are a form of playground bullying, but outside schools, it is often an opportunist snatch. Keeping mobile phones out of sight is a start.'

While ministers and officials have tended to play down phone theft as largely a playground phenomenon, the shooting of the 19-year-old on New Year's Day showed it can be a violent crime.

The girl, who cannot be named because of fears for her safety, was shot in the head by a mugger who snatched her handset in Walthamstow.

thefts, but we need to know more about what happens to stolen handsets,' a spokesman said. 'We aren't recovering large numbers, and there doesn't appear to be a large organised market for stolen handsets, but it is there.

'We think some phones are used for a short while by the thief and thrown away, and others are shipped abroad, while a proportion are resold in this country.'

The Met is deploying extra officers near schools in the late afternoon, when most thefts occur, and is encouraging security marking of phones with ink which shows up under ultra-violet light.

The Government wants the phone industry to equip phones with far better anti-theft technology – action by motor manufacturers has helped slash car thefts.

Two of the largest networks, Vodafone and Cellnet, are unable to block stolen phones using a handset's individual serial number. They can block a phone number, but thieves can get around this by swapping the SIM card.

The various network suppliers do not share information on stolen handset serial numbers, meaning that phones are relatively easy for thieves to recycle and reuse by swapping SIM cards and using a different network.

Perdita Patterson, editor of *What Mobile* magazine, said: 'The networks need to get together and pool data. That should mean that a stolen handset is unusable on any UK network.

'Even then, a significant proportion of stolen handsets ends up overseas.

International co-operation looks a long way off, but it should be possible as the market is dominated by a relatively small number of manufacturers.'

Q & A

Q Why are mobiles so attractive to thieves?

A The handsets are numerous, valuable – worth £150 or more – easily snatched and easy to hide. Among many teenage gangs, the newest and smartest mobile phone is a status symbol. Police believe there is a sizeable market for stolen phones abroad, particularly in Eastern Europe.

Q How do thieves benefit?

A Casual thieves may use a phone for a few hours until it is reported and blocked, then throw it away. Young thieves wanting an 'upgrade' can steal a smarter, new phone and use it by inserting the SIM card from their old handset. SIM cards are the small coded electronic chips fitted in phones which carry the customer's telephone number and account details.

Q New mobile phones are almost given away. Why is there a second-hand market?

A Operators offer new customers attractive deals, but there are no free phones. Customers are tied into contract for a year or more, and end up paying for the handset through the tariff. If a handset is stolen, lost or damaged and the user is not insured, they face replacement costs of £150 or more. Alternatively, they can buy a new SIM card from their network provider for a few pounds and, unofficially, buy a 'used' phone – which may have been stolen.

Q What can I do to protect my mobile?

A Ask the police to security mark your phone with your postcode Avoid using it in crowded public areas – particularly where you feel unsafe. Tube stations are particular theft hot-spots. Keep your phone hidden when not in use.

Always activate the PIN code security option, and make a note of your handset's 15-digit International Mobile Equipment Identity (IMEI) serial number. It is written behind the battery, and most phones display it if you key *#06#. This could help the police trace a stolen handset. They will also need the phone number, PIN and fascia details.

Q Can 'text bombing' help discourage thieves?

A Dutch police cut phone thefts by 50 per cent by bombarding stolen handsets with thousands of text messages, announcing the phone as stolen. Scotland Yard tried to introduce a similar system last year, but it came to nothing because of 'technical problems'. Text bombing only works until the SIM card is changed.

Q Can't the network operators deactivate a phone once it is reported stolen?

A Only up to a point. There are two ways of barring a phone – either by blocking the particular phone number account linked to the SIM card or by barring the handset itself using its individual serial number. The first is easy, but a thief can still use the stolen handset by inserting a different SIM card. One-2-One and Orange can bar an individual handset so that it cannot be used. Vodafone and BT Cellnet are unable to do this, as the technology was not available when they set up their networks.

Q Couldn't the rival operators pool information on handsets?

A Yes – and in theory, this would render a stolen handset unusable in Britain. But they don't. Moves to set up a shared database a few years ago came to nothing.

Taken from an original article

Question 1 – Non-fiction texts

How does the report from the *Daily Mail* (see pages 148–149) try to arouse the interest of readers and inform them about the topic of mobile phone thefts?

You should comment on the following:
• the design of the page;
• the content of the article and the Q&A panel;
• the use of language;
• whether you think the report is successful;
• any other aspects that you think are relevant.

Question 2 – Writing to analyse, review, comment

Either

(a) Analyse the advantages and disadvantages of living in an age of advanced electronic communications.

Or

(b) Write about a visitor attraction that you know, commenting on its appeal to young people aged 14–16.

Question 3 – Writing to argue, persuade, advise

Either

(a) Your head teacher has banned pupils from taking mobile phones to school and is now reviewing this policy.
Write a letter to the head teacher to argue for the ban to be maintained or for the policy to be changed.

Or

(b) A letter to a local newspaper contained the following comment:
'Many schools waste time on organising trips and visits for the pupils instead of concentrating on teaching them to read, write and add up.'
Write a letter to the newspaper arguing **either** in favour of **or** against this point of view.

(Sample answers and Examiner's comments are given for Questions 1, 2 (b) and 3 (a).)

Edexcel answers and comments

QUESTION 1

Grade C response

The large photograph is the first thing I noticed about this page from The *Daily Mail*. The girl is looking down at the display of a mobile phone and keying a number in. Newspapers often use a photograph to grab the reader's attention and often the photograph is of a pretty girl, which is the case in this report. The large headline also stands out and there is an obvious link with the photograph through the words 'mobile phone' and 'teenager'. The headline reads: 'Warning to teenagers as mobile phone thefts soar'. The words 'warning' and 'thefts soar' make you want to read on so that you can find out more about what is happening.

The content of the article is about the increasing amount of mobile phone crime. The first paragraph talks about teenagers being mugged for their phones and the report goes on to say there were '25,000 such robberies last year'. That's bad enough but the report then says a 19-year old girl was shot in the head just so that someone could steal her phone. This would make most readers sit up and take notice! The report also says what the police and the government are trying to do about the problem. Most readers would find this interesting, whether they are teenagers, parents or grandparents. The last part of the article explains that the phone companies could do more to prevent thefts if they got together. Perdita Patterson who is the editor of *What Mobile* magazine is quoted as saying that lost phones could be made useless if the companies got together. Some readers might find the bits about SIM cards and networks hard to understand but they would probably be the ones who don't have a mobile phone. Young people would understand and be interested.

Some of the language in the report is emotive and tries to get readers interested by emphasising the danger. The main headline and the one above it and the caption for the photograph use these words:

Robberies   mugging victims   Warning
    thefts soar   attacked violently

All of these words make you worried and think you could be on the receiving end. A lot more words like this are used in the report to keep readers interested. The first half of the article emphasises the danger to teenagers and most people would find this interesting.

The second half explains what the police are doing and the report is not as interesting because there are more technical words like 'individual serial numbers', 'security marking of phones with ink which shows up under ultraviolet light' and 'SIM card'. The main points of the story are made in the first half so anyone who isn't interested in the more technical side of things could stop reading without missing anything important.

The box with the words Q&A at the bottom of the page also stands out. Q&A stands for questions and answers, and there are seven questions about what can be done to make mobile phones less attractive to thieves. This is a good way of giving readers extra information because anyone who wants to find out more can look through the questions and then decide whether to read the answers. Some of the information is technical and I didn't really understand what all of it meant. By putting this information together in a separate section the main report can be made easier for readers to understand without having all the boring technical bits put in as well.

I think this is a fairly successful report because it looks interesting and most readers would start to read it even if they don't read through to the end. The way the main report puts the most important information in the first half is sensible. Anyone who is a mobile phone geek could find a lot more information in the later sections and in the Q&A section but I don't think most readers would bother unless they had just bought a new phone.

Grade A/A* response

This report takes up a whole page in the newspaper, which tells us that the newspaper regards mobile phone theft as an important and topical issue. This story is tied in with the publication of a government report about crime in four London boroughs, which identified a large increase in the number of street robberies involving the theft of phones.

The focal point of the page is a photograph of a girl using a mobile phone. The fact that she's attractive and wearing a skimpy top isn't merely coincidental – it's a posed photo designed to attract the attention of readers. If you follow the eye-line of the girl, your attention is drawn towards the phone itself and on towards the main body of the text. The most prominent feature after the photograph is the headline immediately to the left of the girl's head. Both the main headline and the strapline above it contain strong emotive language calculated to achieve an immediate engagement of the reader's interest. This is achieved by identifying the precise focus of the report ('warning – teenagers – mobile phone thefts') and by arousing an emotional response.

The report gives a sensationalised impression because it says that there were 25,000 violent thefts of mobile pones and then gives prominence to one case in which a girl was shot. Elsewhere in the newspaper report, we are told that 40 million people in Britain now use mobile phones, so although 25,000 sounds a large number, the risk to an individual is still very low. The newspaper doesn't spell this out, preferring to alarm readers into reading the story by telling us that mobile phones are a 'popular target for thieves'. We are also told that 'thefts soar', that 'many young victims [are] attacked violently' and that 'youngsters [are] the most likely mugging victims'. The first word of the headline is 'warning'. All of this gives the impression that the situation worse than it really is. The report mentions in passing that 'overall recorded crime fell by 2.5% last year' but is far more interested in capitalising on the bad news. The *Daily Mail* is not a newspaper that is friendly towards the present government, so it's quite possible that the story is presented in this way as part of a continuing campaign against the government's policies on law and order; the message seems to be: 'the government is not in control and the country is becoming more dangerous to ordinary law-abiding citizens'. The cumulative effect of stories of this sort on regular readers of this newspaper is probably to reinforce their belief that the government is failing.

The report targets a general, adult readership. The first word is 'teenagers', which is more likely to arouse the interest of parents and grandparents than of teenagers themselves (we don't think of ourselves as teenagers!). The report moves on from the general point about the increase in violent crime to pick up on the Home Office report on crime in inner London boroughs. It deals with the comments of a government minister and a Home Office spokesman's helpful advice to 'avoid using phones in public' (wait till you get home?) and 'avoid showing them off ostentatiously'. The report tells us that ministers and officials 'have tended to play down phone theft as a largely playground phenomenon', but that is not the impression created by the *Daily Mail's* overall coverage. The question that springs to my mind is this: is the newspaper trying to report things objectively or

are they more interested in reinforcing what they think are the views of typical *Daily Mail* readers? The last part of the article is devoted to a question-and-answer sequence in which readers can find concise answers to such questions as:

> Why are mobile phones so attractive to thieves?

> What can I do to protect my mobile?

> Can 'text bombing' help discourage thieves?

The whole section, especially the headline – a distinctive black Q&A lined in white on a grey background – is effective in design terms. There is some overlap of content with the final section of the main report (the quotation from Perdita Patterson of *What Mobile* magazine) but the language of this section seems to be geared more towards readers who have existing knowledge of mobile phones and won't be intimidated by such terms as 'PIN code security option' and 'International Mobile Equipment Identity (IMEI) serial number'.

The question of whether the report is successful must be related to the target readership of the *Daily Mail*. From my point of view, I don't think this report is an example of responsible journalism, but unless my parents suffer a sudden conversion, the *Daily Mail* is never going to be part of our family's daily reading! Does the report deliver what *Daily Mail* readers want and expect? It probably does – it's reasonably attractive in terms of the appearance of the page and it confirms readers' beliefs that the government isn't solving the problem of law and order. What is genuinely successful, I think, is the way in which potentially difficult technical information is presented in the Q&A format in a separate panel at the foot of the page. It's an easily accessed reference section available for those who want this extra level of information about how to avoid phone theft but it avoids cluttering the main report intended for the general reader with material that is either irrelevant to their needs or impossible to understand.

the first four bullet points, but the final one ('any other aspects that you think are relevant') is entirely optional. Most candidates find that they can make all the comments they need to without using the last bullet point heading.

The Grade C answer is sensibly organised and works through the bullet points in turn. It shows:
- some understanding of the design and layout of the report (but ideas are not developed in detail);
- a personal response to the content;
- a recognition that the content is varied;
- an understanding of the use of emotive language, with some limited explanation of its impact on readers;
- an awareness of the needs and interests of the different groups of readers who might see the report;
- an attempt to explain what might be considered successful about the report.

The Grade A/A* answer is also clearly organised, but it sometimes uses an integrated approach in which comments about the effectiveness of the report are incorporated in sections dealing with design, content and language. This can be a very effective method of demonstrating sophisticated reading and thinking skills. This answer shows:
- a close, detailed reading of the report and the way in which it is presented;
- a perceptive understanding of the way in which the design and layout of the page tries to guide and influence readers;
- an awareness of the interconnections between headline, photograph and text;
- the candidate's confidence and willingness to criticise the way in which the *Daily Mail* presents the story;
- the candidate's use of humour to suggest that the views of the Home Office spokesman quoted in the report are unrealistic;
- a detailed understanding of the way in which the content of the report is made accessible to groups of readers with different needs and different levels of existing knowledge;
- impressive insight into the way the candidate brings her own values and assumptions into play in judging the success of the report.

QUESTION 2 (b)
Grade C response

Alton Towers is a very good theme park in England. There are many attractions and all the young people I know mostly enjoy going there. Obviously the main interest will come from school pupils aged eleven to sixteen who prefer a theme park rather than a quieter day out which an older person would choose.

At Alton Towers there are many attractions, there are fast and scary rides as well as the more calmer ride like the log flume. Alton Towers has a hotel and a rather nice hotel it is too. Lots of restaurants like KFC are at Alton Towers to cater for everyone's taste. It is a splendid theme park that gives everyone a good day out, or a couple of days if one decides to stay in the hotel. My friend went to Alton Towers recently and said she really enjoyed it, and I quote:

> 'Really good fun – a great day out!'

My friend is at school, at the age of fifteen, so one can see Alton Towers does appeal to secondary school pupils.

The educational value of Alton Towers is somewhat limited. School pupils will not find much information I wouldn't think on anything in relation to school. I myself haven't been to Alton Towers for quite a while so possibly it has changed a bit but on the whole, theme parks do not really have a good educational value. On saying that, the experience in itself of going to Alton Towers or any other theme park is a good experience and therefore of some value. If also school pupils go to Alton Towers with their school, it may encourage them to work harder at school work to go on another theme park trip.

Alton Towers has a good range of shops to interest school pupils, from candy stores to gift shops, all with the Alton Towers logo. Value for money I believe isn't too bad although it's a known fact that theme parks can be expensive. I would say that the actual theme park is good value for money but the shops, restaurants and hotel could be more expensive.

School pupils aged fourteen to sixteen will enjoy their day at Alton Towers I would guess because the rides will be great fun and they can look around the hotel, as well as eating the food they like and buying friends gifts from the shops.

Grade A/A* response

Blenheim Palace in Oxfordshire might not be the first choice of venue for most 14–16 year-olds contemplating a day out. For them, the label 'stately home' could conjure up images of middle-aged and elderly people trooping slowly in hushed lines through dark galleries, pausing to admire family portraits of a succession of forgotten earls of this and viscounts of that. For me, though, a visit to Blenheim Palace transports me into a living world of English history. Yes, I love history, and anyone who enjoys GCSE History would find so much at Blenheim to enjoy.

Blenheim Palace was built for John Churchill, the Duke of Marlborough, as a reward for his great victory over the French at the Battle of Blenheim in the early years of the eighteenth century. From the distance, the palace is elegant, but you have to enter the rooms open to the public to really appreciate its full splendour. Only a small proportion of the palace is open to visitors, but of those rooms, the Great Library alone would make the visit worthwhile. This long room is beautifully decorated with intricate mouldings and family portraits hanging from the walls. This is my favourite room, although some people prefer the more lavish décor of the State Rooms. What I find so unforgettable about Blenheim Palace is not just the fact that I am walking through rooms that are beautiful in themselves. These rooms were also the home of the first Duke of Marlborough, a soldier, and of Winston Churchill, a politician, who were two of the most important men in our history.

Because I live quite close to Blenheim Palace, my family and I sometimes walk in the grounds. There are public footpaths that enable you to walk freely through the extensive grounds and to enjoy the view of the lake with its famous bridge leading to the grand main entrance to the house. The parkland has avenues of trees and a tall stone monument to the first duke with inscriptions in Latin and English describing his achievements at the Battle of Blenheim.

If you pay to enter the private parts of Blenheim's gardens, there is much else to see. There are various themed gardens in which lavender and herbs and roses are arranged in formal displays. There are also fountains and other water features, as well as a maze and a butterfly house. Blenheim Palace and the grounds attract thousands of visitors each day, but I prefer to go when I know it's less likely to be crowded. If you're looking for a theme park, it might be best to go to Thorpe Park or Alton Towers. But if you are interested in history and enjoy beautiful surroundings, my advice is to visit Blenheim Palace at least once in your lifetime.

Examiner's comments

Questions 2(a) and 2(b) are alternative **writing questions** which test the ability of candidates to **analyse**, **review** and **comment**. The two examples given are by candidates who chose to answer 2(b).

The Grade C answer sets out and explains the choice of Alton Towers as a visitor attraction reasonably clearly. It shows these qualities:

- clear organisation into paragraphs although some are under-developed;
- a focus throughout on the needs of the target age range of 14–16;
- clear expression on the whole, despite some weaknesses (e.g. 'more calmer ride' and 'If also school pupils go to Alton Towers ...');
- some thoughtful comments on the possible benefits of organising a school trip to theme parks which do not have obvious 'good educational value';
- generally sound control of spelling and punctuation.

The Grade A/A* answer describes an attraction which may be a more surprising choice as an attraction for 14–16 year-olds, but the candidate presents a convincing justification. The writing is:

- confident and mature in its style and approach (look again at the opening paragraph);
- ambitious in the range of vocabulary and sentence structure;
- well structured, with effectively developed paragraphs;
- technically assured throughout.

QUESTION 3 (a)

Grade C response

Dear Mr Gray

In response to your notice this week about the ban on mobile phones, I am writing to you to voice what I feel should be done about the situation. My opinion along with many of my fellow students is that the school should take back the rule of banning mobile phones completely.

My reason for this is because, students need to be able to make contact with parents, if something has happened at school or if you have left something at home etc. Mobile phones are simple to use and require alot less effort than walking to the nearest pay phone and using it.

Mobile phones may also come in handy if you need to remind yourself to do something. I do feel that the use of mobile phones is not just a maybe, I feel that they are needed for a lot of things in and out of school. I'm sure my fellow students will agree with me in saying that it's hard to live without the use of your mobile phone.

However, I do agree with you that they should not be used during a lesson, because they can cause distraction to your fellow classmates and also prevent you from doing your work. I feel that mobile phones are needed during the school day but not during lesson time.

My advise to you sir is that you should not ban the use of mobile phones at school, unless used in lesson time. I feel that the use of mobile phones at lunch and breaktime should be allowed for what ever reason. However if a mobile phone is being used in a lesson for the wrong reasons, it should be confiscated.

I do believe that if a pupil decides to bring a mobile phone into school, it is their responsibility and no one elses. If the phone gets lost or stolen, it is their own fault and not the schools. That is the risk they take for bringing an expensive and valuable item into school.

I sincerely hope that you listen some of my suggestions and hopefully put them into practise as I feel this will benefit in many different ways. Thank you very much for reading my letter. If you feel you need to discuss any of my points then I am willing to speak to you.

Yours sincerely

Robin Maddock

Grade A/A* response

Dear Mr Gray

With the greatest respect to you, I do not support your decision to review our school's policy on mobile phones. I believe any change to the current arrangements is unnecessary and would not be welcomed by the majority of staff and pupils, and could even be counter-productive.

The system works as well as any system I have encountered. The banning of overt phone use yet unofficially tolerating their presence makes good sense for several reasons. The ban on their overt use means they do not disrupt lessons; the unofficial tolerance allows the pupils to be happy – flouting the rules is a massively satisfying thing (for some!). It also saves the staff from wasting precious time every day (for it would be every day) enforcing draconian regulations. Also, importantly I feel, the 'official' ban exonerates the school from responsibility in the event of theft or damage. It is enough to say that relaxing the rules on phones to the point where they are allowed would be a retrograde step.

To make the rules stricter would not, I feel, affect the presence or use of mobile phones. If six hundred people come to school today with mobile phones, they will rightly realise that the school cannot punish them all or confiscate all of the phones.

The current rules in our school leave the way open for temporary tightening. In the case of general disorder or misbehaviour, the rules can be used against individuals and send out warning messages to act as a deterrent against those who are tempted to go too far.

My final point is this: mobile phones are not affecting teaching, or learning, or lessons in general as things stand. You can't get better than that. To ban mobile phones would be to impersonate King Canute. And that, with the very greatest respect, would be ridiculous.

Yours sincerely

G McDonald

- an attempt to persuade the head teacher to accept the writer's point of view;
- generally accurate expression and technical control, although some lapses are present (e.g. 'the school should take back the rule of banning phones', 'it requires alot less effort', '... no one elses'). It does, however, contain a number of spelling mistakes and punctuation errors.

The Grade A/A* answer is an engaging, ambitious and effective letter. The candidate shows wit and flair in his attempt to persuade the head teacher not to change the school's policy on mobile phones. The candidate's writing shows these qualities:

- a concise style and sharp focus on the issues;
- subtlety in arguing that not upholding rules to the letter is the policy most likely to achieve the desired outcomes;
- an adventurous and precise vocabulary (e.g. 'draconian', 'exonerates', 'impersonate King Canute');
- a very high standard of expression and technical control;
- the confidence (some might say foolhardiness!) to imply that the head teacher would look ridiculous if he chooses not to accept the writer's advice.

ANSWERS
Check Yourself Answers and Comments

UNIT 1: READING
1 Fact and opinion (page 3)

Q1   **Facts**
- entertainments, special events, music, workshops, canal walks, boat trips and eating facilities
- it's free
- 30 shops, open seven days a week
- a festival market (up to 60 additional stalls) every Saturday, Sunday and Bank Holiday Monday
- shops open 10 a.m. to 5.30 p.m.
- Granary Wharf is behind the Hilton Hotel in Neville Street
- access is via the Dark Arches
- illuminated sign under the railway bridge
- parking
- special arrangements for coaches
- address/telephone number

Opinions
- a unique place
- for all tastes
- there's always plenty to see and do
- it's friendly, it's fun
- a fascinating selection of original goods and gifts
- right in the centre of Leeds
- just two minutes' walk from Leeds railway station
- small (illuminated sign)
- ample (parking)

Comments You should have found that task quite straightforward: words and phrases such as 'unique', 'for all tastes', 'always plenty to see and do', 'friendly', 'fun', 'fascinating' and 'original' are almost always going to reflect opinion rather than fact.

There are some less obvious expressions of opinion, however. Not everyone would necessarily agree that Granary Wharf is 'right in the centre of Leeds', and since not everyone is able to walk at the same speed, it can't be 'just two minutes' walk from Leeds railway station' for everyone. The 'small' illuminated sign might appear to be anything but small if it shines into someone's bedroom window at night; and whether the parking is 'ample' or not will presumably depend on how many visitors turn up on particular days.

Q2 a The writer hopes readers will want to visit Granary Wharf because it will be a new experience for them. It will be enjoyable for the whole family because there are shops and entertainments and places to eat. The writer hopes that readers will think it is easy to get to Granary Wharf because it is 'right in the centre of Leeds'.

b The writer uses colourful photographs to attract the reader, and large, eye-catching headlines. The language is easy to understand and makes Granary Wharf sound different and interesting. The name of Granary Wharf is printed at the top of both pages and is mentioned twice in the text. There is also a logo at the bottom of each page and details of the address, so the name and place becomes fixed in the reader's mind.

Comments A better answer for part (a) would quote 'unique'. A reference to the photos which show different attractions and people of all ages enjoying them would help. Add specific detail, e.g. Granary Wharf is close to the railway station and there is parking for cars/coaches.

In part (b), you could point out that the headlines are in a larger-size print than the text, and the text on the left-hand page (which is the text mostly designed to attract) is larger than that on the right-hand page (which is mostly information). Comment on specific uses of language, e.g. the memorable effect of repetition and alliteration in 'it's friendly, it's fun and it's free'.

2 How information is presented (page 8)

Q1   To prevent accidents to swimmers at the seaside.

Comments This is a basic 'D-ish' answer. To move safely into Grade C and beyond, a more detailed answer would also suggest: to encourage more people to learn lifesaving and rescue skills, and to educate the public about the meaning of flags and other signs seen near beaches.

Q2   By telling swimmers what to do and by showing information about seaside warnings.

Comments Another basic answer. It could be improved by being more specific: swimmers (and potential rescuers) are given clear, bullet-pointed instructions; the flags and signs are shown in their exact shapes and colours. The cartoons should be mentioned: they attract attention because they make the page layout look more appealing, and some people will find them amusing.

Q3 To make them think about being more careful when swimming.

Comments But also to be aware when others might be in difficulty and to learn to avoid possible dangers by recognising warning signs.

Q4 People who go swimming on the beach.

Comments A good answer will recognise that information may have more than just the most obvious audience: this would also be of interest to parents, to people who might be attracted to train as lifesavers, to surfers who want to avoid causing problems to swimmers, and to members of the general public who want to know the meaning of warning flags at the seaside.

3 Following an argument (page 14)

Q1 a The argument is that if you give £2 to Oxfam, it is put to good use because it funds projects which encourage people in the Third World to help themselves and so become less dependent on charity. It gives examples of projects, and ends by stating outright the main theme, that helping people to help themselves gives them dignity and independence.

Comments This is a good, detailed answer of Grade C standard. To raise the grade further, you could mention that the photographs show people working on projects, rather than people suffering, and so emphasise the positive message of the leaflet.

Q1 b The first implication is that you may be surprised at how much a £2 donation could achieve, when that amount won't buy much in our society. A second implication is therefore that anyone reading this leaflet would have to be very mean not to donate £2.

Comments Again, a sound Grade C answer. To achieve a Grade A, you need to spell out the deeper implication that, as it goes towards projects which encourage self-help and independence, refusing to make a donation is not just harming the charity, but actually preventing people in the Third World from achieving dignity and independence which will make them less dependent on charity in the future.

Q1 c There are no obvious inconsistencies in this page, except the lack of clarity about the monthly £2 donation: the page makes three claims about what £2 a month will achieve, but does not say for how many months the £2 needs to be given to achieve these outcomes.

Comments You might additionally point out that the leaflet is in fact very consistent by sticking to the theme of the £2 donation and illustrating (through the three photographs as well as in the text) what this can achieve. Do not be afraid to 'reverse' a question in this way to show that you have appreciated the structure of a text.

4 Collating and cross-references (page 17)

Q1 Holidays are offered to two different destinations: the Nile and Lake Lugano in Switzerland. The Nile holiday costs £100 per person more than the Swiss holiday, although both trips are for eight days. There are only three departure dates for the Nile cruise, but you can go on the Lugano trip any Tuesday or Wednesday in August.

The Nile trip is full board, and there is the opportunity to extend the stay by seven days in one hotel or by four days in one hotel and three in another. The Lugano holiday is half board, and you cannot extend the stay. The trips are organised by different companies, but both are offered at a discount to GLC members if you quote a membership number.

The photograph of Lugano shows you the attractions of the area, while the Nile holiday offers excursions accompanied by a qualified Egyptologist. We recommend the Nile holiday to readers who are interested in a more active holiday looking at historical remains, while those in search of a relaxing holiday in a pleasant climate will prefer Lugano.

Comments This answer meets the requirements of the task – it compares the holidays, suggests a suitable clientele for each and is the right length (just over 180 words). A mention of actual prices would be helpful in this context. Basic departure/return details are compared. There is a useful comparison of what you actually get with each holiday. Although the discount is important, there is still no mention of what the actual price is. There is an appropriate summary of what the holidays offer.

The model answer here is of Grade C standard. To achieve higher, you would certainly need to remember to mention the actual price of the holidays and you might have made the holidays sound more appealing by giving a little less dull, factual detail and by using some of the descriptive language from the advertisements themselves, e.g. words such as 'exclusive', 'wonderful', 'excellent' (the Nile) or 'flamboyant warmth', 'cool efficiency', 'lovely climate', 'unique cultural mix' (Lugano).

5 Uses of language (page 21)

Q1   **Opinion made to sound like fact**
- few have come further than the average English hostelry
- can assure you that they are all the same substance

Humour
- hostelry
- emptied into it … moisturising creams

Addressing the reader
- if you stop to think about it for even a moment you'll see that …
- don't be alarmed

Effective descriptive language
- a fiesta of airy bubbles
- layout out … prom
- a long wallow … Joan Collins movie

Comments This is a 'recognition' exercise. If you were asked to spot similar features in an examination, you would be asked to explain them as well to gain a Grade C or higher. Here are some suitable explanatory comments.
Opinion made to sound like fact
Either of these examples would do; Bryson states these opinions very firmly, as though there is no possible argument with them – but they are opinions none the less.

Humour
You could have chosen either of these. The first example is of humorous language, using a consciously old-fashioned word. The second example is of visual or 'situational' humour. If you noticed that the whole passage is written in a mockingly humorous way, so that picking out individual examples of humour is difficult, then you are achieving a level of response and analysis worthy of a Grade A.
Addressing the reader
Again, either example will do. What Bryson achieves here is to make it seem as though he is talking directly to you, and this means that a) you believe him, and b) you feel honoured.
Effective descriptive language
The word 'fiesta' sounds lively, fun, exotic and fits in with the general air of self-indulgence which Bryson is describing. In the second example, Bryson makes himself sound like an eager, handsome young teenager rather than the weary middle-aged traveller. The third example conjures up visions of expensive and far-fetched lifestyles such as those seen in American TV mini-series.

6 Structural and presentational devices (page 25)

Q1   The leaflet is aimed primarily at business people, but also families who are travelling. The text is in short sections, so it is easily understood, and the main features of the rooms in the Lodge Inn are bullet-pointed to make them stand out. Some headings are used, with frames around them, so that the reader's attention is drawn to the name of the company, the price of the rooms and the convenience of the facilities. The photographs make the reception area and the restaurant look very welcoming, and emphasise that the rooms are for men and women, although children are not shown. The photographs are of smart, smiling people, giving the idea that the Lodge is somewhere for successful, happy people.

The map gives clear instructions for reaching the Lodge, and show that the expected audience for the leaflet will be travelling by car, as the instructions only work if coming off the motorway. The leaflet is effective: it is colourful and gives all the information someone would need to decide if they wanted to stay there, and what to do and how to get there if they did want to stay.

Comments This is correct, but a more analytic answer would have commented on the colour of the bullet-pointed text: it mirrors the colours of the company logo and so links the listed features with the company name. An A-Grade answer would comment on the font used for the 'Lodge Inns' name: it is slightly ornate, to give the impression of somewhere smart, but is not 'over the top'.

An additional point about children would be that their accommodation is only detailed in a small-print footnote, so presumably families with children are not the main audience.

A more analytic answer would comment that there is too much small print on the map for a driver to read.

A more critical answer would say that the leaflet is quite cluttered, and would question why some information about eating is in the section headed 'The Best Pubs & Restaurants' and why some is in the white panel after the map. A top-class answer would go on to suggest that this may be to try and capture trade in food and drink, even if the person reading the leaflet decided not to stay there. The answer given would merit a Grade C: the additional comments suggested here would raise the level of performance to that of Grade A.

8 Different types of media texts (page 32)

Q1 a Both covers are in colour, and the titles stand out in white on a coloured background. Both magazines have pictures on the cover and both have several headlines in a range of bright colours which 'trail' stories inside so as to capture the interest of browsers in a shop, and both use some frames around these pieces of text. Both covers include date, price and barcode information.

Comments You should make the point that the overall colourful effect is intended to be eye-catching and cheerful; explain as well as describe in answers to questions like this.

A good explanatory comment – don't overlook obvious features such as this.

You might have added that both covers refer to holiday offers/competitions.

Q1 b The main illustration on the cover of *Woman* is a photograph of two well-known soap characters, looking straight at camera and so catching your eye. Two smaller photographs are also of smiling people looking at the camera. The illustration on the cover of *The Lady* is a line drawing of part of a stately home in subdued pastel shades, and it is the only picture on the cover. The whole of the cover of *Woman* in bright colours.

Comments You could also have commented on the facts that all the typefaces on the *Woman* cover are modern, but *The Lady* uses traditional typefaces for the title and main headline; and text and illustrations are mostly separate on *The Lady*, but on *Woman* they run across and into each other, to give a much busier effect. An analytical answer would comment that the size and positioning of the main photograph on *Woman* suggests that the imaginary relationship is likely to be of more interest to readers than real-life stories, and therefore that gossip or stories about film/TV characters (and the actors who play them) may be a significant aspect of the contents.

Q1 c The cover of *Woman* suggests the contents are mainly about homes ('kitchen and bathroom makeovers') and relationships, both real ('Happily married …' and 'After 28 years …') and in the world of soap opera ('It's payback time!'). Health matters related to women are also included ('9 years …' and 'Phew'!'), and two competitions are mentioned, one for a holiday and one for car, cash and a holiday. The cover of *The Lady* suggests that articles about cultural pursuits (such as literature, landscapes and architecture) and finance are the main contents, although a holiday is also trailed. An important aspect of the contents is information about jobs, holiday and retirement homes.

Comments You might have commented that in the case of *The Lady*, it is a holiday offer, not a competition.

Q1 d *Woman* is for an audience of young to middle-aged women who are interested in the make-believe world of television, their own health and relationships, and who aspire to 'dream' holidays, better cars and more money. *The Lady* is for two quite different audiences: one of well-off women who pursue a cultured lifestyle, and the other of those looking for employment with the first group. A third audience, really a subset of the first, is those elderly women who are seeking retirement homes.

These audiences are suggested by the content and layout of the covers; *Woman* is bright and breezy and puts a soap-opera scandal centre-page, while *The Lady* is dignified and subdued; the use of a traditional font for the title and main headline reinforces this quality.

Comments You could take this analysis further and say that the audience for *Woman* is probably not rich, but comfortable (i.e. middle income), and may have aspirations to 'improve' socially, e.g. through home improvements.

A sophisticated answer would raise the issue of whether the first audience of *The Lady* is quite as comfortable and secure as it might seem: the words 'The very special weekly magazine' on the cover are perhaps an attempt to reassure the readers that they are still special, and the prominence given to the classified advertisements box suggests that a number of fairly desperate people will be among the readership. Another audience might be of women who don't belong to any of these groups, but aspire to the kind of lifestyle which the illustration on the cover suggests.

9 Poetry – sound effects and imagery (page 38)

Q1 a A city is full of buildings and lots of people, a place which is civilised. Night time is when everyone's indoors and it's quiet, but the writer makes it full of life, but not happy life. Everything in this poem is violent. He makes cars and motorbikes seem like animals in the jungle. In the night, ordinary things around the streets are afraid of the savage creatures around them. Objects are like people being picked on – they 'cough' and 'flinch' as if nervous and afraid of all the nasty things around.

Comments This is a good statement about the mood of ferocity and fear. For a higher grade, there could be more sustained comment on language which animates or personifies the scene. Even the rain is shown as something sharp and destructive – it 'splinters' – and cars are not only compared with living creatures in the metaphor 'lizard cars', but they seem to have feelings too, enjoying their own power (suggested by 'grin'). The motorbike sounds like a jungle creature, and the lights, which should make things less like a jungle, are also part of the savage scene, described as 'staring', looking boldly or 'baring their teeth'. The effect of all this savagery is to create fear and nervousness so strong that even buildings feel it, as suggested by the metaphorical description of a house being 'hunched' and coughing. The description of litter makes even this seem nervous and glad to get away, 'shuffling' off with its hands in its pockets. This detail could be developed into an account of the poem as an extended metaphor.

There is scope to refer to the sounds of words chosen here: it is a violent scene, and there are rough sounds in words like 'cars cruise', 'hunched', 'cough', 'gargle', 'snarl' and 'lash'. Short vowels in 'Dustbins flinch' and 'cat-black tongue lashes across' make things seem abrupt and sudden.

Q1 b It makes me think that there's more going on than I see, or perhaps there's more than I want to see. I think some of the poem is amusing – I liked the idea that a dustbin could be frightened and that an old newspaper could want to get way from the hassle and bother.

Comments This adds some personal feeling in response. Although one comment is about a serious aspect of the poem's thought, there is also comment on something which the reader found amusing. For a higher grade, there could be further exploration of the humour or seriousness of the poem, and of the view it gives of urban life.

10 Poetry – purpose, tone and attitude (page 41)

Q1 a Ted Hughes compares these plants to fierce warriors – Vikings, etc. They are like warriors because if they are attacked, they fight back and grow again (or their sons do). When he says that they have 'weapons', he could be thinking of their prickles, which are used to defend themselves and hurt people who come too close.

Comments This response makes a valid point about the similarity between weapons and prickles. To obtain a higher grade, there could be more sustained comment on words which link the plant with warriors and weapons. Some of the words he uses are intended to suggest human qualities of mood and intention, such as 'revengeful'. Verbs like 'spike' and 'crackle' give a sense of roughness and activity. There are lots of harsh consonant sounds in this poem, making the plant seem as primitive-sounding as the old Icelandic warriors whose voice was 'guttural'.

Metaphors link the plant with violence, such as the description of 'a grasped fistful' and 'blood'. It could develop this point by explaining the use of animating and personifying language.

Q1 b He makes out that they are rough plants, not nice like flowers, but they are still special in their own way. They are strong enough to stand up to cows and men, so he thinks you should respect them for being tough.

Comments This makes a good point about the poet's attitude of respect. There could be more sustained comment on the language that suggests respect, such as 'resurrection' and 'feud' which make the plants seem magically reborn after a long-lasting battle. Discussion of the poet's attitude could be developed by explaining that plants are usually valued for their beauty or what we get from them, but Hughes is finding something to value in the plant in its defiance of humans, its ability to withstand harshness by being tough itself. There could be a an attempt to explore Hughes' use of the plant to make us think of human qualities that we should admire.

Q1 c I think the poet is right when he says thistles are rough. They live on waste ground and they don't have flowers or fruit – they're just weeds and they can hurt if you try to pull them up. I suppose he's got a point about them being like soldiers because humans try to get rid of them and they have to stand up for themselves.

Comments This is an honest response, but it is more about thistles than the poem called Thistles. To obtain a higher grade, you need to pick out some features of the writing that helped you grasp the poet's ideas, such as the surprising admiration for a weed, or the use of animating or personifying language.

11 Prose – responding to character (page 46)

Q1 Jenny is not a person who is fascinated by her shoes! She is looking at her shoes because she does not want to look her questioner in the face. This may be a sign of her guilt or sorrow, or unwillingness to show any emotion.

Comments This is very clear, stating that her motive for looking at her shoes has nothing to do with shoes. This answer looks for a motive to explain the lack of face-to-face contact. Offering some possible explanations shows ability to explore a text for implied meaning and a range of alternative interpretations.

Q2 Fothergill is fussy and uneasy about the people he has encountered. His gesture shows either that he takes care over his appearance or perhaps shows fear or mistrust of the bag-ladies, securing himself against contact with them.

Comments Again, this answer looks for reasons for behaviour. Offering 'either ... or' interpretation shows willingness to explore. There could be more sustained close reference to details such as 'picked', 'carefully', 'tight' and the odd habit of flicking dust off his sleeve. Pointing out that 'picked' and 'carefully' suggest choosiness and caution would tie the comment to the evidence, and the reference to 'tight' suggests that he wants to keep himself covered up, protected from people or from dirt.

Q3 The questioner is confident and poised, carefully using words to avoid directly saying that Mr Cornwall is lying. Mr Cornwall is nervous, and his emphatic denials are perhaps a sign that he is bluffing and has been caught out.

Comments This is clearly stated, but there is no sustained close reference to the words which create the impression. 'Respect' and 'humbly' are words used by the questioner, but the questioner is actually more confident and not as humble as the other person. The relationship between the two could be explored. The questioner seems to be using these words ironically, as he does when he says that the man 'may' not be speaking the 'entire' truth, rather than accuse him outright. Reading for his motives, this comment could be developed. It is as if he is making it easy for him to confess that he has lied a bit. He seems skilful at this. Note that it is quite all right to say in your examination answer that a gesture may 'perhaps' mean something or other – it is perfectly in order to venture an interpretation, not just facts.

12 Prose – responding to setting (page 49)

Q1 This is not so much a description of a place as an account of the way a child sees the environment around him. The setting is described from a child's point of view, making ordinary things seem quite exotic and unusual, as if experienced for the first time. Water, for example, is something that adults take for granted, but the child sees it as magic.

Also making this seem like a child's observation is the detail of things found at ground level, perhaps not noticeable to an adult. Things which an adult may not notice are made to seem exciting and interesting – the hole in the wall where snails gather is described as a 'grotto', which is usually a place where treasures are found.

Another thing which makes this description of a place suggest the mind of a child is the way that the senses are used – smell and touch, for example – and the exploration of the environment is physical, rather than just visual – putting his head under the water.

Comments This answer is very successful in showing how the setting works to illustrate a child's discovery of the environment. It could develop the idea of discovery showing that it is ugliness, not just beauty, which the child encounters, and that this is an evitable part of the experience of venturing outside the safe 'haven' of the home. There could be sustained comment on other words which suggest 'voyaging', such as 'oceans', 'harbour mouth' and the sisters who seem to 'sail past like galleons'. A child's sense of growing power is suggested by 'captured', making the world beyond exciting but also a little bit menacing because of the reference to death. If you included this, you would demonstrate close attention to the writer's choice of language.

The child's way of finding out about his environment is amusing because it is play, but it is also a sort of scientific testing of the properties of things around him. The description of water is like an analysis of its properties. The close observation of the insides of broad-bean pods and the comparison of carrots with coins shows a child's attempt to categorise objects in his universe. Exploring this description as typical of childhood development, not the unique experience of one child, would show your ability to make generalisations and appropriate comment on style and meaning.

13 Prose – narrative devices (page 56)

Q1 a Mrs Rutter seems like a typical lonely, old lady. She seems friendly and cosy because of the descriptions which make her harmless, like 'cottage-loaf', 'creamy, smiling pool of a face'. She smiles a lot, which is friendly. She likes little rabbit ornaments and offers the visitors tea, so she is kind and homely. Her garden is overgrown and untidy, so perhaps she isn't fit enough to look after it or she hasn't got a husband to do it.

Comments There is good use of details. There could be sustained reference to roundness which seems cosier than something linear or with angles. There could also be more sustained and developed comment on her smiles, which come so quickly that one 'folds into' the next, as if her face is always moving. She seems very concerned to make them feel at home – offering sugar, for example. The comment could be developed by using her surroundings and her possessions as clues to her nature. She doesn't have expensive tastes – some of the things she has kept are not worth much but seem to have sentimental value to her. There is a good attempt to explore the implications of the untidy garden, offering two possible interpretations.

Q1 b She uses friendly phrases, like 'my duck' and 'dear', and she says nice things to the visitors, such as 'You're pretty', and she is concerned about getting the jacket messy. She asks questions and takes an interest in her visitors and is a bit of a gossip, remembering Susie from last week.

Comments This is apt and makes use of details, but for a higher grade there would need to be sustained comment on her tone and language, for example referring to the inviting way she promised to make 'us' a cup of tea. She talks fondly about the flowers in the wood. This adds to the impression given by the ornaments that she likes pretty things and is a peaceful, homely person. For a high grade, there is scope for exploring what she means by saying that working in a garage is all right 'if you've nothing special in mind'. Is she being kind and making him feel it's worthwhile, or is she saying it's not much of a prospect?

Q1 c Her eyes 'snapped and darted', which makes them seem quicker and more active than the rest of the description. Although her smiles 'folded' into each other, her eyes above the smile 'examined' him, which makes you think she knows what she is doing. Her face seems to be doing two things, and perhaps this means she is 'two-faced'.

Comments This answer makes good use of material to show contrast. There could be more sustained comment about the eyes being as 'quick as mice', and how she 'glittered' at them, which could be developed by showing how the detail counteracts the cosy sleepiness of the rest of the impression. Penelope Lively uses many of the words which immediately create a stereotype of a dear, old, harmless biddy, but she writes this story to show that not everyone is quite what they seem if we trust to stereotypes. There is an attempt in this answer to explore contrasts and make meaning from the details.

14 Reading beneath the surface (page 62)

Q1 In this passage, some readers may take pity on Becky because she has suffered bad luck and cruelty. She seems to be an innocent victim. She pours out her suffering, her lack of love and family, her loneliness, and she finally breaks down, unable to go on because she is so upset. This impression is caused by words such as 'tender' and 'despair'. Thackeray seems to add to this sentimental and sympathetic view of her by narrative detail by making her seem weak and vulnerable – her littleness and frailty are frequently mentioned.

Although she seems a victim, she is not that helpless or innocent. At the beginning of the passage, the author refers to her 'archness and mischief', and this fits the way she overacts the part of innocent victim. Everything she does is designed to get sympathy – like referring to her lost husband and child. When she breaks down in tears, she just happens to use a handkerchief with a letter J on it, which is the first letter of the name of her visitor, who she describes as the first man she ever saw. This suggests she has kept it since their first relationship.

The writer makes us look below the surface of appearance. He reminds us that she has hidden some things in order to appear innocent and charming. She hides her real motives just as she hides the signs of her real life – her make-up, her alcohol and her cold snack. In reality, her looks are now in need of help from cosmetics, her happiness comes from a bottle and she's living on junk food. The fact that these are below the surface reminds us that she is putting on a show. When Thackeray mentions the clinking of the bottle or the 'sausage', the reader is reminded of the real nature of her life which she is trying to hide. In the last line, he uses the word 'moved' literally to mean that the objects were displaced, but also to suggest that her speech was so emotionally moving that it could affect a brandy bottle and a sausage. This is such a comical thought that it stops us being sentimental or sympathetic. At first glance, this could be a romantic scene, but I think it shows Becky Sharp as a cunning woman trying to trap a man. Her life may be a bit of a wreck, but her 'poor me' attitude is only a façade.

Comments This is a very good answer. It is well structured, the first part dealing with what may be thought, and the second paragraph looking more closely at motivation and behaviour. The last paragraph looks at the writer's narrative methods. This structure is well suited to discussion of different interpretations.

There is sustained comment on Becky's speech and actions and the writer's use of language. There is developed comment on the handkerchief and the connection between concealed objects and concealed motives. There is close attention to language, particularly to 'moved' and the reference to smallness. Discussing the passage as one which could be sentimental or not shows ability to evaluate different interpretations, and there is analysis of Thackeray's methods in the references to the objects in the bed. As well as showing these strengths, there is a personal judgement at the end which shows strong engagement and insight.

15 Making effective comparisons (page 66)

Q1 The attitudes of both writers are similar. They both see something good about a plant that is a weed. They both seem to think that Nature is a place of battles, but Hughes makes the battle with man more obvious.

The two poems are similar in the ways they use language. Both of them use lots of metaphors which make the thistles seem like animals or people not plants. They both talk about the thistles as if they are an army, using words like 'weapons' (Hughes) and 'armour' (Stallworthy), but Jon Stallworthy does not make them seem as dangerous because the farmer is not bothered by them.

Both of the poets use verses to separate parts of the poems, but Jon Stallworthy uses rhyme ('seen' and 'keen', 'stand' and 'hand'), and Ted Hughes does not.

Comments This response has structure because it deals with attitude, language and verse as required by the question. It also shows similarities and differences in each of these. However, it is not a developed answer because it does not give enough range of detail to support comparison and it describes the similarities and differences rather than explaining them.

The answer would be improved if it included more features to support comparison, and said more about the significance of the differences between the poems. It could have referred to some or all of the following:

Similarities
Attitude and ideas
Respect for savagery and survival of a natural species
Nature a battleground

Language suggesting warfare
Hughes: 'spike', 'weapons', 'feud', 'fighting', 'plume of blood'
Stallworthy: 'armour', 'swords', 'warrior', 'infantry', 'purple plume'

Animating language
Hughes: 'revengeful', 'fistful', 'hair', 'sons'
Stallworthy: 'boldly', 'challenge', 'head', 'meeting', 'writhe', 'sons'

Differences
Verse
Hughes: capitalised line beginnings, blank verse
Stallworthy: not capitalised at line beginnings, so looks informal, but has firm rhyme structure, varied at the end

Attitude and ideas
Hughes: connection with warriors/invaders of the past – Vikings
Stallworthy: present-day warriors without a battle to fight

Hughes: resurrection/rebirth
Stallworthy: spirits live on

Hughes: thistles resist a farmer's chopping
Stallworthy: thistles accept being chopped down in old age

Hughes: revengeful against man
Stallworthy: warrior-like but not sure who their enemy is

Hughes: makes them carry on the battle through their offspring
Stallworthy: makes them appear longer-lasting than man, rather than in conflict with man

16 Selecting and using textual reference (page 70)

Q1 This poem is about a teacher who doesn't like his job. He seems tired [1] and he doesn't want to go on. Their work is really bad [2]. He uses words for controlling them that make it seem like hard work [3]. The class have been hard to handle and he can't control them because they've been fighting against him [4]. I don't think he likes them much because he thinks of them as animals and him a trainer [5]. He uses a metaphor in lines 2–5 about him having to hunt knowledge with them, but he can't any more [6]. He uses metaphors again when he talks about his energy like a fire burning, but he's running out of fuel. There are lots of words to do with fire there [7]. His attitude is that his life is precious to him [8] and the kids don't seem to care about him [9] so why should he bother. He thinks it's a waste of time trying because he can't get through to them and they can't get through to him, so it's pointless and can only lead to getting hurt [10]. I think he should get a grip because he's paid to teach them and they need exams.

Comments This response sustains comment on the teacher's feelings but doesn't develop comment on the stated or implied attitude of the children.

There could be comment on the implications of 'tugging the leash' as a metaphor for resisting control or a sign of enthusiasm for other things they find interesting. His view of their blotted and scrawled writing is that it is an insult to him, rather than a sign of their ability or needs.

There is a lively personal response at the end which relates to his attitude, but it is better to look at motivation from two angles rather than one. He may seem not to care about his job or the children's futures, but there could be exploration of what has caused his loss of interest.

It is worth analysing the poem for the frequency of words related to hunting, and exploring the appropriateness of this image and its effect on different readers. Lawrence's intention may have been to gain sympathy as a weary pack leader, but his view of children as pack, and knowledge as something to hunt as if it is the prey, may tell us of Lawrence's attitude to children and to learning, as well as to teaching. The final comment could therefore be developed, pointing out its implications for real life. The answer is particularly weak in supporting comment with appropriate textual detail.

Check your choices of supporting textual detail against these examples, which would make the sample answer much stronger.

1 'weariness' or 'no longer ...' or 'I am sick'
2 'blotted' or 'scrawl' or 'slovenly'
3 'haul' or 'urge'
4 'tugged' or 'strained' or 'unruly'
5 'My unruly hounds' and 'hunt'
6 'I cannot start them again on a quarry of knowledge ...'
7 'fuel', 'kindle', 'flame'
8 'my last dear fuel of life'
9 'insults', 'dross of indifference'
10 'beat our heads against the wall of each other'

UNIT 2: WRITING
1 Using accurate spelling (page 73)

Q1 **a** 'chiefs': exception to the pattern that words ending with a single 'f' or 'fe' change the 'f' or 'fe' to 'ves' to form the plural

Comments It is a good idea to learn the exceptions carefully.

b 'deceive': 'i' before 'e' except after 'c'

Comments The 'i' before 'e' except after 'c' pattern is fairly reliable.

c 'shopping': words ending with a single vowel followed by a single consonant double the last consonant if adding an ending beginning with a vowel

Comments Another regular and reliable pattern.

d 'hopeful': 'full' and 'till' drop one 'l' when added to another syllable

Comments 'Putting double 'l' on the ends of words like this is a very common spelling mistake.

e 'weigh': 'i' before 'e' does not apply when the sound is 'a'

Comments Not, therefore, an exception to the pattern; look carefully at the explanation on page 71.

f 'although': 'all' followed by another syllable drops one 'l'

Comments A regular, reliable pattern.

g 'driving': drop the final 'e' from a word before adding an ending beginning with a vowel

Comments Remember, however, to keep the final 'e' if the ending begins with a consonant.

h 'funnily': if a word ends with a consonant followed by 'y', change the 'y' to 'i' before endings

Comments True of all endings except 'ing'.

i 'leaves': words ending with a single 'f' change the 'f' to 'ves' to form the plural

Comments There are exceptions – remember 'chief' and the others.

j 'question': 'q' is always followed by 'u'

Comments The only exception is the name of the country, Iraq.

Q2 My neighbour[1] is hopeful[2] of returning to the land of her birth[3] one day, and she is driving[4] me mad with her constant chatter[5] about how much lovelier[6] than England most other countries[7] are. She has been all over the far and middle east, including Iraq[8], where[9] her best friend[10] lives. I would happily[11] take a leaf out of her book – several leaves[12] to tell the truth – and visit foreign[13] places, but I'm always[14] kept very busy at my job. I mend roofs[15], and after this winter's storms, I've been busier[16] than ever. I'm hoping[17] to get a holiday soon, but it won't be until the better weather[18] comes. I'm dying for a break[19], but I'm a bit short of money at the moment – I hardly have enough to keep the wolves[20] from the door, never mind exciting holidays.

Comments
1 Exception to 'i' before 'e' as it's pronounced 'a'.
2 'Full' loses one 'l' at the end of words.
3 Homonym: think of 'birthday' for the correct spelling here.
4 Drop the final 'e' from a word ('drive') before adding an ending beginning with a vowel ('ing').
5 Words ending with a single vowel + single consonant ('chat') double the last consonant if adding an ending ('er') which begins with a vowel.
6 If a word ends with a consonant followed by 'y' ('lovely'), change the 'y' to 'i' before all endings.
7 Words ending 'y' after a consonant make the plural by changing the 'y' to 'ies'.
8 The only word in English where 'q' is not followed by 'u'.
9 Homonym: 'where' refers to a place, 'were' is the past tense of the verb 'to be'.
10 'i' before 'e' except after 'c'
11 See point 6 above.
12 Words ending with a single 'f' change the 'f' to 'ves' to form the plural.
13 An exception to the 'i' before 'e' pattern.
14 'All' followed by another syllable drops one 'l'.
15 An exception to the pattern mentioned in point 12 above.
16 See point 6 above.
17 See point 4 above, and beware of doubling instead of removing the 'e': that would give 'hopping', which has a totally different meaning.
18 and 19 Homonyms
20 See point 12 above.

2 Using appropriate punctuation (page 79)

Q1 a • separating items in a list
  • separating phrases
  • marking pauses for sense
  • in direct speech after 'he said', etc.

Comments The comma is a particularly useful device for helping readers make sense of written text. Take care, however, that you use full stops to indicate the end of sentences. Note a special use of the comma in the previous sentence: the word 'however' should always be followed by a comma and have a comma before it if it is not the first word in the sentence.

Q2 It would then mean that the success of more than one candidate had depended on the votes of the women.

Comments Remember that the position of the apostrophe is crucial, particularly in words which could be plural or singular, as in this case.

Q3 But the men did not go unscathed either. Three of them had their heads broken by blows from Boxer's hoofs; another was gored in the belly by a cow's horn; another had his trousers nearly torn off by Jessie and Bluebell. And when the nine dogs of Napoleon's own bodyguard, whom he had instructed to make a detour under cover of the hedge, suddenly appeared on the men's flank, baying ferociously, panic overtook them.

Comments Orwell's own version is shown here. It would be possible to punctuate this as two sentences only, the second starting at 'Three of them' and continuing right to the end, with commas rather than semi-colons after 'hoofs', 'horn' and 'Bluebell'. However, it would then be a long and very complicated sentence, and this is a good example of how semi-colons and commas can be used together to make meaning clear. Note that Orwell begins his last sentence with 'And': this is often supposed to be an error, but used carefully, it can be a striking stylistic feature – here, it draws your attention to how the men were eventually driven away in panic.

3 Using different sentence structures (page 84)

Q1 a In Folkestone, I met old Walter Dudlow as I was crossing the Leas, heading west.

Comments This is how the sentence actually appears in Paul Theroux's *The Kingdom by the Sea*. There are other ways of joining these sentences; for example, a straightforward compound sentence could be 'I was heading west and crossing the Leas in Folkestone and met old Walter Dudlow'; alternative complex sentences could be: 'Heading west and crossing the Leas in Folkestone, I met old Walter Dudlow' or 'I was crossing the Leas in Folkestone, heading west, when I met old Walter Dudlow'. All are equally acceptable, and much more fluent than the three separate sentences. Look at

some examples of your own writing, and if you tend to write in short, separate sentences, practise ways of joining them.

Q1 b When I came upon the diary, it was lying at the bottom of a rather battered red cardboard collar-box, in which, as a small boy, I kept my Eton collars.

Comments This is how the sentence actually appears in L.P. Hartley's *The Go-Between*. Again, you could have done it differently; for example, 'I came up on the diary lying at the bottom of a rather battered red cardboard collar-box, where I had kept my Eton collars when I was a small boy.

Q2 I was able to overcome my fear of heights through climbing and abseiling. Through taking part in a potholing expedition, I tackled my fears of darkness and claustrophobia, and demonstrated leadership qualities when I had to guide a group, some of whom were more scared than I was, through one tunnel.

Comments You will not have written exactly this, but you should have used some complex sentence structures. Notice how the complex second sentence links the activity, the writer's fears and achievements, and other people's fears. The choice of language (e.g. 'overcome', 'claustrophobia') supports the formal style of the sentence structure.

4 Using paragraphs (page 88)

Q1 My longing to talk to someone became so intense that somehow or other I took it in my head to choose Peter.

Sometimes if I've been upstairs into Peter's room during the day, it always struck me as very snug, but because Peter is so retiring and would never turn anyone out who became a nuisance, I never dared stay long, because I was afraid he might think me a bore. I tried to think of an excuse to stay in his room and get him talking, without it being too noticeable, and my chance came yesterday. Peter has a mania for crossword puzzles at the moment and hardly does anything else. I helped him with them and we soon sat opposite each other at his little table, he on the chair and me on the divan.

It gave me a queer feeling each time I looked into his deep blue eyes, and he sat there with that mysterious laugh playing round the lips. I was able to read his inward thoughts. I could see on his face that look of helplessness and uncertainty as to how to behave, and, at the same time, a trace of his sense of manhood. I noticed his shy manner and it made me feel very gentle; I couldn't refrain from meeting those dark eyes again and again, and with my whole heart I almost beseeched him: oh, tell me, what is going on inside you, oh, can't you look beyond this ridiculous chatter?

But the evening passed and nothing happened, except that I told him about blushing – naturally not what I have written, but just so that he would become more sure of himself as he grew older.

When I lay in bed and thought over the whole situation, I found it far from encouraging, and the idea that I should beg for Peter's patronage was simply repellent. One can do a lot to satisfy one's longings, which certainly sticks out in my case, for I have made up my mind to go and sit with Peter more often and to get him talking somehow or other.

Whatever you do, don't think I'm in love with Peter – not a bit of it! If the Van Daans had a daughter instead of a son, I should have tried to make friends with her too.

Comments The first paragraph is a statement of the theme of the diary entry, and so the end of this opening sentence is a logical first break.

All of the second paragraph belongs together, as it is about Peter and his 'mania for crosswords'.

The third paragraph is all about Anne and her thoughts about Peter. You may have inserted this paragraph break one sentence earlier on the grounds that 'I helped him ... on the divan' is about Anne and not Peter. However, that sentence describes something that actually happened, while this paragraph is about inner feelings. A better alternative would be to put the sentence about Anne sitting opposite Peter in a paragraph by itself.

The fourth paragraph is a sentence which belongs by itself, as it describes what actually happened during the rest of the evening.

The fifth paragraph is another section on Anne's feelings – these two sentences clearly belong together.

You might argue that the sentences in the final paragraph could be part of the previous one, but while there is a logical connection between the subject matter, they form a neat, separate conclusion to the passage.

5 Presenting your work (page 92)

Q1 1 An appropriate title, especially in a different style or size of lettering, attracts the reader's attention.

2 Sub-headings are useful to guide readers through the different parts of the material.

3 Bullet points can clarify lists and also make important points stand out.

4 Simple diagrams, e.g. of a typical school site where there are hidden corners for smokers together in.

5 If statistics are used, graphs and charts are an economical and easily understood way of re-presenting them.

6 The whole article could be framed or written in two columns to make more visual impact.

Comments

1 The title is often forgotten – but it's where people begin to read, and it may either attract them or turn them off.

2 You might add that using underlining or frames or upper-case letters for sub-headings is even better.

3 Remember that you can use different styles of bullet point, indent them differently, etc.

4 Good – always look for opportunities to 'lift' the writing with appropriate visual material.

5 Yes – you can draw bar graphs or pie charts fairly accurately by hand.

6 The overall appearance is often forgotten, and even in the examination answer book, you can make your work leap off the page.

6 Using vocabulary and stylistic features (page 97)

Q1   1 festooned   2 flash   3 bole   4 crawled
5 scrambled   6 squirrel   7 wings   8 eating
9 gnaw   10 irresistible   11 jaguar   12 belly
13 fledged   14 flapped   15 foliage
16 nimbly   17 flaring   18 capering
19 savage   20 drum-roll

Comments Don't be disheartened if only a few of your answers match the words used by Golding. This is a complex extract, and there are many possible words for each gap.

1 You may have suggested 'covered'; 'festooned' gives a more vivid picture of great hanging loops, like decorations.
2 Creates an effective alliterative and visual effect.
3 You may have put 'trunk'; 'bole' means the same, but is a useful variant.
4 Suggests the animal-like qualities of the tree.
5 You may have suggested 'climbed': 'scrambled' suggests more effort, and reinforces the comparison of the fire with animals.
6 A clue to this is in the next but one sentence! It is a surprising but apt comparison, given the way squirrels leap about in trees.
7 Alliterative effect.
8 Continues the animal image.
9 You may have suggested something like 'spread'; 'gnaw' is more menacing.
10 We now tend to use the secondary meaning of this word (fascinating) more than its first meaning (cannot be stopped).
11 The fire is now more fierce than a squirrel.
12 A stronger, rougher word than 'stomach'.
13 Unusual choice of word: it makes the trees sound like the feathers of a young bird (fledgling) and so reinforces the image of the fire as a jaguar stalking its prey.
14 Notice all the alliteration on 'f'.
15 An original, precise visual image.
16 Another animal image.
17 An alliterative word again.
18 Not a common word, but continues the picture of excited, slightly out-of-control boys.
19 Conveys the emotions of the boys and the effects of the fire.
20 You may have suggested a general word, such as 'noise': the use of a word which is a precise noise is much more powerful.

7 Writing to explore, imagine and entertain (page 104)

Q1   'Hi, Denise. It's Karen. How are you? Is …'

'Fine, thanks. What's up, Karen? You sound different. Is something wrong?'

'Oh … no. I was just ringing to speak to Mum. Nothing important, really.'

'Your mum? Why would she be here at this time? Isn't she at work now?'

'No. She … she said … I thought she said she was popping in to see you this afternoon.'

'No, she's not here. Actually, I haven't seen her for ages. I've been a bit worried, really, and … But I'm sure everything's all right, love!'

'Yes, no problem! It's OK, I must've got the message wrong. See you soon. Bye!'

'Bye, Karen. But are you sure …'

Karen had already hung up. She hoped she hadn't sounded too worried to Denise, but her heart was racing. She had the feeling that today was no longer any old Tuesday, but had suddenly become a very special Tuesday, one the family would remember for ever. Bitter memories they would be.

Comments Karen's concern and confusion make her start to ask about her mother before waiting for an answer to her first question.

Denise notices something unusual in Karen's manner. Karen tries to pretend there's nothing wrong, after being thrown for a second.

Denise is now worried, realising that Karen's mum must have changed her usual routine.

Karen is finding it difficult not to reveal too many of her fears.

Denise expresses her own worries, then realises she ought to be reassuring Karen and changes direction.

Karen also tries to adopt a cheerful attitude and quickly rings off before she is asked any more questions.

Denise is still wanting to find out more.
Karen reflects on how she sounded to Denise – has she given away too much? Then she beings to think about her immediate situation and how – if her fears about her mum are right – their lives will never be the same again.

Q2 a Plot

- School trip to castle – art class – to sketch the ruins
- Teasing on bus
- Pupils told to keep off dangerous high walls, one pupil ignores this
- Boy stuck on high tower – frightened to move, helped down by quiet boy whom he teased on bus
- Both boys quiet on bus on way back, but for different reasons

Characters

- Tom – quite boy
- Jack – the loud, confident one
- some of their friends, who join in teasing on bus
- art teacher – not very strong on discipline
- castle attendant – doesn't like school parties disturbing the peace

Setting

- the bus journey
- the castle (outside – going in – the inside generally – the ruined tower where Jack gets stuck – going out again)
- the return bus journey

Idea

- that quiet people can be brave
- that some people can behave in different ways

Structure

- starts on return journey, told by Tom, flashback to earlier events

Comments

- You need to set the scene: why is the trip happening? Who is on it?
- Establish the main characters and their relationship.
- How does the main incident come about?
- What is the central unexpected happening? This needs to be the detailed focus of the story.
- An ending which will allow contrast with the start, to convey the 'message'.
- Use your plan to work out who is really important: obviously the two boys, some of the other children, and at least one teacher. Including the attendant will bring a second adult into the story and give you extra opportunities for description and dialogue, and he can be part of the plot, e.g. raising the alarm.
- Variety gives you more descriptive opportunities

again, and bus–castle–bus is a pleasing circular structure. How will your description convey the different atmosphere on the return journey in the bus?

- Worth noting how you will convey this, e.g. buy the different way the two boys are treated on the return journey.
- If attempting a complicated structure, it is worth developing a paragraph plan, so that you do not lose track of the sequence of events.

8 Writing to inform, explain and describe (page 111)

Q1

Anytown Comprehensive School
Anything Road
Anywhere
Blankshire
XX9 9ZZ

20 June 2002

VISIT TO THORPE PARK

Dear Parent/Guardian

We are planning to take all Year 7 pupils on a visit to Thorpe Park, near Newtown, on Friday 18 July.

We shall leave school at 8 o'clock in the morning, and we intend to be back at school by 5 o'clock in the afternoon. We shall be travelling by Fred Blogg's Coaches, all of which are fitted with seat belts and other safety devices. Six teachers will accompany the pupils, together with several parent volunteers, so that pupils will spend the day in groups of no more than ten, each accompanied by at least one adult.

If your child comes on this visit, s/he will need to bring a packed lunch and a small amount of spending money in case s/he wishes to buy more food and drink or a souvenir of the visit. No pupil should bring more than £5: all the facilities of Thorpe Park are free once inside, and large sums of money may be lost or stolen. School uniform is not necessary; pupils should wear comfortable, casual clothes and footwear suitable for outdoor activities.

Thorpe Park is a centre where young people can try pursuits such as wall-climbing, abseiling, assault courses, canoeing and caving. All activities are supervised by trained centre staff, and specialist clothing and equipment are provided where necessary. We are arranging this visit as part of the pupils' personal and social education programme, so that they can develop their skills of teamwork and supporting and encouraging each other in challenging situations.

We hope that you will agree to your child taking part in this visit. If so, will you please sign and return the slip at the bottom of this letter together with a donation of £7.50 to cover the cost of travel and use of the facilities at Thorpe Park. We regret that we shall have to cancel the visit if insufficient parents are able to support it.

Yours faithfully

Comments Your letter will probably be quite different from the example, but check to see if you have included all these features. If so, your work should be worthy of a Grade A!

Informing
- where is the trip to?
- who is the trip for?
- what is the date?
- what are the departure and return times?
- what does it cost?
- how do you book a place?

Explaining
- what is the method of travel?
- safety issues (e.g. travel and supervision)
- lunch arrangements
- clothing
- money
- why has this trip been chosen?
- what will happen if there is insufficient interest?

Describing
- what is there for the pupils to do at Thorpe Park?
- what will the pupils gain from the visit?

Language
- formal, but friendly – this example ends rather negatively

Layout
- the school address
- the date (which may be placed left or right)
- a heading to say what the letter is about (best placed after 'Dear Parent/Guardian' rather than before as in the answer shown)
- paragraphs (best to keep them fairly short so that the letter does not look too dense on the page)
- if you refer to a return slip, it's a good idea to actually include it, as it is another opportunity for you to show how clearly you can set out the necessary information

9 Writing to argue, persuade and advise (page 116)

Q1 *This is not the only way to rewrite the beginning of the passage, but see if you have identified similar problems in the original, even if you have dealt with them differently.*

Why do many countries compete over nuclear weapons? Those with successful economies have more effective weapons than poorer countries, but any nuclear weapon could cause enormous damage. Many economically developed countries live in fear of being attacked with nuclear weapons, and so keep them as both protection and deterrent.

Today, a number of organisations are trying to persuade countries to dispose of their nuclear weapons safely, but no country is prepared to be the first . . .

Comments
Content and structure
- Avoid exaggeration: it is not true that 'nearly every country in the world' completes for nuclear weapons.
- The original answer is very repetitive, both at the beginning and at the end.
- The answer needs to be split into two paragraphs and some of the material needs to be rearranged, as there are two different ideas here: a description of the problem and attempts to do something about it.

[Note: from this opening, it appears that the writer is arguing one side of the question only. Remember that to gain a high grade, the argument would need to consider other opinions and viewpoints, even if they are ultimately rejected.]

Style
- Starting with a question is good and worth retaining.
- 'Nuclear weapons' does not need upper-case letters.
- Much of the language of the original is very simple. For example, it is better to use 'successful' rather than 'large' economies; 'more effective' instead of 'bigger and better'; 'enormous' instead of 'a lot of'; 'both protection and deterrent' to replace at least two whole sentences; 'organisations' instead of 'groups'.

Presentation

No presentational features have been added, but it might have been worth considering:

• a title (perhaps something like 'Nuclear weapons: fear or threat?');
• underlined or framed headings for each paragraph (e.g. 'The weapons race' and 'Peer pressure');
• bullet-pointing the reasons given in the first paragraph for why countries keep nuclear weapons.

10 Writing to analyse, review and comment (page 120)

Q1 You probably all remember what a mess the school site looked a year ago. What was wrong with it? Where do I start! Bare patches on the grass at the front entrance, weeds in the flower beds, litter bins broken or overflowing. Yes, you remember! Inside wasn't a lot better, either: bare walls and echoing corridors don't feel much like home, do they? So a group of us on the School Council decided to change this if we could, and the Improving Our School campaign was launched.

We had someone from each year in the action group, and they all talked to everyone who had anything to do with the school, so that ideas for changes wouldn't just come from one part of the community. We didn't have much money to spend, but the Head and the Governors said they could spare about £500 to start us off, and that if the changes worked, we might be able to have more money next year.

We looked at the problems and all the suggestions, and realised that with only £500 to spend, we couldn't do everything. So we decided to concentrate on four improvements: displaying work on the corridors, improving the entrance to the school, encouraging more pupils to eat in the school dining centre, and – the biggest challenge of all – attacking the litterbugs!

The corridors look really attractive now, and I've overheard visitors commenting on them. Of course, they're already impressed by the entrance to the school: the flower beds and what used to be an overgrown area by the car park are tidy and bright with shrubs and trees. I know that doesn't make us a better school, but it certainly gives people a better impression of us.

Once we had persuaded the Cook to survey pupils' eating habits and to provide more of the food they really wanted – not chips, actually, but salads and vegetarian dishes – the numbers staying for school meals shot up. This helped the litter problem, because pupils weren't coming back into the grounds dropping wrappers from food they'd bought outside. A few extra bins in the right places made a huge difference too.

So, it has all gone really well, We think that we've given back some pride to the school, and we're hoping that we can do more next year. If you want that too, make your feelings known to your School Council rep.

In the meantime, keep supporting the dining centre; keep doing all that great work to go on the walls; keep your litter in the bins and keep off the flower beds!

Comments

The answer uses the notes well to:

• analyse the situation in the school before the improvement campaign started;
• review the process which then took place;
• comment on the end results and possible future development.

If you have also done this in one way or another, you have fulfilled the main purpose of the task.

The answer is presented coherently and logically and with a sense of enthusiasm and involvement. The language and tone is appropriate to a school audience. Although it is an easy piece to read, and so would hold the interest of its audience, some of the points made are quite sophisticated (such as the comment 'I know that doesn't make us a better school, but it certainly gives people a better impression of us'). This answer would gain a high GCSE grade.

Published by HarperCollins*Publishers* Ltd
77-85 Fulham Palace Road
London W6 8JB

www.CollinsEducation.com
On-line support for schools and colleges

First published 1998
This new edition published 2003

ISBN 0 00 714634 5

Andrew Bennett and Peter Thomas assert the moral right to be identified as the authors of this work.

British Library Cataloguing in Publication Data
A catalogue record for this book is available from the British Library.

Edited by Catriona Watson–Brown
Production by Jack Murphy
Series and Book Design by Sally Boothroyd
Index compiled by Julie Rimington
Printed and bound in China by Imago

Acknowledgements

The Authors and Publishers are grateful to the following for permission to reproduce copyright material:
© Amnesty International, Amnesty International advertisment, p. 113; © Binatone, 'Binatone' quick reference card, p. 7; Black Swan, Notes from a Small Island by Bill Bryson, pp. 21, 27; Ian Cave, 'Granary Wharf' leaflet, pp. 3, 18, 22; Countryside Magazine, 'British Food is the Best by Far' by Alison Pratt, p. 29; Laurence Pollinger Ltd and the Estate of Frieda Lawrence Ravagli, 'Last Lesson of the Afternoon,' by D.H. Lawrence from The Complete Poems of D.H. Lawrence, p. 70 ; © Crown copyright, p.172; Faber & Faber: 'The Trout' from Death of a Naturalist by Seamus Heaney, p. 36; 'Weeds' by Norman Nicholson from Sea to West, p. 40; The Lord of the Flies, by William Golding, pp. 59, 78; 'Thistles' by Ted Hughes from Wodwo, p. 41; The Guardian: 'London my London,' 1/8/95 by Sebastian Faulks, p. 118; 'Musical facts' graphs 9/5/95, p. 6; Heinemann, 'The Darkness Out There,' from Pack of Cards by Penelope Lively, p. 56; IDG, Internet Explorer 3 for Windows 95 for Dummies, p. 108; IPC Magazines Ltd, front cover of Woman magazine, p.32; The Lady, cover of The Lady, p. 32; Macmillan, 'City Jungle' by Pie Corbett from Sandwhich Poets Rice Corbett & Moses, p. 38; The Observer, 'The Lighthouse Keeper,' and 'The Seafront Attendant,' 6/7/97, p. 15; Oxfam, Oxfam leaflet, p. 14; Jake's Thing by Kingsley Amis, pp. 48-9; Going Solo by Roald Dahl, p. 2; The Catcher in the Rye by J.D. Salinger, p. 51; Cider with Rosie by Laurie Lee, p. 49; The Diary of Anne Frank by Anne Frank, p. 88; A Kestrel for a Knave by Barry Hines, pp. 60-1; The Kingdom by the Sea by Paul Theroux, pp. 2, 4; I'm the King of the Castle by Susan Hill, p. 102; Pergamon, 'Mastering the Craft' from Mastering the Craft by Vernon Scannell, pp. 37-8; Puffin Books Ltd, Daz 4 Zoe by Robert Swindells, p. 53; Random House: The Commitments by Roddy Doyle, William Heinemann/Minerva, p. 52; The Last Enemy by Richard Hillary, Pimlico, p. 120; There was Once by Margaret Attwood, p. 98; RNLI, 'Water Safety Code,' and 'Flags and Signs,' from Beach Safety Guidelines, p. 8; Routledge, 'The Dandelion,' from Selected Poems by Jon Silkin, p. 34; Scottish and Newcastle Retail, Lodge Inns publicity leaflet, p. 25; The Benefits Agency, Income support leaflet, p. 90; The Daily Mirror, 'It's Chelsea FC,' 6/8/97, p. 30; Urathon Bike Tyres, Urathon bicycle tyres leaflet, pp. 10-11; The Women's Press, Push Me, Pull Me by Sandra Chick, pp. 50-1; Chatto & Windus Ltd, 'Thistles' by Jon Stallworthy from Root & Branch, p. 66; 'Dress Sense' by David Kitchen, pp. 40-1; Presents from my Aunts in Pakistan by Moniza Alvi, p.128; Daily Mail, 'Warning to teenagers as mobile phone thefts soar', 8/1/02 by Matthew Hickley, p.148; Department for Education and Skills, 'Dads & Sons', 2002, pp.122-125; Night of the Scorpion by Nissim Ezekiel, p.127; Kidscape, 'Parent of a Teenager?', 2001, p.138,139; Island Man by Grace Nichols, p.127; The Observer, 'Teenagers don't do as they're told,' 19/5/02 by Maureen Freely, p.140.

Photographs

The Author and Publishers are grateful to the following for permission to reproduce photographs:
The Archive Collection/Disney Corporation: p.72; BFI Stills/Canal + Image UK, Ltd: p.74; BFI Stills/Imageworks: p.75; BFI Stills/Polygram: p.98; BFI Stills/Universal Films: p.87; Bubbles Photo Library: p.148; Collections/Michael St Maur Sheil: p.2; Department of Health: p.112; Mary Evans Picture Library: p.61; Mary Evans/Jeffrey Morgan: p.69; Getty Images: p.140; Getty/Telegraph p.105; Imperial War Museum: pp.65, 120; Minerva: pp.27, 52; Michael O'Mara Books: p.26; Christine Osborne Pictures: p.85; Penguin: p.77

Illustrations

Sally Artz, Nick Asher, Peter Byatt, Gecko Ltd, Madeleine Hardy, Michael Ogden, Dave Poole and Nick Ward.

INDEX